The Use of Simulation in Educational Administration

Edited by **DALE L. BOLTON**

College of Education
University of Washington

CHARLES E. MERRILL PUBLISHING COMPANY

A Bell & Howell Company
Columbus, Ohio

MERRILL'S SERIES FOR EDUCATIONAL ADMINISTRATION

Under the Editorship of

DR. LUVERN L. CUNNINGHAM, Dean

College of Education
The Ohio State University

and

DR. H. THOMAS JAMES, President

The Spencer Foundation
Chicago, Illinois

International Standard Book Number: 0-675-09824-6

Library of Congress Catalog Card Number: 75-166973

1 2 3 4 5 6 7 8 9 — 75 74 73 72 71

PRINTED IN THE UNITED STATES OF AMERICA

Preface

The preparation of educational administrators has undergone intensive examination and change during the past ten years. Four dramatic changes have occurred in preparation programs during this time: (a) increased use of inter-disciplinary content, (b) broad use of internships, (c) emphasis on research orientation—even at early stages of programs, and (d) increased realism by use of simulation procedures.

All of these changes have received attention in the professional literature. However, recent developments in simulation procedures have not been discussed in a unitary context. Consequently, the purpose of this book is to describe and discuss recent projects and activities that allow the simulation of real-world events in such a manner that the simulations may be used for research and/or instructional purposes.

The intent of the book is not completely unlike some prior writings;* however, the scope is such that is provides for the reader a sophisticated acquaintance with a broad range of simulation techniques currently in use. Because no single person or institution is using all of these simulation techniques, the book is organized so that each author has written a chapter about a single aspect of simulation in which he is a specialist. Each author has been intimately involved with both the development and use of the simulation that he describes.

---

*For example: Culbertson, Jack & William Coffield, (eds.), *Simulation in Administrative Training,* Columbus, Ohio: The University Council for Educational Administration, 1960; Griffiths Daniel E., "The Case Method of Teaching Educational Administration: A Reappraisal, 1963," *The Journal of Educational Administration* vol. 1, no. 2, (October 1963); Thomas, Jr., Michael P., *Strategies in the Preparation of School Administrators,* a Report of the Seventeenth Annual Meeting of the National Conference of Professors of Educational Administration, 1964.

The primary reader for which this book is intended is obviously the professor of educational administration. However, it will be useful to advanced graduate students as they participate in courses which utilize simulation techniques. Many professors ask students to devise situational problems, cases, or simulated activities during courses for the purpose of analyzing administrative behavior to the degree that an abstraction of it is possible. This book will provide excellent background material for such a course project.

In addition to the above audiences, it is expected that some practicing administrators will find the book useful in relation to inservice activities for administrators. Many of the simulation techniques described have been used in inservice settings as well as preservice university courses, and acquaintance with the *concepts* presented would facilitate communication between practicing administrators and professors of educational administration.

The reader should be aware of the fact that, although the chapters have been independently written and do not depend on each other for their understanding, common topics are discussed by the various authors. This has lead to some redundancy (e.g., definitions and historical development) from chapter to chapter, but this is considered desirable because some readers will not read the book in its entirety.

It is suggested that the first chapter be read prior to reading any of the other chapters because the historical development of simulation provides a context for comprehending the details of the other chapters. The other general chapter, Using Simulation to Conduct Research in Educational Administration, provides a context which is beneficial for interpreting how simulation materials can be used for research purposes.

Dale L. Bolton
Seattle, Washington

Contents

Chapter 1   A POWERFUL BUT UNDERDEVELOPED EDUCA-
TIONAL TOOL, *Luvern L. Cunningham*   1

Simulation: Its Early History, 3
Uses in Educational Administrator Preparation, 5
Simulation in Other Fields Within Education, 7
Approaches to Simulation, 9
The Sensitivity Thrust, 18
Issues, 21
Summary, 26
Notes, 27
Bibliography, 27

Chapter 2   THE USE OF CASES, *Glenn L. Immegart*   30

An Historical View of the Case Method in Educational Adminis-
tration, 34
Using Cases, 39
Illustrations of the Use of Cases in Instruction, 47
Some of the Problems in Using Cases, 52
Some Guides for Using Cases, 56
Developing a Library of Cases, 58
Summary, 60
Notes, 62
Bibliography, 63

Chapter 3   IN-BASKET TECHNIQUES, *Donald P. Anderson*   65

Brief History of the In-Basket Technique, 66
Uses of the In-Basket Technique, 70

Strength of the Instructional Technique, 74
Limitations or Shortcomings of the Technique, 77
Design and Construction of In-Basket Materials, 80
Need for Additional Work, 84
Notes, 85
Bibliography, 86

Chapter 4   SIMULATING THE PROCESS FOR SELECTION OF
            TEACHERS, *Dale L. Bolton*   88

The Need for Simulating the Teacher-Selection Process, 89
Description of an Example, 93
Problems of Simulating the Teacher-Selection Process, 95
Use of Materials for Simulating the Teacher-Selection Proc-
    ess, 101
Background Information and Theoretical Framework, 109
Summary, 142
Notes, 143
Bibliography, 145

Chapter 5   SIMULATING THE PROCESS FOR SELECTION OF
            ADMINISTRATORS,   *Kenneth E. McIntyre*   149

Examples, 151
Other Sources for Examples, 166
Evaluation of Simulation for Selection of Administrators, 167
Notes, 168
Bibliography, 169

Chapter 6   SOME APPLICATIONS OF GAME THEORY TO
            ADMINISTRATIVE BEHAVIOR, *Robert E.
            Ohm*   171

Games and Game Theory, 172
The Laboratory Function of Games, 188
Research Potential, 193
Future Trends in Game Development and Use, 194
Bibliography, 196

Chapter 7 SIMULATION OF COLLECTIVE NEGOTIATIONS,
John J. Horvat 198

The Simulation Device, 201
Techniques of the Simulation, 210
Assessment of the Utility of the Simulation, 222
Additional Training Materials Needed in the Area of Collective
    Negotiations, 227
Notes, 232
Bibliography, 234

Chapter 8 THE USES OF COMPUTERS IN SIMULATION,
Wailand Bessent 235

When is a Computer Called For?, 236
Four Simulation Models, 244
A Word About Languages, 254
Some Causes for Disenchantment, 255
Notes, 256
Bibliography, 256

Chapter 9 USING SIMULATION TO CONDUCT RESEARCH
    IN EDUCATIONAL ADMINISTRATION, *Dale
    L. Bolton* 259

The Need for Research Output, 261
Potential Advantages of Simulation in Research, 274
Potential Problems of Simulation in Research, 281
Examples of Research Within Simulated Situations, 288
Summary, 293
Notes, 297
Bibliography, 300

1

A Powerful
But Underdeveloped
Educational Tool*

Luvern L. Cunningham

Simulation is a method of approximating reality. Its utility is legion especially for educational, training, and research purposes. At present it is appearing in many forms, carrying several labels, and expanding rapidly as a research and educational device. Its potential, despite advancements, remains relatively unexploited by educators.

Simulation as a concept has moved rapidly into common usage. Its widespread utilization in the space programs of the United States and the Soviet Union has not only extended and refined its practical applications but also brought it directly into the living rooms of the world. Moon surface mock-ups, space craft models and role-playing astronauts have become commonplace. The arts and sciences of simulating are so well-developed and useful that television audiences have come to expect

*Some material in this chapter appeared originally in George Barron, Dan H. Cooper, and William C. Walker, eds., *Educational Administration: International Perspectives,* (Chicago: Rand McNally & Company, 1969). Permission to reproduce that material, in revised form, was granted by Rand McNally & Company.

them. The large networks are even compared on the quality of their simulations and channel-changers switch from station to station in search of the most informative simulations. The designers of space exploration use simulation in several ways. First it is used as a sophisticated way of pre-experiencing events. The moon flights are simulated from blast-off to recovery. The integration of computer capability with human performance is highly developed. The linkage of man with cybernetic devices has been popularized in an advanced way through the film *2001 A Space Odyssey* (5). In this motion picture, space pilots interact with HAL, the spaceship computer system. The flight begins with very rational interchanges between the pilots and HAL. As the flight to Mars progresses the relationship between man and machine moves through several emotional states—from respect, even affection, to mild mutual suspicions, to attempts on the part of HAL to eliminate the pilots, to a last-ditch but successful attempt of one surviving pilot to destroy HAL. The scenario is a magnificent blending of man-machine relationships in a setting marked by dependency upon simulation capability.

A second spaceage use, hard to separate from the first, is as a training device. It is highly developed as a training tool for situations which demand sophisticated blending of cognitive and motor abilities as well as understanding of psychological and affective problems of space exploration. These are especially critical in astronaut preparation. The pre-flight simulations include training in elementary features of space flight as well as very advanced, exceedingly complex, pre-experience simulations of entire flights. Small pieces of flights and missions are simulated independently; many of these emphasize manipulations of machines and equipment. Larger segments are simulated in lengthy time blocks approximating larger features of the missions such as blast-off and re-entry. More extended training exercises incorporate encounters with psychological problems as well as cognitive and motor exercises. Some simulations, such as weightlessness, are laboratory based; others are conducted on moon-surface-like environments here on earth, particularly where geological knowledge is important.

A third use is in the mass education of the world's viewing publics. NASA achieves fantastic public relations mileage out of walking every viewer, with the aid of role players, through the features of space travel. Such simulations are augmented with live television from space flight cameras. The degree of realism is substantial and the learning rates of viewers "astronomic," to employ a poor analogy. It is probably true that the people the world over are better informed on the technological, legal and moral issues in space development than on any other single matter. Programming saturated with NASA information, utilizing such a powerful tool as simulation, has effected a major information and mass-education achievement unparalleled in the history of the world.

SIMULATION: ITS EARLY HISTORY

Robinson reviewed the use of games and simulations in war, business and politics and concluded that the applications of these techniques for teaching and training were usually secondary objectives of their creators. Maybe educational uses were even fortuitous. The principal early purposes of simulation and gaming were for research—the investigation of a particular system, process or set of behaviors (16). And so it was in educational administration.

Few if any ideas have diffused as rapidly, or have been adopted with such relish, as simulation. The persons (either to be praised or damned, depending on your point of view) most responsible for the early development and refinement of the concept of simulation in educational administration and its application to the training of administrators were Daniel Griffiths, Richard Wynn, Dan Davies, and Harold McNally at Teachers College, Columbia. It was the thinking of these men, in the mid-1950s, that lead to the now well-known research project called "The Development of Criteria for Success in School Administration." Simulated materials developed for the study of administrative behavior were widely used for administrator preparation in the years that followed.

The University Council for Educational Administration (UCEA), the facilitating agency for the production and distribution of a range of instructional materials including simulation devices, reported the extraordinarily wide adoption and usage of the idea.[1] The range of materials, as well as the forms of their utilization, makes an interesting story in itself.

The precise origin of the concept of simulation is not well known. Its most extensive use has been within military and/or government establishments. In the military it has been adopted almost universally and dates back at least to the Spartan war games. Modern military uses are often rather advanced, ranging from complicated field maneuvers involving thousands of men to laboratory-based simulations where military personnel are trained individually under exacting conditions involving actual performance, evaluation, feedback to the trainee, and repetition of the performance-feedback cycle. Most of us are at least somewhat familiar with these techniques either because we have experienced them ourselves or we have observed their employment in a training exercise.

The term *simulator* is often used to refer to hardware or equipment such as the Link Trainer (used to train pilots in World War II), or the auto console designed for driver-training instruction. Such devices are for refining individual proficiencies under controlled conditions. Each employer of the term *simulation* modifies its meaning to fit his own intent. Gagne defines the notion more or less in terms of what a simulator is designed to achieve (11). The word *simulator* to him does not mean one who simulates; rather it means the hardware and/or software (the total range of physical, social, and political conditions) essential to the training purposes to be satisfied. In brief he suggests the following:

(1) A simulator is developed to represent a real situation in which operations are carried out;

(2) In representing a real operational situation, a simulator provides its users with certain *controls* over the situation;

(3) The simulator is deliberately designed to *omit* certain parts of the real operational situation.

Simulators may or may not involve hardware. The simulation of military decision-making processes often involves the use of representative war plans, operations' orders, messages, and other materials without employing either the equipment of war or computers as partners in the military decision process. There are also human-machine systems simulators; these are complex, involved mock-ups with interrelated and interdependent components which provide settings for the simultaneous training of teams or groups of persons.

The applications of the basic concept are extensive in areas other than the military. They are found in almost every field: business, medicine, transportation, air pollution control, education, international relations, urban renewal, communications, or police work. The fascinating experimentation with business games is worth noting; so are the commercial pilot-training simulators which permit laboratory "flying" of all types of aircraft for training purposes (14). Computerized simulations also permit the advanced design testing of aircraft that have not yet been constructed; the performances of aircraft are simulated while still on the designers' drawing boards. Obviously the world's largest and most comprehensive systems and mission simulators are those employed in the several space flight centers. As stated earlier, simulation is the single, most important mechanism for space training permitting those in training to experience as many of the problems they will encounter in actual flight as can be anticipated or incorporated on the basis of previous flight experience.

Definitions of simulation continue to be imprecise. The word has acquired a broad set of meanings. In its earliest usages it had a negative connotation. "Pretense," "sham," "mock," and "misinterpret" were synonyms. More recently it has been used as an analogue or a developed, accurate representation of a particular reality.

USES IN EDUCATIONAL ADMINISTRATOR PREPARATION

Reference has already been made to the pioneering work of the men at Columbia. They were assisted in the early period by a number of other persons from the field of educational administration as well as from other disciplines. John Hemphill, Norman Frederickson and Glen Stice, psychologists and research design specialists from Educational Testing Service, were members of the DCS (Development of Centers for Success in School Administration) team that created the *Whitman Elementary School, Jefferson Township, Washington County, State of Lafayette.* Their simulation was to satisfy research objectives first, administrator-selection objectives second, and instructional objectives third (13).

The first uses of the research materials for instruction occurred in 1959. At Columbia some experimentation with simulation in instruction went forward during the 1958-59 academic year. Further exploration at Columbia, Stanford and Chicago followed in the summer of 1959, where the materials were used in workshops chiefly for elementary principals (9). Later, *Jefferson Township High School* background data and problems were integrated with the previously prepared DCS elementary school set. Simulated problems (tapes and in-basket items) were eventually prepared for the positions of high school principal, director of instruction, business manager, and superintendent of schools. The *Jefferson Township Public Schools* became well known in the United States and other parts of the world.

Additional simulated materials have appeared since the Jefferson School became so prominent. (The names and roles of Marion Smith, Gayle Jones, Diane Seward, Dr. E. Andrew Donnelly and others became educational household words in the early 1960s. Literally hundreds of persons, in administrator-preparation programs as well as in-service training workshops and institutes, assumed those simulated roles and came to know the Jefferson Schools.) In-basket problems of the *Shady Acres Elementary School* were prepared by Kenneth McIntyre at the University of Texas. The national Department of Elementary School Principals produced a "decision-making kit" composed of a set of in-basket-type problems to be used in local, state and national meetings of elementary principals. The Department of Elementary School Principals devoted whole-day sessions of its national meetings in 1964 and 1966 to the discussion and analysis of simulated problems. Professor Richard Wynn of the University of Pittsburgh was the chief designer of the new materials and the organizer of their use at the 1966 annual meeting in Portland, Oregon. Because of his assistance and the imaginative leadership of the elementary principals' organization itself, memorable in-service experiences were provided for several thousand principals.

Useful new materials continue to be produced through or in cooperation with UCEA. The Jefferson Township battery was updated and revised, and the UCEA Articulated Media Project provided other valuable instructional materials. The Collective Negotiations Game (see Chapter 7) developed by John Horvat, for example, had strong appeal in the 1960s because of the collective bargaining momentum generated by teachers and other professional employees in this country. Special sets of simulated materials for administrators of vocational education programs were developed at the University of Nebraska in the late 1960s. Likewise, there was a collaborative effort to produce materials for leadership training in special education involving several prominent universities with strong special education programs.

A number of professors at colleges and universities around the United States, and in other countries as well, have invented a variety of new materials for their own use: in-basket materials for school board members; socio-drama for community groups. They have also been creative in finding promising ways of using their inventions, or in the adaptation of other simulation materials to new preparation requirements. An excellent example of the latter was the work at Los Angeles State College where the original DCS Jefferson Township materials were modified to fit an inner-city, in-service training need for Los Angeles principals and assistant principals.[2] New in-basket items were developed treating racial integration, relationships with news media in crisis situations, and community problems in changing neighborhoods. Three experimental workshops were financed under Title IV of the 1964 Civil Rights Act; these materials were the chief vehicles for instruction during the three-week sessions.

At the University of Chicago another innovation was attempted, particularly in instructional format. There, in 1965, simultaneous simulated training was achieved involving representatives of several professional groups—administrators, teachers, counselors, adult educators, and school psychologists. For three weeks, forty persons performed in a non-materials-based simulation. Simulated environments were created by participants. Cross-role experiences, confrontations, problem-solving task forces and other experience-producing techniques were employed.

SIMULATION IN OTHER FIELDS WITHIN EDUCATION

The best organized and most comprehensive use of simulation in professional training has been within administrator preparation programs. However, the basic notion of simulation spread rapidly to several other professional areas during the late 1960s.

Counselor training came to feature some simulated exercises. The counseling relationship lent itself to simulation techniques because of the rather narrow range of behaviors expected of counselors. Some insitutions have learned to make excellent use of video- and audio-tapes as well as the filming of the counseling act itself. Such audio-visual tools have provided vehicles for analyzing the substantive problems confronting counselors as well as a method of examining the behaviors of the individuals in training. A tape-recorded case conference, for example, not only prompted a review of the issues revealed in the case, but also offered opportunity to study the behaviors of the participants. When the conference was video-taped, it was an even more powerful tool because it revealed non-verbal behavior too.

In several projects completed in the area of teacher education, simulation was a prominent method of instruction. The INSITE program at Indiana University, a special experiment incorporating new components into the pre-service training of teachers, included several types of simulated activities throughout the teacher-preparation sequence. A variety of simulation materials were prepared, patterned somewhat after those in the Jefferson Township School set. There were simulated exercises in pupil evaluation, reporting to parents, lesson planning, preparation of examinations, learning difficulty diagnosis, and parent-teacher conferences. In-baskets were developed which included such areas as central office memoranda, notes from parents, communications from teachers' organizations, and messages from students. There were extensive background data on pupils, including films of youngsters at work in their classrooms. This information was provided as background for the teacher-trainees prior to their assumption of teaching responsibilities in the simulated school. Materials were created for both elementary and secondary teacher preparation.[3]

At the University of Oregon, several professors developed and tested simulated materials for training teachers to assess children's specific reading requirements and to identify the types of instructional arrangements most appropriate for meeting each need (19). Bert Y. Kersh, at Monmouth College of Education, did pioneering work with *micro teaching,* a type of simulation. Donald R.

Cruickshank, Ohio State University, completed a United States Office of Education project on the use of simulation in the preparation of beginning teachers (8). His techniques, extended to include specific materials for preparing inner-city teachers, were somewhat like those tested at Indiana University.

Still other innovations were underway using simulation in the colleges, high schools, even grammar schools, for the instruction of students at those levels. The work of Guetzkow and Robinson at Northwestern University stimulated the spread of inter-nation simulation as an instructional method at the college and secondary school level (12). James S. Coleman and his colleagues at Johns Hopkins breathed new life into social studies classes with his legislative, life career, consumer, family, and community disaster games (3). The idea had so much appeal that it gained the attention of the popular press. *Life* carried a story on September 30, 1966, of an advanced use of computer simulation in a Yorktown Heights, New York, sixth-grade classroom (7). The experiment involved more than just computer-assisted instruction; it included role playing in which children acted out situations, used data, and tested hypotheses regarding action vis-a-vis the computer.

APPROACHES TO SIMULATION

As the previous discussion illustrates, simulation has assumed several forms. A few of these, either on the drawing board or being used currently in educational-administrator preparation, are here reviewed briefly.

"Saturation" Approach

The UCEA Jefferson Township Schools (later revised and named the *Madison Township Schools*), aspects of the Indiana University teacher-education simulations, and the UCEA-sponsored urban education simulations might best be described as attempts to simulate a comprehensive work environment. Considerable information was gathered and organized concerning the school, the community, the pupil population, the professional and non-professional personnel, the physical environment, and the expectations which the community and staff held for the school. Such data were necessary in order successfully to create a reasonably useful hypothetical school situation.

Advocates of this approach believe a sketchy presentation of a simulated situation in which trainees are to be placed will not provide them with sufficient knowledge to make adequate decisions relevant to that environment. Some argue that the success of simulation is contingent upon the "feeling" that the trainee has for his role as the hypothetical administrator or teacher within the simulated school context. The degree to which the trainee feels himself in his role, and the degree to which he can sustain himself in that feeling, appears to be dependent upon the realistic recreation of a total school and its surroundings.

The excuse for creating a setting of this kind is simply to provide a stage upon which the trainee may perform. The person in training solves problems or makes decisions in response to situational stimuli designed to confront him as they would in reality. Furthermore his performance is partially public so that his actions can be judged. Supporters of this approach maintain that judgments of the adequacy of the trainee's performance are largely conditioned both by the realness of the simulated environment and by the quality and variety of administrative problems with which the trainee is faced. The quality of an administrative problem is difficult to ascertain, but to be useful for training purposes it needs to be typical, and it should incorporate into its resolution a significant number of situational variables. The trainee should be called upon to utilize his knowledge of the situation in which he is working, as well as his knowledge of the science and art of administration. At the same time the trainee should be faced with a broad range of administrative problems. Confrontation with a variety of issues sensitizes the trainee to the diverse demands made upon the practicing administrator. Furthermore, it permits the individual to appraise his personal strengths and weaknesses across a spectrum of administrative responsibilities.

In the early 1960s, as indicated earlier, a series of promising simulations of political phenomena occurred. These, chiefly in the field of international relations, involved extensive sets of background and situational information. These simulations also generated another kind of debate. At the University of Wisconsin, for example, Cohen used real names; political leaders, countries and events were identified (6). On the other hand Guetzkow and his colleagues at Northwestern used fictitious names, places and situations (12). The architects of the two schemes (real *v* pseudo) maintain there are distinct advantages to each. Using real names and situations allows the learner to use what he knows plus what he can acquire from available sources to assist him in his participation in the simulation. Advocates of fictionalizing the simulation argue that it allows teachers more control over situations and avoids the pitfalls of students identifying with unplayable roles such as presidents, kings, ambassadors and the like.

The point to be made here is that the same arguments have occurred in educational administration simulations. Should real persons, schools and events be identified in the recreated environments? Or should they be disguised? Also, how much needs to be known about a given person, act, place or event to allow others to experience the value inherent in what is recreated? Long and rather inconclusive discussions have been held about the amount of background material need for successful simulations.

Although my own views on simulation have altered as a consequence of experience with several approaches, I believe that there is great value in saturation when sustained and intensive simulation is intended. Culbertson (9) made a case for this view when he wrote:

> Comprehensive background information based upon careful study of real school situations is essential to the effective use of simulated materials. Thus, if a letter which a principal has received, is used as an in-basket item, the context from which the letter came is pertinent to its value and an item for instruction. The rich background of facts against which a problem is analyzed and weighed is necessary to develop the student's ability to see the interrelated elements of the total situation. Such comprehensiveness simulates more nearly the gestalt of administration and increases the student's feeling for the 'reality' of the situation.

Micro Approach

The saturation approach is based on data comprehensiveness and multiple-decision stimuli; the micro simulations are more manageable in terms of the extensiveness of the reality required as well as the range of problem stimuli to be incorporated. Micro teaching simulations involve the intensive examination of teacher-pupil interaction, usually between one student and one teacher or, at most, a small group of pupils and their teacher. Using electronic tools, especially audio-visual devices, teaching and learning behavior can be recorded and analyzed under laboratory conditions. Similarly, in administrator preparation, micro techniques are applicable. For example, administrator trainees can be given data relevant to the solution of a single problem. Their total patterns of problem-solving behavior evoked by one stimulus can then be observed for analytic purposes.

Gaming Approach

The business game model, as well as other gaming techniques, are now well established. Reference has already been made to one elementary school game and to the collective-negotiations simulation developed through UCEA. Ohm (see Chapter 6) has advanced useful ideas about the application of gaming techniques to the training of educational administrators. He developed a game rationale for the classification of in-basket items, the construction of gamed situations from such items in the context of a simulated school, and the analysis of responses of trainees as they participate in a gamed, school system simulation training exercise (15). The rationale, to be operational, is dependent upon a saturation approach simulated school system. Extensive background data are needed. The game, as Ohm conceives it, is not dependent upon a computer for information storage although incorporating computer capability into the model is a logical next step.

Gaming requires controlled conditions with most problem-solving behavior options known to the designers of the game. One such game was developed by John Forbes and Darrell Willey at New Mexico State University. Competition is the essential motivational element; a second important element is the availability of feedback to the individual about the results of his decisions.[4] The computer is a particularly effective vehicle for offering immediate and definitive information about how well the play is doing. Bessent (see Chapter 8) focuses on the general function of the computer in simulation.

Non-Materials-Based Approach

At the opposite pole from the "saturationist" school of simulation are those who maintain that you need not have carefully prepared background materials, in-basket items or mechanical simulators to achieve effective simulation. These are the "purists;" that is, they believe you only really simulate when you improvise on the spot the reality necessary for your instructional purposes.

As an example, suppose our purpose was to achieve a first-rate in-service training exercise for a group of professionals in education. Rather than create an exercise for just one group, we would mix the professionals and have principals, psychologists, teachers and assistant principals involved. Since these persons have professional lives which center in schools, we would enlist the group in the immediate task of creating a hypothetical school system. We would record the data which the group considered to be relevant information as far as the performance of the school is concerned. Within a reasonable period of time our small group would have invented their simulated setting. The next step would be to develop simulated problems; these could be produced as was the school. The problems would be drawn from the experience of the participants. With environmental boundaries roughly established and a sense of reality imposed by the school creation process, the business of problem solving would go forward.

Such simulations can serve effectively either for weeks or minutes of instruction. They can be abandoned and replaced; they can be modified or repaired; they can be large-scale or small. They can become intense and intimate. And they are inexpensive.

In the summer of 1965 at the University of Chicago this approach was used for a three-week workshop called "The School as an Operating System." It was as successful as were earlier uses of the Jefferson Township materials in workshops of the same length. My experiences with this technique have tended to modify many of my former views about the instructional uses of simulation. My belief in the need for extensive, carefully prepared simulated materials for training to be effective was sharply altered as were my perspectives on the necesssity of continuity of experience in one simulated setting.

A Non-Material Example: Socio-political Drama

As one devotee of simulation as a training device I see great promise in refining techniques for the efficient use of social, political, even economic dramas. I distinguish these from games although they possess some commonality. Games are more carefully defined with explicit rules, norms and approximations of what winning or losing, success or failure mean. Games, too, sometimes require hardware such as computers. Dramas are less explicit, there are fewer specifications as to role behaviors, and the whole enterprise is deterministic. The parameters are broader, the settings less circumscribed and the numbers of potential dramas almost infinite. Their potential is nearly unlimited.

Kangaroo courts, Girls' and Boys' State, County Government are examples of partial role taking and semi-systematic socio-political simulations. Some participants exhibit rather authentic role playing saturated with affect and having the potential for substantial cognitive development. The seriousness with which young people participate in legislative bodies created as a part of Girls' and/or Boys' State programming is apparent. It is difficult to fault such realism although it defies easy appraisal in either cognitive or affective terms.

To illustrate the flexibility of the concept and the infinite number of dramas available, I have prepared a brief scenario. To pursue a socio-political simulation one needs a director (professor of school administration possibly), persons designated as role takers and some analysts chosen for their capacity to comment on salient events transpiring in the simulation. I could have chosen a scenario that would reflect behavior expected in almost any institutional environment—a hospital, business, military arena, boy scouts, church, mass media, or education. Within education, the sector I have chosen, a similar set of choices is available—a planning event, a cafeteria riot, a school board hassle, a P.T.A. session, a superintendent's selection, a classroom, a boycott. This scenario is not sharply delimited in terms of time—it could, when played out, cover a period of days, months, or even longer. Other scenarios might be more limited—minutes or, at most, hours. Flexibility is available to the socio-political drama director. He may choose to involve a pre-determined number of actors; or he may enlarge the number of persons involved as events unfold. Obviously there are advantages, especially from the standpoint of analysis, in limiting the number and scope of events to be observed. At the same time this may do violence to reality. Those choices depend too on whether the purpose is to present examples of known realities or to produce an entirely unfamiliar set of behaviors in order to test something new.

My example here is multi-purpose: (a) I want to test something new, almost radical; (b) I wish to elicit reactions to substantive ideas from knowledgeable people; and (c) I want to create sufficient affect in the setting to produce both cognitive and affective responses to events for which everyone present has a responsibility.

The scenario is designed for use experimentally with a discussion group interested in community control of education. The directions to the discussion group members, all of whom are to play roles either as "committee members" or analysts, are as follows:

> Rather than proceed in our conventional manner on Wednesday we will go into a modest simulation exercise. Our purpose will be to prepare and examine alternatives to contemporary educational systems. The proposals will be those we generate. And we will indeed have the opportunity to experience "community control" of education.
>
> The memorandum which follows will serve as the introduction to our work on Wednesday. Each of us is invited to be a newly appointed member of the Local Community Education Reconstitution Committee. Those who wish will choose a role at the start of the session from the list of potential roles below. (You might think in advance which role you prefer, but some arbitrary selections may be necessary.) On Wednesday there will be name cards around the table which will help others identify you.

This approach will allow us to approximate a reality (a group of laymen with a tough job), to be creative within those constraints, and to appraise this technique for generating ideas.

The Committee

P.T.A. Officer	Welfare Services Administrator
Community Organizer	City School Board Member
Junior College President	Teacher
Black Militant	Professor of Education
Industrialist	Chairman, Board of Directors,
NAACP	County Hospital
League of Women Voters	Humanities Professor, City College
City Students Association	Parent (female)
Urban League	Public School Principal
Mayor's Assistant	Department Store Executive
Parent (male)	Diocesan Superintendent
Labor Leader	Museum Director

Obviously each person on a Committee such as this would represent a number of interests. The designation of roles here reflects prominent community interest sectors. Certainly not all community perspectives are reflected in these roles but they are conspicuous and might reflect the thinking of a mayor who would be trying to put together a heterogeneous group. As a role player your task is to represent the visible characteristics of the role assignment but not be totally constrained by it.

The memorandum is to be distributed in advance. Members will select roles which they wish to play when the discussion group assembles. Oral instructions, essentially restatements of the directions in the memorandum, will precede the actual convening of the Committee. The background-setting memo appears below:

Memorandum

To: The Local Community Education Reconstitution Committee

From: Temporary Chairman (Assistant to the Mayor)

Re: Background statement for Wednesday's meeting at 1:30 p.m.

On Wednesday we will assemble for an extraordinary purpose. We are to begin the task of remaking educational services for our community, our part of the city.

We need not harangue over the educational deficiencies that have been noted by so many authorities, and nonauthorities for that matter. We should avoid going over old terrain, old arguments. Our task is clear-cut. We have accepted appointment by the Mayor of this City, under legislative authorization, to design a new pattern, system or way of delivering educational services to the people of our community.

Obviously this is a frightening assignment. It is even more onerous since we know that our existing educational systems, public and private, will be abandoned in less than four years. We have approximately forty-two months to do our job and Wednesday is day one. We are in the countdown period and all systems are go.

We must do planning and implementation. We must have recommendations prepared. We must be ready to abandon all existing institutions in less than four years. We must decide the educational futures for generations. And we do not have the alternative of saying the decision to abandon what we have is bad. There is no retreat—we must produce a totally new educational delivery system.

A word about this committee. The Mayor has asked me to serve as temporary chairman. My task is to help set the stage and direct our preliminary discussions Wednesday afternoon. After that we will need to structure ourselves in whatever ways we decide, to enable us to complete this unparalleled assignment. We are all aware of the heated discussions that brought our State legislature to the decision it has just reached. So we are not starting from scratch. Some of us were active in the campaign to abolish our present school system. We have $100,000 per year available to us to aid in our planning. We may need more—if so, we are to let the Mayor know.

Wednesday is "big think" day. As you will note from the membership on this committee many segments of our community are represented. Some of us have worked on educational matters before; some of us would be classed as reformers; some of us have positions of leadership in our present system; and some of us are strangers to such discussions. Our session on Wednesday will allow us to become better acquainted and hopefully to set fresh thought processes in motion. We will not establish our planning structures on Wednesday— that will come later.

As the Governor, Mayor, legislative leaders, and their advisors have thought about this responsibility, they believe discussion should start with four questions:

(1) Who will teach?
(2) Will there be "schools"?
(3) If there are schools, who will operate them?
(4) How will "learning" be financed?

In time each of us will have to deal in great depth with all four—and more. But Wednesday let's deal generally with each of these.

A reminder about some other details. We are to design educational services for our part of the city only. Currently there are about thirty thousand persons living in our community. After considerable consultation with city leaders, the Mayor has chosen our sector of the city as the arena for experimentation. If we can be successful, our ideas will be used as the basis for city-wide educational reform.

I hardly need emphasize the seriousness of LCERC's assignment. As you will remember, the legislature stipulated that LCERC members would receive a token stipend of $1,000 per year (plus expenses). Arrangements are now being made for payroll and other fiscal matters.

The above scenario, which I have used in slightly altered form with two groups (in single two-hour sessions) has produced interesting results. As in most simulations, considerable interest was aroused. Role identifications were easily achieved. The extreme heterogeneity of the interests reflected in the roles caused the "Committee" to flounder initially. Both groups had difficulty in accommodating to what was an exaggerated example of pluralism. Participants were astounded by the difficulties they came to perceive as inherent in achieving substantial reform in one of society's prominent institutions.

THE SENSITIVITY THRUST

During the past decade *sensitivity training* has blossomed in many educational arenas (2). It has produced cultist overtones, rightly or wrongly, which have tended to raise enough eyebrows about its usefulness that its original momentum has been moderately reduced. Nevertheless it is still very big on the American scene, gathering new advocates to its bosom daily, and likely to be around in some form from now on.

In its finer moments the movement has been credited with allowing persons to see themselves as others view them, strengthening self-concepts, leading persons to discover enough about themselves so that they come to possess greater self-confidence.[5] Less attractively for many, sensitivity training has been credited with destroying people, contributing negatively to persons' "effectiveness" and often exhibiting blatantly the evils of charlatanism and chicanery. Probably both views are partially right.

In the beginning the founding fathers of the movement were in charge. Later there were many managing sensitivity enterprises who seemed to have little or no knowledge base to support their activities. They appeared to feed on human frailty. They extended feelings of guilt, inadequacy, self-doubt. They promised new capacities and brighter personalities acceptable to their owners as well as others. They languished in the shadows of love, affection, absolution. At its best (or worst) participants absented themselves from reality, set aside most inhibitions, and searched for love and respect—qualities that were apparently absent in their lives.

Sensitivity trainees did what to the uninitiated appeared to be extraordinary things. They cried, groveled in corners and under tables, withdrew. They learned to enjoy other persons in sensual ways. The orgy label, exaggerated most often, was sometimes applied to such activities. Nudity, sex and drugs quickly were linked, at least in the minds of doubters, with sensitivity and/or encounter sessions.

Negative reports may have tended to tarnish the positive image that genuine sensitivity training seemed to have earned. In the minds of many, persons who participated in the first place were weak, probably a bit sick: "Strong, well-adjusted persons would not allow themselves to be associated with such affairs." A contrary view was that everyone could benefit from enlarged self-insight and improved understanding of human behavior.

How does sensitivity training compare with simulation? In some ways the objectives of the two techniques seem to be similar. Those who recite the virtures of each may sound much alike—better people, more empathic, self-confident, insightful about themselves and others. The principal variation appears to be the extent to which simulation builds on cognitive growth and improvement whereas sensitivity training settles more affirmatively upon affect—attitudes, feelings, emotions. Sensitivists bear down hard on the person. Simulationists acknowledge the significance of the person, but use broader bases of analysis, hoping that learnings extend far beyond self-insight. Developing understandings of social and political phenomena are at least, if not more, important to the simulationist, i.e., knowing the significance of group- and society-wide events vis-a-vis the individual.

Persons who develop socio-political exercises are themselves more politically and organizationally oriented. They see simulation as a vehicle for analyzing social, political and organizational roles. They obviously do not ignore the idiographic domain but seldom do they allow prolonged focus on one person's problems, whatever they may be. In actual experience with simulation, especially where role playing is employed, the elimination of extended attention on the strengths and weaknesses of individuals is not easily avoided. At the same time however, skillful social and political simulation leaders try to by-pass intensive attention to one participant's deficiencies. This is prompted by the obvious dangers of intense examination of personal matters when those in charge may be incapable of dealing with extreme problems requiring psychological or psychiatric treatment.

The power of simulated situations is severe. The boundaries of human feeling and emotion are not easily detected nor predicted. When the human is stimulated in unusual ways his capacity for self-control may be affected. It is criminal to release feelings of weakness or inadequacy unless there are persons present who can restore confidence, repair damage, or, more importantly, lead a person to an improved state of affairs.

Few professors of educational administration are professionally trained sensitivists. A number have attended programs sponsored by such agencies as the National Training Laboratory and as a consequence have had some experience as participants in T-Group exercises (a form of sensitivity training). But short (usually three-week) sessions are hardly sufficient to produce training experts. Those who have participated in NTL sessions, for example, must subdue the temptation to play the expert role. In arenas where the parameters of expertness are ill-defined it is easy for persons to delude themselves into thinking they possess capacities which they do not actually have.

There is danger too in exaggerating the negative features of sensitivity programs. Thus I would opt for studied attention to the contribution that sensitivity training can make in support of what I believe to be a broader, more flexible tool, i.e., simulation.

ISSUES

There are issues in the use of simulation which arise as the concept is considered in administrator preparation. Some relate to the incorporation of simulated approaches into pre-service preparation programs; others are identified with the impact of simulated experiences on the individual. I will focus essentially on the latter.

The Purpose Issue

Considerable emphasis has been placed on the importance of clarifying purposes in the use of simulation. Morris Weinberger found that professors using UCEA materials were trying hard to specify the objectives to which they were addressing their simulated exercises (20). Weinberger credited several UCEA-sponsored new instructional methods institutes for professors with hammering home the crucial responsibility of purpose defining. In polling more than eighty professors he discovered that both general and specific purposes were being articulated. The most frequently cited general purpose was *conceptual learning in a real setting;* the most frequently cited specific purpose was *decision making.* Obviously conceptual learning and decision making are global notions and require further operational specification if they are to serve usefully as instructional purposes. Examination of the actual purposes listed in Weinberger's categories reveals considerable overlap and little or no genuine differentiation between the two classes of responses.

If simulation is to be used in training it behooves professors to begin to specify in some detail the particular behavioral changes they hope to achieve. They need also to become more sophisticated in their diagnosis of trainee qualities so that they can particularize the training experiences in keeping with that assessment. Simulation has potential for strengthening cognitive skills; it likewise has possibilities for effecting changes in trainees' attitude and value structures. Furthermore, simulation can be used as a vehicle for practicing leadership skills such as diagnosing organizational problems, refining communication skills, and acquiring group-process capabilities. The point is simple and obvious: we must focus more directly on purposes and the shaping of simulations in keeping with such objectives.

The Evaluation Issue

From the beginning of my experience with simulation as a training device I have been concerned about the problems of evaluation. We must find ways of adding up the impact of these methods on those who are exposed to them. UCEA, or any member institution, might usefully sponsor a major research effort of this type. Weinberger's study offered some suggested starting points. William Fern, at the University of Chicago, examined changes in participants' problem-perception and problem-solving adequacy in a 1960 workshop. Little change was noted over the three-week period. He found that there was no relationship between perceptions of problem priority (a need for either speed or importance) and number of problems handled; likewise, apparently neither of these was related to adequacy of problem solutions (10). Fern encountered difficult problems in defining the variables he wished to examine, and in developing adequate instruments to measure changes in behavior, as well as in treating data from the small sample which a single workshop provided. James W. Anderson, at the University of Minnesota, studied the effect of simulated experiences on leadership behavior of elementary school administrators. Anderson, like Fern, focused on principals attending workshops where the UCEA Whitman School materials were used. He concluded that little change could be detected in the behavior of the participants, acknowledged the brevity of the exposure as a limiting factor, and urged more attention be given to materials development and appraisal (1).

The evaluation issue has been recognized elsewhere. At the University of Wisconsin, Cohen reported severe misgivings about political gaming in undergraduate classes in political science. He questioned the investment of time and energy in the further expansion of the technique based on the Wisconsin experiments and the results of similar trials at other institutions. His chief discomfort was with the cumbersome, inefficient nature of political gaming as an instructional method when little or no learning advantages accrued (6). Much more optimistic appraisals come from Johns Hopkins. Boocock has noted attractive gains in factual learning (especially from career games) as well as shifts in attitudes. Altered feelings about political efficacy have occurred as a consequence of participation in legislative games (3). Clearly, more attention to appraisal is warranted.

The Behavioral Science Issue

Simulation permits the careful scrutiny of behavior. It provides a standard set of events and a standard situation. Patterns of behavior that emerge when a series of persons have responded to similar stimuli reflect individual differences. If such opportunity is to be capitalized upon, it requires a range of expert observers or extensive expertness within a single observer. This is especially true when the saturation approach is used, in contrast to a micro simulation where both the purposes and the necessary range of training staff expertness are narrower.

Use of the UCEA-distributed materials (Madison Township, for example) permits the application of political, social, economic and psychological concepts in the analysis of problems. Behavioral scientists could theoretically, at least, make a contribution to the training exercise. Several institutions have involved one or more such persons as staff members and with apparent success. However, we need to learn much more about how such resource people can best be involved, keeping in mind the efficient use of scarce talent, timing, purposes, and the like. Above all, we need to keep in mind that many social science concepts are not easily assimilated by trainees and that considerable attention needs to be given to this problem.

The problem is somewhat different when simulation is used as a pre-service technique rather than employed in in-service programs. Greater understanding of social science concepts can be expected from pre-service use because participants should bring to the simulated exercise a richer background of recent reading and discussion of such ideas. Students who have spent a semester in the study of complex organizations should recognize and understand such notions as role conflict, role-personality conflict, incentive systems, goal displacement, and communication barriers more readily than experienced persons confronted for the first time with these ideas.

We should continue to experiment with several instructional formats in which variations in staffing, composition of training groups, position in the preparation sequence, and behavioral science concepts are tried.

The Team Issue

"Team" training through simulation has been attempted at the University of Chicago. As reported earlier, new simulation techniques were tried in the summer of 1965 with the simultaneous training of representatives of several professional groups. More recently aspects of simulation were used with an entire school staff including non-professional personnel. The 1965 workshop was called "The School as an Operating System." Features of an operating, though simulated, system were created with many professional roles represented. Thus the workshop staff was able to generate genuine interaction among professionals with their own discrete role-identities functioning as they do in real situations. All of the barriers of real-life situations were present: role tensions, value conflicts, communication difficulties and informal power relationships that operate in school systems everywhere.

Gagne sees simulation as a powerful technique for developing operational doctrine. By "operational doctrine" he means understanding and acquisition of the behavioral norms appropriate to the enterprise (11). He cites the training of air defense system crews as an example. In those instances teams were involved in simulated exercises which, when observed, indicated that team members were needlessly setting limits to system effectiveness all along the way. Through group critiques following each simulated exercise the team was able to discover and to put into effect procedures which made possible an increasing effectiveness of the operation what Gagne has described was what the University of Chicago staff experienced when they simulated an entire system on the spot and populated the system with representatives of several role groups.

The issue is whether or not team training or the incorporation of several professional roles into a single simulation is too complex to deal with appropriately. In my judgment it is not, but widespread experimentation is again called for before we settle prematurely on an issue position.

The Realism Issue

Realism has been discussed extensively since the first trials with the Jefferson Township materials began several years ago. Launor Carter believes that the realism issue is related to the specific purposes to be achieved (4). If the focus of training is on general principles and these principles are thought to apply to many situations, then no great degree of exactness is required. On the other hand, if precision in behavior is expected in terms of detailed features of the simulated environment, considerable attention to realism is warranted. Astronaut simulations require painstaking attention to realism, whereas simulation of international relations problems may call for less detailed data and more general background.

My position is that there is no shortage of realism; it is everywhere. We also have the capability for packaging it; we have already made superb use of in-baskets, problems taped and filmed, telephone stimuli, and background data, all of which are genuine. The basic question of realism arises in relation to the contexts we invent for the presentation of the stimuli to trainees and the naturalness of the responses we hope to evoke. Drawing on the astronaut example again, space flight can be simulated to such perfection that almost all features of real flight are anticipated and incorporated in the simulation. The behaviors of astronauts in simulation exercises can be evaluated and performance fed back to them with such precision that the trainees can adjust subsequent behaviors. The large scale simulations in educational administration are not yet as real as those used by the space flight trainers. But that is not to say that they cannot become much more real than they now are—if we want them to be.

The designers of the urban simulation project sponsored by UCEA (headed by Troy McKelvey of the State University of New York at Buffalo) are wrestling with the realism issue. The program is ambitious, involving several phases, a number of professors in universities across the nation, and an output of materials unparalleled to date (18).

SUMMARY

My personal view of simulation is that it is the most promising, currently available, single innovation in administrator preparation. Much, indeed most, of its potential remains to be activated; we have only begun to invent appropriate means for its usage. Our beginnings have been instructive: we have some experience; we have become sensitive to some of the training issues; we are exploring some "hardware" adaptations; we are creating new techniques for incorporating aspects of simulation into many aspects of professional education, including administrator preparation.

The University Council for Educational Administration has been the single most important force in extending the utilization of simulated materials in the preparation of administrators. It has also supported the strengthening of new conceptualizations of the role, purpose and function of simulation as a vehicle for training. The UCEA urban school simulation program of the late 1960s involved a large number of professors of educational administration as well as practitioners in its development. New approaches to materials development, as well as their use in preparation, were produced. But much more needs to be done.

We need to invest considerable time and resources in many areas, several of which have been pointed out, or at least implied, in this chapter. Special attention should be given to appraising the impact of simulated experiences on persons in training; the considerable research opportunity which accompanies the use of these devices ought not be ignored; increased attention to creative new approaches to simulation is warranted; and our experience with simulation should be shared more effectively (among those interested in professional education as well as in skill training) in the future than has been true in the past.

The preparers of educational administrators are a conservative lot. We tend to think small thoughts in large quantities; we disseminate weak ideas with abandon; we hesitate in the face of exciting opportunity. Most programs to prepare administrators are much like they were two or three decades ago. They have been adorned with a little social science cheesecake here, a little simulated experience tinsel there. But fundamentally they are the same. In the meantime others have learned how to prepare people to transplant human organs, explore the moon, investigate the prospects of living under the ocean, lead Vietnamization teams in foreign cultures, and de-fuse violence-prone populations. Our schools cry out for vigorous new leadership. The several types of simulation available to us provide the most promising tool now known to meet that challenge.

NOTES

[1] The *UCEA Annual Report,* UCEA, 29 West Woodruff Ave., Columbus, Ohio 43210, 1966. For a comprehensive overview of a range of materials, see John J. Horvat, *An Index of Media for Use in Instruction in Educational Administration* (Columbus, Ohio: UCEA, 1965).

[2] The evaluation of the program at Los Angeles State can be obtained from either John Neiderhauser or Harold Hall, Department of Educational Administration, Los Angeles State College, Los Angeles, California.

[3] Information about the Indiana project can be secured from Dr. Arthur Rice, Coordinator, INSITE, School of Education, Indiana University, Bloomington, Indiana.

[4] This game is discussed briefly in Michael P. Thomas, Jr., *Strategies in the Preparation of School Administrators.* Copies are available through Kenneth St. Clair, Secretary, NCPEA, College of Education, Oklahoma State University, Stillwater, Oklahoma.

[5] Titles in the catalogs of such institutions as the Esalen Institute illustrate the feeling, affective, sensual, and humanistic emphases that surround sensitivity and/or encounter exercises there. "Movement and Massage," "Creative Psychotic, Ecstatic and Meditative States," "Education in the 'Affective Domain'," "The Quest for Love," "Personal Growth, Awareness and Emotional Education," "Intimacy: Encounter for Couples," "Eclectic Encounter," and "A Weekend of Psychodrama" are titles listed in *Winter Programs,* Esalen Institute, IX, no. 1, Winter-Spring 1970.

BIBLIOGRAPHY

1. Anderson, James W. "The Effect of Simulated Experiences on the Leadership Behavior of Elementary School Administration." Ph.D. dissertation, University of Minnesota, 1967.

2. Birnbaum, Max. "Sense About Sensitivity Training." *Saturday Review,* November 15,1969, p. 82.

3. Boocock, Sarane & Schild, E.O., eds. *Simulation Games in Learning.* Beverly Hills, California: Sage Publications, Inc., 1968.

4. Carter, Launor F. "Exercising the Executive Decision-Making Function in Large Systems." In Robert Glaser, ed., *Training Research and Education.* New York: John Wiley & Sons, Inc., 1962, pp. 107-13.

5. Clarke, Arthur C. *2001 A Space Odyssey.* New York: The New American Library, A Signet Book, 1968.

6. Cohen, Bernard C. "Political Gaming in the Classroom." *The Journal of Politics* XXIV, 2 (May 1962), 367-81.

7. Cory, Christopher. "Kids with the Problems of Kings." *Life* XLI: 28-31 (September 30, 1966).

8. Cruickshank, Donald R. "Simulation: New Direction in Teacher Preparation." *Phi Delta Kappan* XLVIII: 23-4 (September 1966).

9. Culbertson, Jack, ed. *Simulation in Administrative Training.* Columbus, Ohio: University Council for Educational Administration, May 1960.

10. Fern, William H. "Aspects of Problem Perception and Problem Solving in Educational Administration." Ph.D. Dissertation, University of Chicago, 1961.

11. Gagne, Robert M. "Simulators." In Robert Glaser, ed., *Training Research and Education.* New York: John Wiley & Sons, Inc., 1962, pp. 223-46.

12. Guetzkow, Harold. "A Use of Simulation in the Study of Inter-Nation Relations." *Behavioral Science* 4 (1959):183-91.

13. Hemphill, John K.; Griffiths, Daniel E.; and Fredericksen, Norman. *Administrative Performance and Personality.* New York: Bureau of Publications, Teachers College, Columbia University, 1962.

14. Link, Edwin A. "Simulation: The Serious Business of Make-Believe." *Airworld* I:29 (September 1966).

15. Ohm, Robert E. "A Game Model Analysis of Conflicts of Interest Situations in Administration." Mimeographed. College of Education, University of Oklahoma, June 1966.

16. Robinson, James A. "Simulation and Games." In Peter H. Rossi & Bruce Biddle, eds., *The New Media and Education.* Garden City, New York: Doubleday & Company, Inc., Anchor Books, 1966, p. 95.

17. Ryan, Doris. "The Raymond School Workshop." Mimeographed. The Midwest Administration Center, University of Chicago, 1967.

18. University Council for Educational Administration. *UCEA Newsletter* XI, no. 1 (October 1969), p. 3.

19. Utsey, Jordan; Wallen, Carl; and Beldin, H.O. "Simulation A Break-through in the Education of Reading Teachers." *Phi Delta Kappan* XLVII:572-74 (June 1966).

20. Weinberger, Morris J. "The Use of Simulation in the Teaching of School Administration." Doctor of Education project, Teachers College, Columbia University, 1965, pp. 81-84.

2

The Use of Cases

Glenn L. Immegart

The use of cases in educational administration typically refers to the case method of instruction or the use of case studies in the teaching of educational administration. Although case study has a multifaceted potential for any field of professional practice, such as for instruction in preparatory and in-service training programs, research, or clinical activity, the basic and most extensive use of the case in the field of educational administration has been instructional.[1]

The case method of instruction is now well into its second decade of widespread use in the training of educational administrators. Although the antecedents for the use of cases in educational administration can be traced back even further to Donham's use of cases in the Harvard School of Business, or to Benz's use of cases in preparation courses for school administrators (7), the real impetus for the general use of cases in educational administrator training followed the 1955 publication of the first case book in this field of specialization (19). Since that time, we have witnessed not only mounting use of cases but also increasingly sophisticated and refined applications of the case method of instruction. Accordingly, Griffiths observed in 1963 that the case method was "more firmly entrenched in educational administration than it has ever been in the past" and that one can only look for "wider use in the future" (7. p. 81).

A case or a case study is, most simply, *a carefully recorded account or narrative of something that actually happened.* It is a "piece of reality" and represents an intensive examination of the characteristics, elements, and dynamics of a "unit"—a person, a work group, an organization, a community, or a culture over a period of time.

Cases are developed for a number of reasons and may therefore take a variety of forms. This is precisely the multifaceted potential that case study has for any field of professional practice. For example, *research cases* are empirical investigations and contribute to the substantive knowledge in a specialized field. As such, they provide data that can be used for description and prediction, and as a base for generalization and the generation of questions and hypotheses for further study. The *clinical case,* a second form of case study, is an analytic vehicle developed for working with a social unit whether it be an individual, a group, or an organization. Serving primarily diagnostic purposes, the clinical case provides the basis either for treatment and/or counselling when working with an individual, or for analysis, development, and/or design when applied to a group or organization. *Instructional cases,* the form of case study we are concerned with here, are developed to serve as teaching tools or vehicles for instructional situations. Use of the instructional case enables students or trainees to grapple with a selected "chunk of reality" until its learning potential for them is exhausted.

In this vein, the instructional case has been clearly defined by Lawrence as follows (15):

> A good case is the vehicle by which a chunk of reality is brought into the classroom to be worked over by the class and the instructor. A good case keeps the class discussion grounded upon some of the stubborn facts that must be faced up to in real life situations . . . it is the record of complex situations that must be literally pulled apart and put together again before the situations can be understood.

Instructional case materials themselves may also take a variety of forms. They may be short or long, open-ended or complete units, behavioral vignettes about individuals or comprehensive narratives of human interaction in complex organizations, or even precipitative or terminal incidents. They may be conveyed through written, audial, or filmed media or any combination of these. In any event, the instructional case is "some kind of written or recorded account of a *real situation* (19, p. 23). As such, it is not reality, but rather a faithful and accurate representation of reality; cases are not fictitious; they are, perforce, grounded in fact.

Bridges has identified and described three generic types of instructional cases—the *issue case,* the *descriptive case,* and the *substantive case* (2). According to this categorization scheme, the issue case involves the open-ended presentation of a problem situation. It is essentially a dilemma case in that problem resolution is not presented. Students or trainees may analyze the facts and dynamics in the case and then project and develop problem solutions. The descriptive case, more of a complete narrative, presents an entire behavioral situation. It includes antecedents, a comprehensive account of the event, and the outcome. This type of case provides a vehicle for situational analysis and the application of concepts and theory to practical situations. The substantive case is primarily a research device and is more extensive than most instructional cases. It is basically an analytic form that goes beyond mere reporting to rigorous and systematic analysis, and an attempt to advance understanding about an aspect, or area, of practice. In such a case, behavioral science concepts typically serve as organizing themes or deductive frameworks.

Similarly, Culbertson, Jacobson, & Reller have noted five general types of cases—the *historical case,* the *problem case,* the *thematic case,* the *process case,* and the *cause and effect case* (5). Thus, according to this classification system, instructional cases are developed to illuminate the temporal sequence of events (the historical case), specific problems or dilemma situations in a field of practice (the problem case), dimensions of behavior such as deviant behavior in organizations (the thematic case), the dynamics of, for example, decision making or building morale in an organization (the process case), or the antecedent events that precipitate a given consequence (the cause and effect case). Also, according to the above authors, any combination of these perspectives yields an additional hybrid type of case.

In addition to the various possible types of instructional cases identified above, case materials vary greatly in length. From the short sketches found in Campbell, Corbally, & Ramseyer's introductory text in educational administration (3) to Goffman's book, *Asylums* (6), cases may range from one or several paragraphs in length to full book length. In between these extremes are the short cases found in Hamburg's and Griffiths' casebooks (8, 10), the moderate or chapter-length cases in the Sargent & Belisle or the Culbertson, Jacobson & Reller casebooks (19, 5), and the longer cases such as the dissertations done at the University of Oregon or Goldhammer and Farner's *The Jackson County Story*.[2] Obviously, the time span and complexity of a situation dictate to some degree the ultimate length of a case. But, in any event, an effective instructional case may vary in length from a single paragraph to a full-sized book.

Instructional cases are presented through a variety of media or communication formats. Most common of all is the written case study. In fact, in the field of educational administration, virtually all of the presently available case materials are in the written format. However, through the efforts of the University Council for Educational Administration, both filmed and tape-recorded cases have been produced. Obviously, the costs involved in producing and purchasing taped and filmed cases is such that, in a profession lacking adequate or abundant financial resources for the development of optimal instructional devices, efforts in this direction are often thwarted. But, as cogently noted by Griffiths (7, p. 87) and attested by case users, filmed and tape-recorded cases have a greater emotional impact than do written ones.

Cases may also take the form of the incident technique as developed by Pigors (15) in the field of business administration. In the case incident approach, students are given a precipitating event and are required to solicit from the instructor, who functions as a repository of knowledge, relevant facts and data about the event. The case is, therefore, the product of student search, a dynamic process of seeking and unearthing relevant data. As yet, no such materials employing situations from the field of educational administration are commercially available. However, some instructors do use a number of the Pigors' materials, and undoubtedly others have developed their own case incidents.

Lastly, case presentation can involve a multi-media approach. For example, the filmed case, "The Conference" (17), is an abbreviated version of a written case by the same title from the Sargent and Belisle case book (19, pp. 189-202). Some instructors use this film for an initial discussion and then have students read the written case as a basis for further in-depth discussion. Others use the film somewhat as a case incident in the Pigors' tradition by encouraging students to elicit additional facts from the instructor after viewing the film. These instructors draw upon the more comprehensive data provided in the written case in a case-incident fashion. In another similar approach, instructors use written cases and supplement that data with tape recordings (such as a taped board of education meeting) or with additional data drawn from their experience in investigating the case. Unfortunately, many of these alternate presentation approaches and multi-media variations are not generally available and thus do not have widespread application. They do, however, offer a real potential for increasing both the usability and impact of case materials. Only the ingenuity and creativity of the instructor limit his ability to modify and devise unique approaches to the presentation of case materials in the classroom setting.

AN HISTORICAL VIEW OF THE CASE METHOD
IN EDUCATIONAL ADMINISTRATION

Historically, the use of cases in the instruction of educational administration evolved as do many instructional innovations. Resulting from a disenchantment and dissatisfaction with existing methods of teaching and the persistent push by instructors and students to make instruction relevant, the case offered an excellent vehicle for alleviating some of the problems of the early teaching of education administration. As this developing profession began to take form in the 1930s and 1940s, the lack of substance or content, and the lack of reality in training, were apparent to instructors and students alike. Already the case method of instruction had demonstrated its potential for teaching those entering such fields as medicine and law, and Donham's use of cases in training business executives in human relations was having a pervasive effect (7, pp. 81-82). In all instances, the case method was being demonstrated in a number of fields as a viable instructional approach for injecting more reality and practicality into the classroom. And, in these fields, the case was proving to be both a source of content and an excellent device for applying substantive content and knowledge to practical situations.

Since, the majority of instructors at this time in educational administration were former school administrators and, therefore, much of their instructional strategy was to inform the neophytes in the field of "what they had done," moving to the use of cases did not represent a drastic departure from the caselike "pearls" of "how they did it when they were administrators." In fact, for those with few effective, exemplary practices and those whose "how to do it" was either not well received or totally without relevance, the case study provided a real and practical vehicle with great potential for use in classroom work with administrators-in-training.

Thus, it was natural that some instructors in education administration who were seeking to have a greater impact, or who were disenchanted with the results of their classroom efforts, began to turn to cases and to the case approach to instruction. Here was a way to bring the real world of administration into their classrooms, to keep instruction practical, and to help students apply substantive knowledge, or experience, to the problems and situations that typically confront the administrator. To expand the historical perspective on the case method in educational administration we can now examine in greater detail three rather distinct periods: (a) the period of inception and early use, (b) the period of the case method's "coming of age," and (c) the period toward more refined applications.[3]

Inception and Early Use

Following Donham's use of cases with business executives and his later move (after World War II) into the field of human relations in general education, along with Burris' and Benz's early use of cases in education, the pre-1950 era of the case method represents a period when the approach was tested by a relatively small number of interested instructors. Although the movement spread from coast to coast and early adherents were energetic and enthusiastic, they were few in number. Also, at this time, there were few opportunities for professional dialogue in the emerging profession of educational administration. No real mechanism was available for disseminating innovative instructional materials or approaches, and the preparation of administrators was undertaken by one or two professors of education rather than a full-fledged department of educational administration in most universities. Instructors, therefore, were introduced to the case method of teaching largely by chance and, to the extent it was appealing and useful to them, they adopted it in their work. Hard historical data in this regard is scarce, and there is little evidence of any concerted push for the use of cases at this time; rather, efforts were sporadic and isolated. Dissemination and adoption of this new approach was based upon existing collegial relationships or passed along from teacher to student.

In this period the case was typically used to assist the administrator-to-be with decision making. Students were confronted with cases, asked to think about and analyze them, and required to arrive at solutions which they would defend in class discussions. At first, little attempt was made to draw upon literature to illuminate the dynamics of the case situations under scrutiny. Instead, discussions and analysis of alternatives and solutions were, for all purposes, limited to the logic of deductive rationality or personal experience. And, since the permissive approach of the early tradition of case instruction gave students virtually full reign in case expolrations (typically the instructor was content at most to ask leading questions, or at least merely to open the discussion), the effect of the case method was obviously bounded by student ability, insight, and experience.

It soon became apparent, however, that the potential of this instructional methodology extended beyond merely improving students' abilities in decision making. Skill in problem and situational analysis was fostered; the range of decision or solution alternatives for a given problem was revealed; the value of group discussion and the evaluation of administrative problems was witnessed; and, increasingly as the inter-disciplinary spirit pervaded instruction, the substantive knowledge from the emerging field of administration and from other social science fields was brought to bear upon the cases under scrutiny. Even though there was little help available for the early case instructor, he intuitively began evolving and refining a useful approach to instruction.

The Case Comes of Age

During the period from the early 1950s through the early 1960s the case method of instruction in educational administration saw its greatest expansion and took its place along with other instructional procedures, such as reading, lecture, and discussion, as a useful approach for training future administrators. Most significant at the outset of this period was the publication of Sargent & Belisle's case book in the Harvard case tradition (19). This and other casebooks published in educational administration in the middle 1950s made, for the first time, a cadre of cases readily available to the profession at large. Also, the writers of these casebooks included in their texts a number of suggestions and guides for those inexperienced in the use of cases. Generally included in the books were the following: a description of the case method and its value, a statement of purposes that could be achieved through the case approach, illustrations of "typical" case discussions, and suggestions for injecting substantive knowledge relevant to educational administration into the classroom setting through the use of the case method.

As the stockpile of administrative cases in education grew and cases were classified to facilitate their use (19, p. 48; 5, p. 50), it was generally recognized that the case approach could be used for many purposes beyond improving administistative decision making and problem analysis. The case was seen increasingly as a device that enabled instructors and students to use the literature and knowledge from the social and behavioral sciences to illuminate the dynamics both of administration and of social organization, the context for administration. Also, cases were seen as vehicles for probing relationships within and between groups. Further, even the research value of the case was seen as attested by the University of Oregon doctoral investigations in educational administration which were, in effect, case studies. The case as a pool of data for empirical analysis in the instructional setting was acknowledged along with the inductive potential of a case or group of cases as data for use in drawing conclusions and in generalization within the classroom.

In this period, as the value of the case for the instructional situation was extended and as the relevant knowledge (theory and research) about educational administration was expanded, instructors' strategy shifted increasingly to more structured approaches. Cases were chosen and used for explicit purposes and with more precise instructional payoffs. Instructors became more prominent in case discussions, actively taking the lead in the dissection of a case or in determining the focus and/or structure of the analysis of a case. This is not to imply that the unstructured or student-centered case approach was abandoned. Actually, some instructors continued in this way while others moved to more structured approaches or utilized whatever approach (structured or unstructured) best fit their particular objectives at a given time.

During this period, the case method indeed became a widely accepted and effective instructional approach for training school administrators. Cases were being written for local and general consumption, and instructional methodology was being expanded and improved. It was during this time that the University Council for Educational Administration (through its institutes on "new methods and materials for preparing administrators") actively sought to help professors with the instructional applications of cases, began its own written case series, and, in numerous other ways, spurred along the growing case method momentum.

Toward More Refined Applications

Since the early 1960s and the general acceptance of the case method as a useful approach to administrator training, we have experienced a period of moving toward, or generating, more refined applications of the method. Cases are used not only for more numerous and more precise objectives but also in increasingly effective ways. In regard to the former, cases now form the heart of entire workshops, courses, and programs of preparation, whether these be directed toward practical or con-ceptual learnings. Regarding the latter, we are beginning to see the evolution of filmed and taped cases (which have even greater intrinsic appeal) as well as a number of other variations on the *instructional case* approach. For example, there are cases and case sequels (13, 14), structured role-play situations that are in reality open-ended, dynamic cases,[4] adjunct case analyses and commen-tary by social scientists incorporated in or appended to case studies (1), and an array of simulated (expanded) case materials for various educational administrator positions.[5] More than ever before, case users are testing and experimenting with newer and more effective strategies and applications of the case method.

In a capsule, we are well into an era of case use in educational administration that is highly individualized, relevant, and stimu-lating; an era in which instructors are creatively extending and refining a beneficial instructional approach.

USING CASES

Although any treatment of the historical development of the case method in educational administration touches on the instruc-tional use of cases, it is necessary to be more explicit about the instructional applications of the case approach. We can now turn directly to the purposes and objectives of case instruction, criteria for selecting an instructional case, and to an examination of where cases are applicable in administrator preparation.

Purposes of the Case Method

Many of the purposes or objectives of case teaching have already been mentioned. Obviously it is a means for bringing reality into the classroom and for making classroom activities relevant for a of practice. Also, it is a procedure for developing and extending within the administrator such analysis and other practice-relevant skills as decision making and grappling with problems in the group context. Finally, it has been suggested that through the analysis of cases, the substantive aspects of a field of practice, along with substantive content from the social and behavioral sciences, can be utilized to illuminate and make more understandable the full array of phenomena and situations with which the administrator must work. In sum, it is a methodlogy for making instruction about administration relevant, practical, and enlightening.

We can, however, be more specific about instructional purposes. In an earlier document on the development of cases in educational administration (12), this writer identified five primary instructional purposes relative to the case method. In this sense, the case can be viewed as a means to each of the following ends:

1. To illuminate social or behavioral science concepts (the concept case)
2. To develop and practice decision making or problem resolution skills (the dilemma case)
3. To analyze and assess relationships between persons, groups, or variables in behavioral situations (the relationship case)
4. To discuss, dissect, or analyze a unit of human behavior or interactions (the event case)
5. To gain skill in seeking information and gathering data from a precipitating incident about a typical administrative problem (the incident case)

These purposes, originally conceived to facilitate the development and classification of cases, illustrate well the range of objectives that can be pursued through case approaches to instruction.

Even more specifically, we can set forth some typical and more operational instructional objectives that can be realized through the case method. In so doing it should be noted that such objectives can be developed and organized in a number of ways—according to *skills* to be developed, *understandings* to be gained, specific *content* to be taught, and so forth. Further, the use of cases can be directed to numerous other ends such as criterion achievement or behavioral change. Since the specific objectives that instructors pursue through the case method are virtually limitless, the following outlined example of objectives *are illustrative only,* and in no way attempts to exhaust the full range of objectives to be achieved through the case method. The three areas illustrated are both a bit discreet and somewhat overlapping, not logically interrelated and at best arbitrarily chosen. They are simply indicative and suggestive.

I. Skill Objectives

    A. Technical Skill

        1. To improve decision-making ability
        2. To improve deductive and inductive reasoning abilities
        3. To improve communication skills

    B. Human Skills

        1. To gain insight into human behavior
        2. To gain a better understanding why members of an organization are affected by others or by their environment as they are
        3. To gain skill in working with others in analyzing and solving administrative problems

    C. Conceptual Skills

        1. To improve the ability to identify and define complex problems
        2. To improve the analysis of relevant factors and dynamics in problem situations
        3. To improve the ability to deal with complex problem situations

II. Understandings

    A. About People

        1. To analyze human motivations
        2. To analyze role conflict between the private and social sectors of an administrator's life
        3. To analyze personality structures and their effects on others

    B. About Organizations

        1. To analyze the formal and informal structures of an organization
        2. To analyze communications within an organization
        3. To assess the effects of change on an organization

    C. About the Relationship of Individuals and Organizations

        1. To analyze the effect of social organization (or *a* social organization) on an individual
        2. To analyze the socialization patterns and processes in small and large social organizations
        3. To assess the status and reward systems in a hierarchically organized association

III. Content
  A. School-Community Relations (a typical administrative task area)
       1. To assess the nature and extent of conflict between a school and its community
       2. To analyze the varying demands placed on the school
       3. To analyze the effect of information from the school on parents
  B. Political Science (a typical relevant discipline)
       1. To explore the interrelationships of governmental agencies
       2. To examine voter preferences
       3. To determine the effects of partisanship on school levy or bond issue elections
  C. Communications (a typical process)
       1. To analyze the effects of mass media on taxpayers
       2. To examine the effects of feedback on messages
       3. To delineate communications barriers
  D. Theory (a typical logically related body of concepts)
       1. To explore Coleman's stages of conflict in a school-community problem setting
       2. To analyze intended and unintended consequences using the Gouldner model
       3. To characterize leadership styles using the Getzels-Guba model of organizational behavior in a social system

In addition to such purposes and objectives as set forth above, the case method of instruction can be used to realize other instructional advantages. Through this method students are able to work individually on problems at their own pace and to analyze situations to the degree each student derives value. In the class setting, instruction is facilitated in that all members of a class are dealing with the same situation and data, and thereby are not using idiosyncratic or unknown situations in class discussions. The case is also a flexible device; it can be used in a short or long class session, over a series of sessions, or along with other cases. In this regard the instructor has great discretion in his implementation of this instructional approach. Lastly, a good case can be used for many purposes and can be reopened, or revisited, as often as is deemed desirable.

The case method, therefore, can be used to pursue an extensive variety of instructional purposes and objectives, and offers a number of distinct advantages for the instructional situation.

Criteria for Selecting a Case

In selecting a case for instructional use in educational administration a number of criteria can be employed. First, does the case encompass problems or issues in education, or the society in general, bearing upon organization and/or administration? Second, are the roles, functions, processes, and behavior of administrators central dynamics in the case? And, third, can the situation under consideration serve as a means for illuminating knowledge or concepts relevant to education or administration? Obviously case materials developed within, as well as without, the field of educational administration will meet such criteria. Certainly the instructor should not limit himself to just those cases from the field of educational administration; he should look to other areas as well. For instructing in education administration, cases from business management, sociology, political science, psychology, and law have a potential. And, since educational administration is an emerging field with sparse resources for case development, the stockpile of cases in this field can be assumed to have gaps and voids. Even if there were breadth of case coverage, outstanding and tested cases from other fields should not be overlooked. What ever the sources, cases should be scrutinized for relevance, pertinence, and practicality.

Once a case has passed the above general criteria of relevancy, more explicit criteria such as the following relating to the case's instructional potential can be applied:

1. Is the case of relatively universal significance to the practice of educational administration?

2. Does the case deal with emerging practice in, or with dynamics of import to, the field of educational administration?

3. Does the situation reveal something significant and/or unique in regard to the old, the ordinary, or the common place?

4. Does the situation have potential for getting at skills, competencies, content, processes, job dimensions, or concepts related to educational administration?

If the potential case user is still satisfied with the relevancy and instructional potential of the case, criteria relating to the kind of case, the specific objectives sought, and the length of time involved can be applied. It is at this point that the user examines his own precise objectives (e.g., skills to be developed, understandings to be learned, and/or concepts to be taught) and examines the case in terms of its appropriateness for his specific objectives. In this regard, the case must also be assessed negatively in order to ascertain that it does not contain anything which will get in the way with this group and these objectives. Then, if the case is appropriate in kind (e.g., concept case, incident case, dilemma case, relationship case, or event case) as related to the instructional goals at the time, it remains only for the user to determine if the length of the case is appropriate—that is, that the case situation can be grappled with in the time allotted for instruction.

The above discussion is not intended to imply that every case is assessed in the chronological order indicated. Often the criteria will be employed out of order and, due to the particular instructional objectives at a given time, some criteria may not be appropriate. For example, one may decide at the outset to look for a dilemma or incident case, or a short or long case. Or, one may decide that, with the specific needs of a particular group, general professional relevance or uniqueness is not a valid criterion.

In any event, the test of a case is ultimately as much pragmatic and subjective as it is objective (in terms of the criteria already identified). Thus, the big question in selecting a case is: *Does the case work?* And equally important are such questions as:

1. Is the case readable (well written)?
2. Does the case have adequate factual information for productive discussion?
3. Will these students react constructively to the case?
4. Can these students grapple with the dynamics and complexity of the case?
5. Am I, the user, comfortable with the case?

Cases, like old shoes, get comfortable as the instructor gains experience in using them. As one works with a good case, its relevancy and payoff are enhanced. In the end, the mesh of case with purpose and objectives, instructor, and students is most critical.[6]

Applications

Of all the newer instructional approaches for making administrator training both real and practical, the case is the most widely adaptable and flexible. At present, no other instructional device or methodology has such a possible scope of applications for learning situations. It can be used in "mini" time blocks (10 to 30 minutes in length), in regular class sessions, in short two- or three-day workshops, in week- or two-week-long workshops, or in semester-length courses. It can be read on the spot, beforehand, or dramatized or as a case incident. Thus, regardless of the time element or the purpose to be pursued there are or can be developed case materials that can be used to facilitate instruction. Only the instructor's knowledge of these materials and their potential limit applications of the case method in educational administration.

It has been suggested that available resources and the recent application of the case method in the field of educational adminstration have resulted in a less systematic and comprehensive stockpile of cases in this field than in other fields. This is not meant to imply that there are not adequate materials for classroom use. Actually, there are ample cases available for the training of educational administrators. To give some idea of the existing resources, Bridges, Horvat & Sroufe, in 1965, catalogued some 221 cases in this field (11). Since this time other cases have been developed. Further, many pertinent case materials can be drawn from other relevant social science disciplines. There are, further, numerous unpublished but useful case materials in the files of instructors or practitioners in this field. To apply and use the case method skillfully and wisely, the instructor must be a collector, evaluator, and constant user of cases. In this way his reservoir of materials can be built to such an extent that the case will be one of his most valuable, if not *the* most valuable, resources. Ample materials exist or can be developed to form an extensive and comprehensive file for the instructor in education administration.

With a knowledge of extant materials, some "feel" for using the case with a group of students, and a precise instructional purpose the case instructor can select appropriate materials for any need. With consideration to his particular group of students and to his precise instructional purpose he may select a vignette for a 30-minute discussion, a ten-page or chapter-length case for a 2-hour discussion, or a longer substantive case to focus course discussions over a several week, or semester, period. He can ask students to read and think about the case materials before the instructional session, wait until the last opportunity before instruction and provide a vignette, short case, filmed or taped case, or use any other efficient way to convey case data in order to expose students to the case immediately before discussion.

The case instructor may decide that his students need experience in seeking and synthesizing facts and, therefore, will use incident cases in the Pigors tradition. If students need experience in making decisions with scanty information the instructor may draw upon short dilemma cases. If students need experience with group approaches to the solution of complex organizational problems, the instructor may use structured role-play situations or open-ended cases that require group interaction, discussion, or analysis.

Also, the instructional case can be used as a supplemental or diagnostic device in working with individual or small groups of students. For the student who is really naive about administration or a particular administrative position, the reading and subsequent individual student-instructor discussion of cases is an excellent way to introduce the field itself or a particular position to the student. A student's awareness of administration or an administrative position as well as his understanding of some of the dynamics and forces surrounding either can be thus increased. Likewise, for a student who has trouble with situational analysis or who evidences problems with decision making, the case provides an excellent, readily workable situation whereby an instructor can diagnose individual student problems and can work with the student to gain skills and understandings necessary for the actual practice of administration. Particularly, the case's advantage of minimum personal involvement with the situation is advantageous when working at a diagnostic or introductory level and such use of a case offers the potential for the instructor to get to know his students better in a relatively non-threatening situation.

Cases can also be used in evaluation or testing situations. The case can be used to determine the competency and potential of candidates for job positions or for entrance into advanced programs of study. And, in courses or programs where an assessment of practical or conceptual skills and insights is necessary, the analysis of a case (written or oral) is an excellent way to assess student insight into a typical situation along with his ability and his methods of coping with similar problems. A note of caution should be extended here: conformity to the instructor's way of thinking should not be the goal; rather, the student's ability to analyze and deal with the case, practically and intelligently, should be the concern.

Finally, if students are encouraged or required to develop case studies, they are afforded an opportunity to come in contact with people and situations in the real world. By researching and preparing a case study, whether a written, recorded, or even incident-type case, the student is able to examine intensively and extensively a "chunk of reality." As a student's case is discussed and analyzed in class or training sessions he is able to contribute uniquely to class deliberations as well as to profit from the insights and reflections of other class members regarding his case. To the extent that students, in preparing cases, are able to develop the case to illuminate a concept or theory, to organize their cases around emerging dynamics, or to develop scholarly commentary about the case situation, to that extent is the viability of the instructional setting enhanced. The intimate contact with a real situation which is required in developing a case study provides a rich learning situation in both pre-service and in-service training. For example, the child study movement, the study of medicine, and training for the legal profession are all based on student development *and* analysis of cases.

The case has, therefore, a potential for use in both formal and informal training, in pre-service and in-service preparation, in large and small group (even individual) instruction, and at the school district (or "in-house"), professional association, or university program levels. It seems likely that, as the use of cases in educational administration is further refined in the future, the horizon of the case method will be continually extended.

ILLUSTRATIONS OF THE USE OF CASES IN INSTRUCTION

The instructional strategy in the case method at a generic level is simply that of involving students actively in classroom instructional sessions. Student involvement is somewhat circumscribed by both the case and purpose to be sought, but it is nonetheless an involvement with the real and practical side of a field of professional practice. Since cases are "faithful representations of something that happened," students are able to grapple with, dissect, and analyze a "piece of reality" until instructional goals and objectives are realized.

In this present period of refining the use of cases in educational administration, three specific instructional strategies have evolved. These can be labeled (a) the unstructured (permissive) approach, (b) the structured approach, and (c) an approach which may be any one of a variety of combinations of the structured and unstructured approaches. We can now turn to a brief description of each of these strategies. Apparent in the discussion will be a number of sub-strategies within each of those noted.

The Unstructured Approach

The unstructured approach to the use of cases is the oldest instructional strategy and, although some instructors today are moving toward more structured approaches, it remains a valid strategy, preferred by many. In this approach students are exposed to case materials, asked to consider them on their own, and then led in group discussion in a class or workshop setting. The instructor's involvement in this approach is minimal; in fact, he seeks entirely to exclude himself from the case discussion. His involvement is limited typically to an opening remark such as, "What do you think about this case?" or "Do you have any observations concerning this case?" If the case at hand is a long one or if some time has elapsed between the reading of the case and the discussion, the instructor might have a student summarize the case before proceeding. From this point on, however, he limits himself to clarification, critical comments, or leading questions to stimulate and prompt further discussion. Often he does not speak unless requested by the class to do so; in many instances, even when the class attempts to involve him, the instructor returns the discussion to the class with a question, comment, or no reply. Students are thus left to explore the dynamics and variables in the case situation in terms of: (a) their interests, (b) their thoughts about the case, (c) their past experiences, (d) their background of knowledge, and (e) the will of the group. Discussion is an opportunity to share ideas, insights, and conclusions as well as to test these and probe for others' reactions to the case. With some cases, such as open-ended or dilemma cases, the unstructured approach enables students to see how others resolve problems and even to test interpersonal skills in reaching consensus in terms of group conclusions. With other cases, the unstructured approach provides maximal opportunity for students to test and exchange ideas and insights with one another.

There are two sub-strategies in the unstructured approach and these apply basically to the termination of the case discussion. In one sub-strategy the class exploration is merely left open-ended; there is no attempt to summarize or pull together the group's discussion. In this approach the discussion is seen as a valuable end in and of itself and individuals are not forced prematurely to effect closure; the case is, in a sense, always open for additional analysis or a "revisit." Here a premium is placed on individual student reflection on and consideration of a case, and the students' personal development through the use of cases. In the second sub-strategy of the unstructured approach an attempt is made to summarize class deliberations. Here students may be asked to highlight the case discussion, to identify the major points of consensus or divergence, to pinpoint what they benefited from in the case discussion, to draw conclusions from the discussion, or simply to summarize it. In this approach these are seldom, if ever, done by the professor. It is his task to stimulate and provoke class discussion but not to focus or direct it totally, to expound his views, or to effect closure as he sees fit. Most important are student involvement, interaction, and growth in dealing with the dynamics of the real world.

The Structured Approach

The structured approach to the instructional use of cases has evolved as the case has come of age in educational administration. It obviously results from the availability of more and better knowledge with relevance for this field of practice and, particularly, the desire of instructors to inject content or substantive knowledge into classroom discussions and to pursue highly specific instructional objectives. The structured method of case instruction enables discussions to focus upon more precise instructional goals and to pursue them efficiently. Thus, the often wide-ranging and sometimes rambling discussions characteristic of the unstructured approach (especially with groups unfamiliar with the case method of instruction) are replaced by directed analyses in the structured approach. With this strategy the instructor has explicit instructional goals or objectives, definite content (a skill, process, theory, or concept) to convey, and precise standards of learning or performance outcome.

Under the rubric of the structured approach are two definable sub-strategies with many possible modifications in between. Since the possible variations of the polar sub-strategies are numerous, we will describe only the two extremes of the structured approach spectrum to case teaching.

At one extreme of the structured strategy is the approach in which the instructor selects a case, such as "The Conference (17), for teaching a given theory or set of concepts. He may wish to use the case for any of the following purposes: (a) to illustrate concretely Gouldner's model of anticipated and unanticipated consequences (16), (b) to demonstrate Coleman's stages of social conflict (4), (c) to examine the conduct of a disciplinary interview, or (d) to illustrate the dynamics of the three-person group. Whatever his purpose, the instructor would first expose the class to the case and then so lead the discussion as to facilitate the learning of particular content or concepts. If for example the instructor were using this sub-strategy to teach the Gouldner model of anticipated and unanticipated consequences, he would explain the theory with the help of illustrations and perhaps the pictorial representation of the model itself. He would then apply the model to the case showing how the use of "impersonal" organizational rules sometimes results contrarily in an increase of tension in the organization and actually yields a negative resultant rather than the positively intended harmony sought by those who applied the rules in the organizational setting. Class discussion of the case and the model would follow. In such a discussion the class would seek to refine their understanding of both the theory and the case situation. The case would be used to clarify and illustrate the theory; the theory would be used to illuminate and explain the case.

The other extreme of the structured case approach represents an attempt on the part of an instructor to elicit a given theory or concept from the group discussion. Here the instructor would expose the class to a case (such as "The Conference") and then lead the discussion in order to teach whatever content he chooses (such as Gouldner's model). Either more or less directly in the discussion, he would 'prompt the class to educe the dimensions and relevant data necessary to develop the theory under consideration. For example, in using "The Conference" to teach the Gouldner concept of anticipated and unanticipated consequences, the instructor might seek to develop the model through such questions as: "What is the principal trying to do in this case?" "But what actually happened?" "Why did it happen that way?" "What were the results of this conference?" and so forth. Through such questions the instructor and class together could sketch, outline or otherwise develop the basic dimensions of the Gouldner theory. Then the real theory itself could be presented and analyzed as such. This inductive procedure for drawing a theory from a real case situation is most effective in illustrating the practical relevance of and in overcoming resistance to theory on the part of practitioners in a field such as educational administration. It achieves the same general theory-practice linkage and interplay goals of the more deductive extreme of the structured continuum; it is, however, more difficult to achieve since, in a sense, the classroom agenda is hidden and students may be prone to wander off in discussion or may miss the point entirely until the instructional goal becomes evident. Nonetheless, it does enable students to grapple maximally with the case situation and, to some extent, to develop their own skills of conceptual analysis and generalization.[7]

In between these two extremes, of course, lie a number of variations that are more or less structured. Such possibilities allow for the adaptation of structured case methodology to particular instructors' interests and styles.

Combination Approaches

Obviously, not all instructors using cases employ one or the other of the distinct strategies discussed above. Many use one strategy at one time, and another strategy in other situations. Some instructors even combine the strategies in probing one given case. For example, an instructor might open up a case discussion along the unstructured lines with: "What do you think about this case?" Whenever an opportunity arises, he then could employ the structured strategy to teach content or to develop a theory. He might subsequently return the discussion to an open format and await other opportunities to teach content.

Or, the instructor may begin the discussion by illuminating the case through a theory and may then move toward an open discussion along the lines of the unstructured approach. As can be seen, the distinct strategies identified above can be modified, varied, and linked in a number of ways according to the purposes, preferences and abilities of the instructor. Each must feel his own way with the case method and will undoubtedly perfect his own style which maximally yields results within his particular group.

SOME OF THE PROBLEMS IN USING CASES

To this point our discussion of the use of cases in educational administration has emphasized the positive side of case methodology. But the use of cases, like any other instructional approach, has its shortcomings as will as its strengths. We would be remiss if we failed to point up some of the problems in using cases. These problems can be discussed in terms of those related to the methodology itself, the case as an entity, the instructor, and the students or the targets of case instruction.

Looking first at case methodology in educational administration, it can be observed that, although we are well into the second decade of extensive case use, the methodology is still being refined. Many instructors have developed and perfected their instructional strategy to a high level. Unfortunately, the details of their exemplary use of cases are not readily available to the new instructor or, for that matter, to most instructors in the profession except by word of mouth or by accident. Thus, the results of experienced and effective case instructors are not common professional knowledge. Case instruction has tended to develop idiosyncratically and has not even yet become the subject of extensive dialogue in the professional literature. Also, as is so true in most instructional innovation, little empirical study has been undertaken to determine in what ways and to what extent the case approach is better than other instructional strategies, which training purposes can best be pursued through the use of cases, or which approaches for using cases are best. Some have developed an intuitive feeling regarding the instructional potential of the case approach and there is considerable subjective evidence that the case method is effective. It remains, however, to determine for what, how, or when. Hopefully in the coming years of refining the use of cases, the methodology will be systematically studied and the evidence about it adequately disseminated.

Of course, there are problems with cases themselves. The case is a "snapshot," not a moving picture and is, therefore, time-bound. The case being a snapshot (representation of reality) causes the student to interact with the representation and not with a live situation (unless he is developing a case). Although the student can take the situation apart, revisit it, and look at it as long as he likes, he is not a part of it (again, unless he is developing the case). A case is not reality; it is not interactive; nor does it permit feedback. Thus, the student cannot really find out what would happen in a case if something were done differently or if the situation were modified in some way, There is no way that the student's unique insights into a case or his ideas for handling a situation can be tested for their real effect on the situation as such. The student can only conjecture as to the effect of alternate courses of action relative to the case situation. He has no feedback on what would happen, only the subjective assessments of other members of the discussion group. The use of role-playing and case incident materials, however, provides for greater student interaction with the case and for some feedback. But even here a case is not "alive;" it is merely a more or less dynamic representation.

Some case situations have sufficient intrigue to captivate students. Others, for a variety of reasons, do not. Ultimately these reasons are related either to the case situation itself or to the case writer. Little can be done about a case situation since, as a representation of reality, it is what it is. On the other hand, case writers can increase their skills. The case writer (developer) has an imposing charge in conveying a situation truthfully but in such a way as to captivate and stimulate reader interest. Case presentation is both a science and an art. To the degree that a case writer is competent at both dimensions of his task—the ability to gather accurate data and communicate it effectively—his work will be ultimately useful.

Also linked to case writing is the data dilemma in case preparation. Since it is seldom that all data can be put into a case, the case developer must be selective. Enough data must be given to enable users to grapple with the case and feel its dynamics, but too much cannot be used for the quantity an/or complexity might inhibit analysis. In the balance achieved between too much and too little data, some students may want more data while others may have problems separating the relevant from the extraneous. In that cases are most often used by someone other than the developer of the case (except for instructor- or student-developed cases), it would be better to have too much data than too little. This will not silence those who want less, nor will it always be enough for others, but the extent to which case data is used in the case presentation can be problematic. If students always lack enough data to come to grips with case situations, or always have too much, they will soon reject the case approach. In selecting cases, instructors should be cognizant of this problem.

In looking at our growing stockpile of cases in educational administration, it can be observed that the growth in numbers over the past decade has been impressive. However, we do not yet have an abundant supply of cases and obvious gaps and uncovered areas do exist. While we can and should supplement our case pool with studies from other fields, one present need is for a systematic assessment of case coverage in educational administration and a planned program of case development to overcome deficiencies in the years ahead. Cases, being time-bound, tend to become dated. In any emerging, dynamic professional field new arenas are frequently opened up wherein instructional cases must be developed.

Further, case materials in educational administration need to be made more readily available to potential case users and to those already experienced in the practice. The sporadic and idiosyncratic nature of the use of cases in educational administration and the method's scarce treatment in the literature suggest that it is possible that few have an extensive knowledge of the existing case materials and many know only the cases they have found accidentally or by extensive searching. Users of cases much become aware not only of methodological refinement but also of the professional case stockpile itself—its composition, extent, and growth. It behooves any user of cases to develop a personal library, to follow and review the development of case materials in his and related fields, and to contribute to the case stockpile by developing materials. As well, methodological refinements and innovations, along with new and unique case presentation formats, should be disseminated by the case user through appropriate professional channels.

Instructors themselves pose problems in the professional use of cases. Many are reluctant to attempt new approaches to instruction and are content to rely on the tested ways to which they have become accustomed. Some will try new approaches but will fail because they lack information about how to use the newer methodology. Thus, there is a great need to communicate the potential of and possible products from the use of cases to instructors, and to provide opportunities for them to learn how to use this method and to keep up-to-date as the method and materials are refined. It is crucial with any technique to avoid malpractice and to foster and insure successful use. Otherwise, adherents will fall prey to the misuse of the skeptics or the uninformed. It is still important in educational administration to seek acceptance of this instructional approach and to help instructors to use cases better.

As student problems in the case method are relatively few (and related to many problems above), it is the rare student group that is not quickly caught up in and stimulated by the use of cases. Whether the student sees this as relief from the instructor's lectures or rambling stories, or as relief from a student who always wants to talk about his particular (and ususally non-typical) school setting or background, or as an appropriate way to come to grips with reality, cases have intrinsic appeal in the instructional setting. Other than realizing that students must learn to use cases just as they earlier had to learn how to profit from other approaches to teaching, the case instructor should anticipate few student problems with cases. Students do, in fact, need to be introduced to the case method—exposed first to easy and then increasingly more difficult cases, and given the opportunity to gain confidence with this classroom approach. For many it is a drastic departure from instructor-centered lecture or discussion. However, students quickly catch the flavor and value of the instructional case; the instructor's problem is primarily to select relevant cases in order to stimulate learning in the direction of sound training purposes.

Lastly, the inclusive problem of "fit" bears mentioning. As indicated earlier, the mesh of classroom purpose, instructor, students, and case is crucial to the successful instructional use of case studies. This is really the instructor's problem since it is his responsibility to blend all aspects of the instructional situation. The case method itself aids in this task but it is not an end in and of itself. A case will do no good if other aspects of the instructional situation are at odds; if however, "fit" is realized, the case does facilitate instruction in a field of practice like educational adminstration where the values of the case have been subjectively, if not objectively, demonstrated.

SOME GUIDES FOR USING CASES

It is difficult in the confines of a written statement to tell someone how to use a case. Case use is, of course, best illustrated by demonstration and discussion. Throughout this chapter an attempt has been made to show something of how cases have been, and are being used in educational administration. It can be generically concluded that cases in this field are used in increasingly more ways for more numerous purposes and objectives. This will continue to be so as the use of cases in educational administration matures. Even though a standard operating procedure is not possible, a number of guides (some already implicitly or explicitly set forth) can be indentified for the inexperienced case instructor. The guides which follow are somewhat general but should be relevant regardless of why, or in what way one uses a case.

1. *Have a purpose for using a case.* Whether an instructor wishes to teach a theory, to discuss a problem area, or to enable students to explore human behavior, the instructor should know for what purpose he is using the case.

2. *Read cases widely and collect an extensive case file.* It behooves any case instructor to be constantly aware of all possible case materials and to have these readily available.

3. *Pick a case study in terms of particular outcomes to be achieved.* The more explicit one's instructional objectives, the better able he will be to select the best case. Outcomes may be skills to be mastered, understandings to be gained, content to be taught, or a combination of any of these. Before selecting a case the instructor

should determine what outcomes he desires and then use appropriate criteria in picking the case.

4. *Permit ample class time for case discussion.* Good cases usually beget productive discussion, in fact, discussions which tend to snowball. Thus, sufficient time should be available for a class to explore the case leisurely although not wantonly. There is nothing as frustrating as leaving a case when it is just being opened up. Discussions can be carried over to subsequent sessions but, unless planned and systematically worked out, there is some loss in leaving a case prematurely or at the wrong time.

5. *Know the case intimately.* Whether using the structured, unstructured or some combination approach, the instructor must read and consider a case until he has full command of it. This permits him to stimulate and evaluate class discussion, and to maximize the full range of pay-offs from the case.

6. *Allow students to grapple with the case.* Again, regardless of approach, the case is vehicle for getting reality into practical training. The key to success in the use of cases is student involvement. Instructor domination of a case is little more than a lecture or sermon. Cases are for students; it is the student that needs to come to grips with the reality of practice in his field. The instructor's task is to foster and permit this.

7. *Start with easy cases and move to more difficult ones.* Do not start a new group on a long, complicated case. Rather, pace them through interesting, productive explorations of more simple cases before leading them into the full complexity and dilemmas of a field of practice. Case analysis is a skill itself that is developed through successes in the classroom. Ultimately, this skill in situational analysis is beneficial to the practitioner.

8. *Use cases from a variety of sources.* Cases, like anything else, can become routine and dull unless the instructor injects variety into the setting. Cases by different writers, of different lengths, and from different fields of study help maintain student interest and provoke discussion. It is far beyond the time in educational administration when anyone need be confined to a single source.

9. *Vary the forms of cases and the purposes for which cases are used.* For additional variety in case instruction use different kinds such as dilemma cases, incident cases, concept cases, and so forth. Also, use cases for varying purposes in the classroom (e.g., for developing skills, understanding concepts, teaching content, analyzing situations, and so on).

10. *Use a new case in different ways.* When using a new case try it out in different ways and for different goals. Some cases may be used in many ways for many purposes; others must be experimented with in order to discover how and for what they can best be employed.

11. *Evaluate your use of cases.* Like any other methodology, perfected use of cases depends on precise assessment of the effect of instruction with cases. Instructors should assess their own use of cases and also seek student evaluations and empirical evidence on their use of cases. Only in this way can ultimate refinement and skill in the case approach be realized.

12. *Realize that the success of case instruction, as any instructional approach, is tied to the fit of purpose, instructor, students, and (case) method.* Unless the case is relevant, instructional purposes are clear, students are prepared and the instructor is comfortable with the case and method employed, the case approach can little be expected to maximize instruction. Case instruction is not a panacea; it must be consciously devised with attention to the mesh of all of its elements to ensure maximal success.

DEVELOPING A LIBRARY OF CASES

It has been suggested that the user of instructional cases ought to be a collector of case materials. In order to utilize the best and most relevant case situations, the instructor must be constantly aware of what is available and familiar with those cases most relevant for his work. As he collects case materials he will need to exercise discretion; criteria for case selection, as already discussed, will help in identifying potentially useful case materials. But in the end, the best test of a case is the pragmatic: "Does this case work for me with my students?" and "Can we reach our training goals effectively and efficiently with this case?" Thus, the instructor must constantly test and experiment with cases to assess fully their worth and ensure their best usage.

In addition to collecting case materials from commercial sources or from other users of cases, some instructors add to their libraries by developing their own cases or by having students develop case materials. The latter adds not only to the stockpile of cases for instruction but also, as noted earlier, can be used to enhance the instructional situation. Student case development is a valuable learning activity and instructional facilitator. Given the current situation in educational administration (that is, ample but not abundant cases, gaps in case coverage and kinds of cases, and limited prospects in terms of support for systematic professional case development) these are invaluable means for adding to a library of cases.

However, since the · case is both a research and literary endeavor, a case preparer ought to be aware of the full complexity of this task. The following outline of the steps in case development should be of help to the inexperienced (12). The interested reader is referred to the source of these guides for further elaboration on the development of case materials.

Some Guides for Preparing Case Materials: An Outline

1. Initial stage in the development of a case study
   a. Follow up lead and seek information
   b. Identify basic sources of data
   c. Contact basic data sources and enlist cooperation
   d. Gather additional information from the basic sources of data
   e. Assess whether or not the case might be cleared for instructional use
   f. Develop a brief case abstract or précis
   g. Develop a rough outline of the case in greater detail than the abstract
   h. Circulate the abstract and rough outline for reaction by
      i. Several experienced case users
      ii. Several of those "close" to the situation
2. Clearing the case and preparing for data collection
   a. Seek approval (in writing) of the case from those involved
   b. Select a case purpose or perspective (or combination thereof)

Purposes	*Perspectives*
i. To illuminate social science concepts	i. Historical
ii. To describe human behavior or interaction	ii. Problem
iii. To explicate relationships	iii. Thematic
iv. To provide a decision situation	iv. Process
v. To precipitate the collection of data for situational analysis	v. Causal

   c. Identify main characters and develop character sketches
   d. Determine needed sociological background data
   e. Develop a chronology of events

    f. Prepare a comprehensive and detailed outline of the case to guide data collection

    g. Identify all possible data sources

    h. Delineate kinds and extent of data needed and appropriate sources for

        i. Factual data

        ii. Biographical data

        iii. Sociological data

        iv. Data about opinions, attitudes, and feelings

    i. Identify appropriate data gathering procedures and techniques

3. Gathering the data

    a. Contact all data sources and schedule interviews, meetings, observation periods, or time to study written documents

    b. Review notes and materials at the end of each day

    c. Organize data daily according to the comprehensive outline

    d. Systematically review all data in relation to the case outline at the conclusion of comprehensive data collection

4. Drafting the Case

    a. Review the logic of the selected case purpose and/or perspective for presenting the case

    b. Determine the length of the case

    c. Revise the comprehensive and detailed outline for use in writing the case

    d. Select case content from the available data and original materials

    e. Use objectivity, clarity, and creating reader interest as guiding principles in writing the case

    f. Use a narrative and expository style in writing the case

    g. Use standard manscript form for the case report

5. Preparing the final case report

    a. Circulate the case draft for

        i. Review by experienced case users

        ii. Review by key participants in the case

        iii. Testing in several instructional situations

    b. Make necessary revisions

    c. Submit the final case draft for clearance

    d. With any necessary revisions made, seek an outlet for the dissemination of the case

SUMMARY

The use of cases in educational administration typically refers to their use in *teaching* educational administration. A case is a carefully recorded account of something that actually happened. As a "piece of reality" the case is an excellent means of making instruction real and practical. There are many kinds of cases, and the case is a most flexible instructional device.

Historically, the use of cases in educational administration had its antecedents several decades ago in a disatisfaction with traditional instructional methodology and in the lack of substantive knowledge in this field. Drawing upon the case tradition in other fields, particularly business administration, the case approach came of age in the 1950s and presently is in a period of moving toward more refined applications of case instruction.

Many valid instructional purposes can be realized using the case method of instruction—developing skills in situational analyses, teaching concepts, illustrating practice, and illuminating the real world of practice. The case is, in fact, a most useful device for linking theory and practice, and for injecting interdisciplinary content in instruction. Criteria for case selection for instructional use relate to purposes to be pursued and to case relevancy, reality, and ultimately the pragmatic criterion of usability. Cases are applicable in preservice and inservice preparation, in formal and informal training, and in small or large group settings for both short and intensive training programs.

There are three basic strategies in the case approach to instruction in educational administration—the unstructured, the structured, and the combination approach. The unstructured approach is an open, student-centered strategy wherein the instructor is permissive and non-directive. In the structured approach, learning goals and outcomes are more precise and the instructor directs the class activities toward the desired ends. Between these polar approaches are many potential combinations and variations of the pure approaches termed the combination strategy.

Although the case approach has many advantages, there are limitations as well. There are problems with cases themselves in that the case is at best a representation of reality, it is time-bound, and does not allow for feedback. Also, in educational administration there is not yet an abundant supply of cases or comprehensive coverage of the field by existing case materials. Other problems with this approach relate to the instructor, the student, and the "fit" of classroom purpose, instructor, students, and case.

Even though it is difficult to prescribe how to use the case method there are guidelines for the inexperienced user of cases. For example, the case user should have an explicit purpose, select the best case in terms of outcomes to be achieved, permit ample time for case discussion, know the case intimately, allow students to become involved with the case, vary his use of cases, and evaluate the results of using the case approach.

Most important to the case instructor is a library of case materials. Numerous cases are available commercially, but instructor- or student-developed cases are valuable and necessary additions to any instructional case library.

In sum, the use of cases in administrator preparation is well established and gives evidence of only greater use in the years ahead. The potential and viability of the approach have already, at least subjectively, been demonstrated.

NOTES

[1] It should be observed that certain universities, such as the University of Oregon, have also pursued the research potential of the case study in their program of doctoral studies in educational administration. In this regard, the frequency of doctoral studies at that institution using case methodology can well be noted.

[2] For example, John D. O'Donahue, "The Green River Teachers Association: A Case Study of the Decision Making Process," Ed.D. thesis, University of Oregon, 1958; William T. Ward, "An Analysis of the Decision Making Process in an Oregon High School: A Case Study," Ed.D. thesis, University of Oregon, 1959; and Keith Goldhammer and Frank Farner, "The Jackson County Story," Eugene, Oregon: CASEA, University of Oregon, 1964.

[3] Throughout this discussion we are indebted to Griffiths, "The Case Method of Teaching. . . ," treatment of the history of case use in educational administration.

[4] See, for example, the five role-playing problem episodes in the "Simulation Materials for the Madison Public Schools Superintendency," Columbus, Ohio: The University Council for Educational Administration, n.d.

[5] See the various simulated training materials for educational administrative positions available from: The University Council for Educational Administration, 29 West Woodruff Avenue, Columbus, Ohio 43210.

[6] It should be noted that one needs to ascertain the "truthfulness" of a case as well. The case method annals are well documented with the problems of

using fictitious or contrived situations. Only real, factual cases stand the test of time in the instructional setting.

[7]A good example of this classroom approach is available from the University Council for Educational Administration in tape-recorded form, made available by Daniel E. Griffiths of New York University.

BIBLIOGRAPHY

1. Alford, R. R. "Community Resistance to School Reorganization." Columbus, Ohio: The University Council for Educational Administration, Case #11.

2. Bridges, Edwin M. "Case Development in Educational Administration." *The Journal of Educational Administration,* vol. 111 (May 1965).

3. Campbell, Roald F.; Corbally, John E., Jr.; and Ramseyer, John A. *Introduction to Educational Administration.* Boston: Allyn & Bacon, Inc., 1966.

4. Coleman, James S. *Community Conflict.* Glencoe, Illinois: The Free Press, 1957, pp. 9-13.

5. Culbertson, Jack; Jacobson, Paul; and Reller, Theodore. *Administrative Relationships.* Englewood Cliffs, New Jersey: Prentice-Hall, Inc., 1960.

6. Goffman, Erving. *Asylums.* New York: Doubleday & Company, Inc., Anchor Books, 1961.

7. Griffiths, Daniel E. "The Case Method of Teaching Educational Administration: A Re-appraisal, 1963." *The Journal of Educational Administration* 1, 2, (October 1963), 81-82.

8. Griffiths, Daniel E. *Human Relations in School Administration.* New York: Appleton-Century-Crofts, 1956.

9. Griffiths, Daniel E. "Class Discussion of the Filmed Case, 'The Conference'." Taped Instructional Techniques. Columbus, Ohio: The University Council for Educational Administration, n.d.

10. Hamburg, Morris. *Case Studies in Elementary School Administration.* New York: Bureau of Publications, Teachers College, Columbia University, 1955.

11. Horvat, John J.; Bridges, Edwin M.; and Sroufe, Gerald E. "Case Studies in Educational Administration: An Information and Retrieval System." Columbus, Ohio: The University Council for Educational Administration, 1965.

12. Immegart, Glenn L. "Guides for the Preparation of Instructional Case Materials in Educational Administration." Columbus, Ohio: The

University Council for Educational Administration, 1967.

13. Immegart, Glenn L. "The Unadorned Building: A Community Saves Its High School." Columbus, Ohio: The University Council for Educational Administration, Case #18.

14. Immegart, Glenn L. "A Permanent Solution: Midville Saves Its High School." Columbus, Ohio: The University Council for Educational Administration, Case #18a.

15. Lawrence, Paul. "The Preparation of Case Materials." In Kenneth B. Andrews, ed., *The Case Method of Teaching Human Relations and Administration.* Cambridge, Mass.: Harvard University Press, 1953, p. 215.

16. March, James G. & Simon, Herbert A. *Organizations.* New York: John Wiley & Sons, Inc., 1958, pp. 44-46.

17. Photography Department. "The Conference," (a 13-minute black and white film). Columbus, Ohio: The Ohio State University.

18. Pigors, Paul & Pigors, Faith. *Case Method in Human Relations: The Incident Process.* New York: McGraw-Hill Book Company, 1961.

19. Sargent, Cyril G. & Belisle, Eugene. *Educational Administration: Cases and Concepts.* Boston: Houghton-Mifflin Company, 1955.

3

In-basket Techniques

Donald P. Anderson

Since 1959, the use of the in-basket technique in the preparation of educational administrators has become commonplace. This chapter will review briefly the history of the in-basket technique, the uses of the technique with special emphasis on its strengths and limitations in the area of instruction, and the design and construction of in-basket materials.

The instructional technique draws its name from the stimulus items which are its key element. In-basket materials consist of letters, papers, memoranda, and other notes and messages which an administrator might find in his incoming mail or in-basket. The in-basket technique is basically a decision-making exercise structured around a model of a school system in which participants assume the role of a decision-maker and are asked to react to stimuli provided them. The most common use of the technique requires that decision-makers react individually to the stimulus item in writing and to identify their reasons for taking such action. Feedback from the instructor and other participants then becomes a vital element in the instructional technique.

The in-basket technique is similar in some respects to the case study technique. Unlike the case study, however, participants are called upon to assume a role in a currently developing problem situation which simulates reality rather than to discuss and analyze problems which have been faced by others. Another related instructional strategy is the critical incident process. In this process, the participant is confronted with a stimulus item and has at his disposal a data bank from which he may call up relevant data before responding to the item. Many users of the in-basket materials utilize some modification of the critical incident process.

The in-basket technique is generally used to teach or demonstrate certain skills, concepts, or principles. Use of the technique represents an effort to provide laboratory experiences for students of administration comparable to those obtained in the natural sciences. Science laboratory experiences are designed to reinforce the principles and concepts taught by traditional lecture or discussion methods and to provide opportunity to learn by discovery; the in-basket technique provides students of administration with these same learning opportunities. Much concern is expressed about the irrelevance or unreality of many programs to prepare educational administrators, and undoubtedly much of this criticism is deserved. Lecturing about or discussing the process of decision making on some esoteric level will not fare well in breaching the theory-practice gap. The in-basket provides a device to make the concepts and skills more meaningful and relevant.

BRIEF HISTORY OF THE IN-BASKET TECHNIQUE

While isolated use of such real-world instructional materials to teach potential administrators and decision makers dates back many years, it was not until the 1950s that use of the technique became very prominent in a number of management training programs. Since using real administrator-decision problems in instruction is such a simple concept, there was undoubtedly widespread use of this concept prior to 1950, but materials developed for such utilization were not shared with the profession and therefore not reported in the literature.

Reality-based instructional materials found their way into preparation programs in educational administration through the research route. In the mid-1950s personnel at the Educational Testing Service were involved in a test-construction process designed to evaluate the effects of instruction in the Command and Staff School of Air University (4). The mission of the Command and Staff School was to increase the administrative proficiency of field grade Air Force Officers; administrators at the School were interested in designing an instrument to test the effectiveness of their instructional efforts. Representatives of Educational Testing Service worked with them in the development of an instrument called the "In-basket Test," a situational test presented in written form and administered to a group of officers. The setting for the simulation was an imaginary Air Force Wing, and each participant was provided a large quantity of background information on the operation of the Wing. The testing involved responding to such in-basket items as letters and memoranda. Participants were asked to respond as if they were really playing the role and to record their responses in writing. Each participant reacted to in-basket items which might have come across the desks of those filling four key decision-making roles in the Wing.

A short time later, Educational Testing Service was involved in the preparation of "The Business In-Basket Test" (11). Norman Frederiksen and John Hemphill played a role in the development of this test which was designed for use primarily by the American Telephone and Telegraph Company in middle management training programs. Like the Air Force's in-basket test, background information was provided the subjects, and they were asked to respond to the in-basket items. In that this was a research endeavor, the responses to the items were subjected to a content analysis of the responses to the items. While the American Telephone and Telegraph Company was the primary company involved in early stages of this project, a number of other large organizations including Westinghouse, Standard Oil, Proctor and Gamble, and Chrysler Corporation, soon began to cooperate and support the endeavor.

In 1957, the cooperative research branch of the United States Office of Education made a $250,000 grant (O.E. contract #214-6905) for a study entitled "The Determination of the

Criteria of Success in Educational Administration" (DCS). [1]
Located at Teachers College, Columbia University, the study was
sponsored by the University Council for Educational Administration (UCEA). Professors from ten universities participated in
selected phases of the study. Again personnel at the Educational
Testing Service played a major role in both the design and conduct
of the study.

In order to study the administrative behavior and personality
factors of elementary school principals in a controlled context, the
research staff gathered data on an actual school district in a school
system called "Jefferson Township." A number of background
materials about the Whitman School and the Jefferson Township
School System were gathered in the actual school and community
through careful and thorough investigation. Filmstrips, tapes,
printed materials, and motion pictures were developed to provide
information for those subjects in the research project.

In the project, 232 elementary school principals from various
parts of the United States become principals of the simulated
Whitman Elementary School within the Jefferson Township
School Stystem. Following an extensive period of familiarizing
themselves with background information about the Whitman
School and its community, each subject was provided an in-
basket and asked to respond in writing as if he were the principal
of the Whitman School. A total of 103 in-basket items was
presented to each of the 232 subjects; each wrote memoranda,
made notes in preparation for interviews, planned meetings,
drafted letters, and took other action which, in his opinion, was
appropriate for the case.

In addition to the in-basket items, there were other problem
situations presented on tape or on film to which each subject
reacted. The materials were used in integrated fashion to create as
nearly as possible the settings and problems of Whitman School.

Although the major objective of the project was to achieve
better descriptions and explanations of selected administrative
behaviors of elementary school principals, another important
objective was to produce simulated situations and problems which
could be used for instructing prospective educational leaders. As
the materials were being used in the research project in various test
centers, professors of educational administration began to recog-

nize the potential the materials had for improving instruction. Interest in having the materials available for instructional use increased particularly after they were used on a pilot basis in three universities in the summer of 1959 (3). During 1960, professors from a number of universities requested that UCEA find ways of making materials available for use in preparatory programs for educational administrators.

As professors began to use the Whitman Elementary materials for instructional purposes, they became increasingly interested in creating simulated problems and situations for other levels and positions in the Jefferson Township District. In the summer of 1963, materials for the school superintendent were made available, and during that same year, professors at Columbia University, in cooperation with members of the American Association of School Business Officials, developed simulated problems and situations for the School Business Manager in the Jefferson Township School District. During the period 1961-63, professors at the University of Chicago made available materials for the Jefferson Township High School Principal. It is unlikely that those responsible for designing the DCS Research Project could possibly have envisioned the impact the materials were to have on instructional programs.

In 1966, the University Council for Educational Administration received another USOE grant to revise and update the Jefferson Township materials. Twelve professors from seven UCEA institutions were involved in this revision project. Personnel in the school district used as the basis for the Jefferson Township materials again cooperated in the provision of background materials. The team collected updated background materials, revised and added to the in-basket materials that were part of the original Jefferson set, and provided other kinds of simulated exercise for instructional purposes. As was true with the Jefferson Township materials, these new Madison materials rely heavily on the use of the in-basket as the stimulus item for instructional use. Materials are now available in the Madision School simulation for the roles of school superintendent, assistant superintendent for business affairs, assistant superintendent for curriculum and personnel, elementary school principal and secondary school principal. Since the completion of the Madison materials, a team at the University of Nebraska has built on the background materials by providing some special in-basket items for training vocational school administrators. Others are designing materials to be used for training administrators of adult and special education programs.

In addition to these major Jefferson and Madison school simulations, a number of other in-baskets have been designed and are available primarily through the University Council for Educational Administration.[2] Many of these in-baskets do not require the great quantity of background data that is part of the major simulations. Examples of such are the *Shady Acres In-basket,* the *Midville In-basket* and the *Community College Presidency In-baskets.*

USES OF THE IN-BASKET TECHNIQUE

In-basket materials have many potential uses, one of which is to collect data about respondents. In the DCS research project mentioned earlier, the subjects were asked to respond to the in-basket items and these responses were subjected to rigorous analysis. It was intended that this analysis would yield a measure of success. In other words, the responses were to serve as the dependent or criterion variable in the study. The independent or predictor variables were personality and biographical data collected from each of the participants during the early part of the simulation sessions.

It is also possible that the in-basket technique might be used in collecting data on the independent or predictor variable. As an example of this usage, part of the admissions procedures in some universities calls for responding to in-basket materials. The assessment of these responses is used together with other data in the process of selecting candidates for degree programs. This technique is being used in a similar manner for selecting candidates for administrative positions in a few large city school systems.

The in-basket provides a unique opportunity for collecting data about participant behavior. Subjects can be asked to respond to very realistic stimuli, not unlike those problem or decision situations faced in actual practice. It would be difficult, if not impossible, to collect some of these data by observing individual subjects as they behaved in a real administrative setting. The in-basket technique allows for data to be collected from a relatively large group of participants operating under similar conditions. It is assumed that, if participants are provided standard background data, some of the variables affecting their behavior can be controlled.

There are, of course, limitations to this method of data collection. The assumption that standard background data will provide experimental control is subject to question. Another limitation is that background data are provided subjects without their first identifying the information needed; this factor may detract from the realism sought in an in-basket exercise. Yet another shortcoming is the fact that the only record one has of subject behavior is provided through writing; it is difficult to collect data on non-verbal and/or non-written behavior using this technique. These kinds of behaviors are exceedingly important to the administrator and are missed using this data collection technique.

Another serious problem for the researcher, much like that found when collecting data utilizing the case study approach, is that of analyzing the responses. With the lack of structure for the responses, the identification and modification of a framework for analysis and the analysis itself can be very time consuming. A more extensive description of the research uses of the technique can be found in Chapter 9.[3]

The most common use made of in-baskets is to provide actual clinical experiences for those preparing for administrative positions. In a comprehensive survey of the uses of simulation in training programs, Weinberger stated that professors from more than ninety institutions reported the major purposes for which simulation was used were conceptual learning, practice in skills, involvement, illustration of administrative materials, and self-evaluation of administrative behavior (10). The specific concepts of decision making and group dynamics were emphasized. Professors also reported that the most effective parts of the simulation exercises were the in-basket items.

While there are a variety of objectives sought in instructional efforts utilizing in-basket materials, it is clear that one of the central values of the simulated positions and problems derives from their reality orientation and their capacity to provide opportunities for students and professors to test concepts against the facts of administrative life. Two quite different types of teaching objectives can be realized through use of in-basket materials. The technique might be used, for example, to provide cognitive learning experiences related to some of the problem areas which administrators face. An in-basket item might provide an entry into substantive learning experiences about problems such as school desegregation, church-state relations, accounting for school funds, or providing learning opportunities for exceptional children.

A more common use is related to the processes of administration. The in-basket item in this mode of instruction provides stimuli to introduce concepts related to morale building, decision making, goal setting, initiating change, negotiating or resolving conflict, or similar processes. That the instructor must first of all decide upon the objectives of the learning experience before instructional materials can be selected is a very old and over-worked cliché. It bears repeating, however, in regard to in-basket materials where substantive content is not built into the materials.

The technique can be used in a number of settings. Weinberger found that in-basket materials were used most frequently in regular classes, but those professors surveyed strongly favored the workshop setting (10). The more complex in-basket packets, such as those related to the Madison school, were designed for use in a workshop setting of one to three weeks. Many users feel this kind of concentrated time involvement is essential if students are going to be able to take advantage of the wealth of materials available. Others claim to have used these complex simulations effectively in regular class sections meeting from one to three times per week. It is much more difficult under the latter arrangement to keep students in the role.

Use of the less complex, shorter form of in-basket is much more varied. It is possible, for example, to deal with a simple set of concepts using a single in-basket item in a regular class period. These shorter forms share many of the advantages of the case study in this respect.

Another setting in which in-basket materials are being used more frequently is in the field. While the classroom and workshop use of materials tends to bring together administrators who hold or are training for the same position in a school system (i.e. elementary school principal, superintendent of schools), it is possible to bring groups of administrators from the same school system together and have them play different roles in the organizations. The in-basket situation then forces participants to play under different sets of rules. There is some research to support the hypothesis that players take more liberal and sympathetic attitudes towards these roles after such experiences (1). Boocock also reports that such role playing provides persons with a better feeling of political efficacy, a sense of being able to understand and control their environment.

Related to the setting is the mix of participants involved in the exercise. While some of the more commonly used materials are designed for use with persons preparing for a particular role in the organization, there is also the question of mixing the experienced administrator with the inexperienced. Because of the socialization and narrowing of decision alternatives with more experience in a position, many users would argue for mixing the novice with the experienced administrator. Both will profit, the novice from the experience of the master, and the master from the less constrained choice of alternatives on the part of the inexperienced.

In terms of instructional strategies, there is much variance among professors using the technique. The strategies are directly related to the objectives sought and the skills and competencies of the users. Strategies will range from a simple share-and-tell operation in which each participant describes the action taken in response to a specific item, to a very complex analysis of the behavior of participants using some form of theoretical formulation. A commonly used warming-up exercise is to have participants indicate their responses to a particular item with little or no analysis of the responses. While this share-and-tell procedure will be unproductive if not accompanied by some feedback or discussion, it does allow participants to recognize the wide range of alternatives possible to a decision maker.

At the opposite extreme to this strategy is the introduction of concepts describing organizational and/or individual behavior coupled with the use of clinical experiences to illustrate the theoretical model or formulation. As an example of such utilization, Item A-13 in the original Whitman In-Basket materials provides an excellent device for illustrating principal behavior using the Getzels-Guba social systems model of organizational behavior. The item is a mimeographed letter to be sent to parents by two kindergarten teachers; the teachers have forwarded a copy to the new Whitman School principal as a matter of record and not necessarily for his approval. The letter contains a number of grammatical errors, including the misspelling of the word *kindergarten* every time it appears in the letter. Responses to that stimulus will provide excellent examples of idiographic, nomothetic, and transactional behavior.[4]

Normally users of the in-basket technique will mix the analysis of item responses with some other form of instructional input. They may, for example, provide some content or experience with decision-making theory or communication to follow or preceed work with the in-baskets. The in-basket is used then to provide the reality base for the more theoretical content. One major caution bears repeating; the in-baskets very seldom contain much of a cognitive or substantive nature. While they provide an excellent vehicle to introduce content or substance that content is not built in.

Just as the setting and strategies of instruction are functions of the objectives sought, so too is the scoring of the responses. While it is difficult and probably inappropriate to score responses for grading purposes, it may be desirable to analyze the kind of responses using some type of scoring mechanism.[5] One of the outcomes sought quite often through use of in-basket materials is a self-evaluation of behavior. Those users seeking this objective normally have students score their own responses.

STRENGTHS OF THE INSTRUCTIONAL TECHNIQUE

In order to understand the growing use of the in-basket for instructional purposes, one must examine some of the more recent assumptions underlying graduate programs in educational administration. Included among these assumptions are the following: most significant learning takes place (a) when subject matter is perceived by the learner as having relevance for his own purposes, (b) when learning is acquired through doing, (c) when learning is facilitated by active and responsible student participation in the learning process, (d) when learning involves the whole person—

feelings as well as intellect, and (e) when self-criticism and self-evaluation are built into the learning process. The in-basket technique provides a vehicle for capitalizing on the strengths claimed by such experiential learning.

Greenlaw, Herron, & Rawdon relate the rapid growth of simulation to an increase in knowledge about the process of learning (5). They give the following learning concepts as examples.

1. *Contiguity.* The learner gets feedback as a result of his performance and this feedback provides reenforcement.
2. *Effect.* There is an intense involvement of participants in these exercises.
3. *Intensity.* Simulation provides an illusion of reality which results in a full range of human perception being brought into play.
4. *Organization.* Since simulation replicates reality, the learning experience is very relevant for the participants.
5. *Exercise.* The participant has an opportunity to practice some of the skills and knowledge previously acquired; this reported occurence is favorable to learning.

Research endeavors focusing on the value of in-baskets and other simulation devices as instructional tools provide rather inconclusive support, however. Cherryholmes, after examining six major research efforts designed to test the value of simulation procedures, concluded (2):

1. Students are more interested in simulation activities than in conventional classroom exercises.
2. Students did not learn significantly more facts and principles in educational simulation than they did in conventional classroom exercises.
3. Students did not retain more information learned in simulation than in conventional classroom exercises.
4. Students did not gain more critical thinking or problem solving skills than in conventional classroom exercises.

In spite of the fact that the use of simulation materials has produced little better than "no significant difference" in the research attempts, the use of the technique continues to grow. The only evidence of significance in the Cherryholmes study is the fact that use of clinical instructional materials stimulates the learner.

While the in-basket technique has little research to support its effectiveness, the same must be said for the more conventional instructional techniques. Richard Wynn reported the following potential strengths of the technique (11).

1. The evident face validity of the situation stimulates interest and motivation in learning and encourages the subject to behave as he might in reality.
2. The written record of performances results in the accumulation of normative data and permits clinical examination and comparison of 'on the job' behavior in identical situations.
3. Simulation permits the learner to profit from mistakes that might be disastrous on the job.
4. The instructor in a simulated situation can provide the subject with concepts, research evidence, models, or other information which he can't always send in during the actual game.
5. Simulation provides an opportunity to see the whole picture, to view each problem in broad context.
6. Simulation permits a degree of introspection rarely provided on the real job.
7. The Jefferson School situation presents a subject with an interesting object lesson in simulation as a medium of instruction which he may find useful in his own school situation.
8. Simulation presents an extremely useful research medium, providing the collection of normative and comparative data on behavior and performance in identical situations.

The in-basket provides stimulus items for the participant much like those found in that very ambigious world administrators face each day on the job. Participants practice skills that are quite unlike those included in previous educational experiences. Besides reading and talking about these skills, they actually utilize them. Participants gain experience in working with others, in recognizing multiple solutions to problems, in attempting to sell others on their own ideas, and in evaluating the ideas of others.

As students are forced to face real problems, their interest and awareness of trends and activities in actual practice increase. Students are given opportunity to seek pertinent factual information and acquire certain analytical tools including defining problems, weighing evidence, and collecting data—all of which are important in actual practice.

If one accepts the assumptions about learning reported earlier in this section, it is easy to understand the growing use of the in-basket as an instructional technique. Through the technique, learners become individually involved in the exercise. Each learner commits himself in writing to stimulus items knowing that he may be asked to defend this action to his peers. This provides an emotional involvement in an exercise which is not to be found in the more traditional lecture or classroom-discussion learning situations. This individual and emotional involvement in the learning experience is a necessary prerequisite for learning.

LIMITATIONS OR SHORTCOMINGS OF THE TECHNIQUE

Wynn lists the following limitations of the in-basket technique (11):

1. The use of simulation depends heavily upon the competence of the instructor using it.
2. Simulated materials are expensive to produce and are subject to obsolesence.
3. Considerable uninterrupted time is needed for full comprehension of the background materials before the in-basket items can be undertaken.
4. There is also a serious question of transferability of learning from the simulated situation to others.

Expanding on the capital cost limitation noted above, an important consideration is that of time or opportunity invested in utilization of in-basket devices. In calculating costs of instruction, we often omit the cost related to student time; to disregard such "opportunity costs" would be a serious omission in considering this particular technique. If, for example, one wants to impart large quantities of rote knowledge in short periods of time, the technique is certainly not appropriate.

Another of the technique's limitations is that its use may artificially simplify the system or universe. By singling out a few variables and dealing with these in the in-basket technique, participants may not realize that there are few situations in the field where only a few variables are at work. It is also possible that

the use of in-basket materials may encourage conservative behavior. If participants are allowed to be very critical of persons
who take risks and experiment with new approaches, there will
probably be a tendency to conform toward a normative kind of
behavior.

One of the limitations advanced by Professor Wynn relates to
the competency of the instructor. The lack of content in the
material demands even more skill on the part of the instructor
than in most other instructional techniques. The tendency on the
part of some users to identify the "correct" response to an
in-basket item is evidence of a lack of understanding of the
technique.

In spite of frequent warning, some users tend to view the
materials as if they held all the content to be covered, the
concepts and skills to be learned. While one can gain skill in
writing memos or responding to telephone inquiries based on the
in-basket, the skill will have to come from some other source than
the materials themselves. In almost all cases the materials are
simply stimulus items which can be used to illustrate some of the
content or concepts to be learned.

Another shortcoming is related to the fact that in-baskets are
not readily available for all the kinds of problems facing administrators, and it will be necessary that some be constructed to
illustrate particular concepts or processes the instructor feels
important. Most of the in-basket materials available are designed
to focus on decision making while the instructor might wish to
focus attention on goal setting, morale building,   long-range planning, assessing the product of the enterprise, or other processes.

One of the more serious limitations of the materials is the fact
that the capacity to gather data in order to respond to an in-basket
item is normally not dealt with adequately in the sets of materials
presently available. Even in the Madison simulation, the availability of a large amount of background material presents an artificial
situation in that participants get the information without asking
for it. In order to handle this particular problem adequately it will
be necessary to store information in either a more complex set of
file drawers or in some form of computer-based information
storage and retrieval system. Availability of data stored in this
manner would remove this limitation of the technique in that

participants then could seek out information much the same as they could in an actual school setting.

One shortcoming of the common in-basket materials is the fact that administrators very seldom make decisions without conferring with other people or at least collecting data from them. In other words, most major decisions are made by involving teams of people. The fact that participants are forced to act as individuals and do not come into contact with other persons in the simulation makes for an unrealistic situation. It is often difficult to respond to an in-basket item without having opportunity to contact another person in the system. While an attempt was made to provide some team problems when the Madison materials were revised, much more needs to be done in this area.

In this writer's opinion, the most critical limitation to existing in-basket materials is the fact that feedback is not built into the items. While users can and normally do allow for feedback in the instructional setting, the materials are not developed to a point where feedback is automatic. When a participant responds to an in-basket item, he does not get immediate feedback to his response. If, for example, the participant decided to invite a teacher in and talk with him regarding what he interpreted to be unsatisfactory behavior on the teacher's part, it would be desirable to have role-playing instructions available so that someone could read them, play the role, and allow the participant to carry his initial decision one step farther. Similarly, there are many opportunities to provide the participants with additional written materials based on their response to an initial item. While participants make a number of decisions, they are not forced to live with their consequences; they can go on to make additional decisions in the later stages of the exercise with no feedback resulting from prior actions.

Because of the large number of alternative solutions to any problem posed, the computer provides the only possible branching mechanisms which would allow feedback to become an integral part of the materials. In order to program the computer, one would have to collect empirical data to predict the consequences of some of these initial decisons. It would be possible, for example, to test a stimulus item in a real setting to see what happened as a result of a certain kind of behavior on the part of the administrator, to analyze the data, and to provide the feedback to the participant using the same probabilities found in this real-world setting.

DESIGN AND CONSTRUCTION OF IN-BASKET MATERIALS

Steps involved in constructing in-basket materials include first the gathering of information and building the basic structure materials, and then creating and designing the actual stimulus items. Using the DCS project as an example of that construction strategy, the researchers attempted to identify those variables which they felt would contribute to a successful administration (6, pp. 39-62). They then went into a school district and collected background information about the system. The selection of in-basket items was based on a two dimensional grid with one dimension consisting of the skills of an effective administrator—technical, human and conceptual. The other dimension related to the task areas of an elmentary school principal—educational program, development of personnel, community relations, maintenance funds and facilities. In-basket items were created to fill each of the cells on this two-dimensional grid.

In the creation of in-basket materials, the key is to design some kind of conceptual framework which will give direction to the kinds of materials to be included. There are a number of different possible conceptual frameworks to be used in selecting from that multitude of stimulus items those which might be used. In the paragraphs which follow, a few examples of such frameworks are identified.

In structuring the in-basket materials, some assumptions have to be made about the way administrators behave and the key problems with which they must deal. In the recent revision of the Madision materials, five roles were simulated, and each was structured differently by those individuals responsible for the development of materials. A two-dimensional framework was used in designing the materials for the Assistant Superintendent for Instructional Service (7). One of the dimensions consisted of some selected task areas including instructional evaluation, curriculum development, in-service education, instructional staffing, development of materials, pupil personnel services, community relations and non-instruction-related tasks. The other dimension on the grid dealt with leadership processes—controlling, influencing, coordinating, facilitating, stimulating, and initiating.

The Madison materials for the High School Principal were designed using a three-dimensional grid with one dimension being the task areas of the administrator-staff personnel, pupil personnel, school community relations, etc. The second dimension related to administrative processes such as planning, programming, stimulating, coordinating, and appraising. The third was concerned with a modification of the decision-making locus categories identified in the DCS study.

The Superintendent's materials were structured on a three-dimensional grid with the first dimension being the locus of discretion—personnel discretion, coordination discretion, shared discretion, complete discretion or authority, and delegation discretion. The second dimension was labeled *function* and included personnel, administrivia, extra organizational relations, policy, organization, program, finance, and facilities, and the third dimension was processes of coordination, communication, controlling, delegating and decision making. These are but a few illustrations of the many different kinds of structures which might guide the creation of in-basket materials.

An excellent source of both background information and in-basket items is a real school system. It may be possible, but it would be very difficult, to simulate a situation without going into a school system to collect data. One of the major problems with attempting to build a simulation without gathering these kinds of data is that of the inconsistencies one is likely to build into the materials. In the Madison simulation, the background materials were built around an actual school system, and a good bit of assistance was gained from the persons in the field in providing potential in-basket items. The professional associations—National Association of Secondary School Principals, American Association of School Administrators, Department of Elementary School Principals, Association for Supervision and Curriculum Development, and Association of School Business Officials—were most helpful in identifying people who in turn provided the material developers with in-basket items which had crossed their desks. These were filtered, using the conceptual schemes described earlier, and became part of the packets.

There is some controversy regarding the amount of background material necessary for effective use of the in-basket technique. Some would argue that it is not essential to have a large amount of background and that the participants might simply respond to items presented with little or no background. The amount of background material, like everything else associated with the technique, is related to the objectives sought. In research projects, it may be desirable to have subjects participate from a common frame of reference, hence the need for a very elaborate set of backgound materials. This may not be as essential in the instructional utilization of materials. Those who argue for the inclusion of a large amount of backgound data do so in an attempt to introduce some uniform base from which decisions can be made. This can be desirable if one wants to make any kind of sophisticated analyses of responses. If each of the participants draws upon his own experiences and material about the district with which he is most familiar, it may be difficult to make any kind of comparison of reponses.

There are some difficulties inherent in the provision of background materials for an in-basket. One of the more serious problems in the traditional materials development is that the background materials are provided to the participant without his calling for them. In other words, he is given a package of information and is asked to become somewhat familiar with it prior to the time he responds to in-basket items. While he can go back to this packet of information in making his responses to the items, this is a very unreal situation. An administrator functioning in actual settings must identify data requirements and seek out data which are provided for him in this simulation setting.

In a computer-based simulation, this problem can be handled by asking the participant to call up materials from the computer storage instead of giving him all of the materials initially. If this capability exists, there can be some kind of penalty for drawing too much information from the data bank. In many of the present computer simulation exercises, the participant is not penalized for calling up all available information. If participants have this freedom to call for data without penalty, they might as well be handed a packet of materials just as they are when using the traditional in-basket items. It is possible, however, in a computer simulation to ask the particpant to "pay" for such materials. Time might be one method of payment. He may have, for example, an amount of time allotted to respond to the stimulus item, and every time he makes an inquiry into the data bank, he sacrifices some of that allotted time.

On the opposite extreme is the possibility of providing no background materials and allowing participants to use their own background experiences. This may be a very desirable procedure in using a single in-basket item in a traditional class-type setting. Those users who advance this strategy as the most profitable way to use the materials argue that the time participants spend on familiarizing themselves with background materials is time wasted. They claim that little use is made of those background materials, and they question the use of the time for such activity.

A variation of using no prepared background materials is to allow participants to go to a real school system and let that setting provide the background for the simulation. The schedule, school policy, manuals, student handbooks, and other materials used in that system can provide a very realistic setting for the participants to use as they approach the in-baskets. This is suggested as the strategy for using the Community College Presidency In-Basket Items.

Providing opportunities for students to construct a simulation or create some in-basket items can be a very effective instructional technique. Designing a simulation raises problems of building some explicit theory about the system. Selecting the variables, relating the variables, and relating the parameters are the work of a scientist in building theory. There is great instructional potential in having a learner play the role of theorist. In order to design a simulation, it is essential that one understands the way the system operates. The Midville In-Basket materials were designed using this strategy.

To have students write their own in-basket items after they have some experience with such materials also has great payoff. This strategy works especially well with participants in workshops in the field. Participants are given opportunity to project their own problems and let colleagues respond them. Through utilization of this strategy, these problems, which are many times real but implicit, are brought out into the open. For example, a principal who is concerned about the blocking effects a central office administrator has on the the program in his school can communicate this concern through the in-basket item he writes. The fact that he is able to project himself into a role gives him more freedom to explicate problem situations than he has in his regular role.

NEED FOR ADDITIONAL WORK

Additional efforts need to be expended to make in-basket materials more widely applicable to administrator preparation programs. It is necessary that a number of new in-baskets be developed, each designed to fulfill a particular educational purpose. Most of the in-basket materials currently in use were designed to improve the decision-making skills of administrators. Many would agree that the in-basket technique is a moderately successful strategy to achieve this goal. The decision-making opportunities provided have been restricted largely to reacting to immediate problem situations with little attention given to long-range problem solving. In order to focus on the new technology of planning and programming, a different kind of in-basket material must be developed.

Also, the problem situations facing educational administrators are changing rapidly and dramatically. The increasing demand by school client groups—students, parents, teacher, and community members—to get involved in the decision-making process is an example of this change. Existing in-basket materials do not take into account these newer problem areas. Likewise the setting for most in-basket materials is the rural or suburban school system; many of the materials are irrelevant in urban settings. The data generated in the constant study of school organizations will give clues to the kinds of materials which might be developed.

Additional resource materials need to be developed to supplement the in-basket items. The materials made available by UCEA consist primarily of transparency masters. Included among these masters are a number of models and concept descriptions plus some of the background materials; all of these materials can be shared with the participants via an overhead projector. In addition to the masters, these materials include a bibliography, role-playing exercises, scoring devices, and other such supplemental materials created by some of the users of the in-baskets. Just as the in-basket materials need constant revision due to new knowledge about the educational enterprise, so too do the resource materials.

A key limitation of simulation, lack of automatic feedback, is one that can be coped with now that the technology problem is being solved. Additional resources need to be made available so that computer simulations can be developed for instructional as well as research purposes.

Since the major decisions in an organization are not made by individuals, additional attention must be given to the development of materials that can be used by teams of administrators. Most of the existing in-baskets are designed for use by one member of the decision-making team. Also, it is essential that materials be developed for persons other than those whom we traditionally see as line administrators in this system; examples of such persons might be school board members, planners, and evaluators.

In addition to materials development, additional attention must be given to an assessment of the instructional technique itself. Research projects should be designed to test relationships between the way materials are designed and used and their instructional utility. More than five hundred professors and a substantial number of practicing educational administrators have participated in one of the fifteen UCEA-sponsored institutes offered to familiarize potential users with the materials. The time has come to assess the need for continuing and/or modifying such training experiences.

In-basket materials are the most commonly used of all simulation materials in educational administrator preparation programs. In spite of the fact that available in-basket materials are limited, their impact on administrator training has been substantial. The current materials development activities, plus more experience in using the technique, should yield even more significant outcomes.

NOTES

[1]For a report of the results of this study, see John Hemphill, Daniel Griffiths, and Norman Frederiksen, *Administrative Performance and Personal-*

ity (New York: Bureau of Publications, Teachers College, Columbia University, 1962).

[2] Throughout this chapter, numerous references will be made to specific in-basket sets, most of which are available from the UCEA. This chapter is not intended to be an advertisement for UCEA materials, but no other organization or publisher has developed and published much in the way of in-basket materials for training educational administrators.

[3] In-basket materials are also being used in testing new patterns of organization. As an example of such utilization, in-basket items were designed and used in a workshop setting in the fall of 1967 to test the viability of two quite different patterns for organizing the College of Education at The Ohio State University. In-basket items were presented to the faculty groups and the responses to the items were channeled through the proposed governmental structures—Faculty Senate, Executive Committee, etc. Assessment of this in-basket role-playing experience played a key role in the internal organization of the College. The same technique was used in a recent organizational study of a county school system in Ohio.

[4] For an illustration of commonly used models, see "Madison Resource Packet" (Mimeographed), The University Council for Educational Administration, Columbus, Ohio.

[5] A number of scoring devices are available in the Madison Public Schools Resource Packet; the devices are based largely on the analysis of responses in the DCS project.

BIBLIOGRAPHY

1. Boocock, Sarane. "An Experimental Study of the Learning Effects of Two Games with Simulated Environments." In Boocock and Schild, *Simulation Games in Learning.* Beverly Hills, California: Sage Publications, Inc., 1968, pp. 107-33.

2. Cherryholmes, Cleo. "Some Current Research on Effectiveness of Educational Simulation: Implications for Alternative Strategies." *American Behavioral Scientist.* vol.10 (October 1966). pp. 4-7.

3. Culbertson, Jack & Coffield, William (eds.). *Simulation in Administrative Training.* Columbus, Ohio: University Council for Educational Administration, 1960.

4. Fredericksen, Norman; Saunders, E. R.; and Wand, Barbara. "The In-Basket Test." *Psychological Monographs.* vol. 71, no. 438, 1957.

5. Greenlaw, Paul S.; Herron, Lowell W.; and Rawdon, Richard H. *Business Simulation in Industrial and University Education.* Englewood Cliffs, New Jersey: Prentice-Hall, Inc., 1962, pp. 46-69.

6. Hemphill, John; Griffiths, Daniel; and Fredericksen, Norman. *Administrative Performance and Personality.* New York: Bureau of Publications, Teachers College, Columbia University, 1962.

7. "Instructor's Guides for Madison Materials." Mimeographed. Columbus, Ohio: The University Council for Educational Administration.

8. "Madison Resource Packet." Mimeographed. Columbus, Ohio: The University Council for Educational Administration.

9. Ward, Lewis D. "The Business In-Basket Test: A Method Assessing Certain Administrative Skills." A mimeographed report of the Educational Testing Service, Princeton, New Jersey, April 1959.

10. Weinberger, Morris. "The Use of Simulation in the Teaching of Educational Administration." Unpublished Doctoral dissertation, Teachers College, Columbia University, 1965.

11. Wynn, Richard. "Simulation: Terrible Reality in the Preparation of the School Administrators." *Phi Delta Kappan* (December 1964), pp. 170-73.

4

Simulating the Process for Selection of Teachers

Dale L. Bolton

This chapter includes a discussion of the purposes and advantages of simulating the teacher-selection process, an example of the development of simulation materials, some problems involved in devising and using simulation, the use of simulation for research and instruction in teacher selection, and a theoretical basis for developing materials. The discussion of the need for improved instruction and more significant research is provided to clarify the motivation for simulating the teacher-selection process. Since simulation is the *representation of reality via a set of materials and/or activities*, the example provides information regarding the nature of these materials and activities. Problems of determining what should be included in the materials and activities and how elaborate and real the simulation should be are discussed in relation to objectives of instruction and research. Cautions and guidelines are provided for using the simulated materials for research and instruction. The theoretical section is included for the reader who is interested in a complete background for simulating the teacher-selection process.

THE NEED FOR SIMULATING THE TEACHER-SELECTION PROCESS

Simulation of the teacher-selection process is important to instruction and research. Instruction should be real enough to ego-involve learners in the task and to facilitate transfer of skills to real tasks, and research should test hypotheses regarding crucial elements of decision theory.

Instructional Needs

It is possible to learn *about* the selection of teachers by reading research reports and scholarly opinions, listening to lectures, and participating in discussions with people who have had experience in selection. However, learning *how to select* teachers may not occur via these procedures. It is assumed that the actual experience of selecting, combined with feedback regarding results, is a more effective way of learning how to select teachers.

A simulated situation provides the experience of selection without the hazards of the actual situation. Likewise, it offers a better opportunity to provide feedback because of the absence of time factors and pressures which are normally part of the real selection situation.

The potential advantages of using simulation to teach the selection process are the following:

1. It provides sufficient realism to develop interest and ego-involvement on the part of the learner. The increased commitment to the task is related to the reliability and validity of the performance.

2. It provides experience with the selection process under conditions that are relatively non-threatening to the learners and where the consequences of the decisions are not damaging to pupils or to a school system.

3. It provides an opportunity for a learner to acquire feedback regarding his performance and to perform a similar act following this feedback. In addition, it allows an instructor to determine whether additional practice is needed before modifying certain elements of the task.

4. It provides these opportunities in a variety of settings and at any time of year regardless of the availability of actual applicants.

Each of the first three potential advantages has a possible disadvantage in that the simulation may not appear realistic to some people; the absence of consequences of the decision may cause decisions to be made differently; and the feedback, although it may be adequate for the simulated situation, may develop skills that are non-transferrable to the real situation. However, simulation makes it possible for university professors and school administrators to provide a precise experience previously not available for practicing and future administrators.

Generally, the purpose of using simulation materials is to teach individuals how to process information about a number of applicants and how to make consistent decisions in the selection of an applicant for a position. Specific behaviors desired in individuals participating in the simulated activities can be illustrated by the following objectives:

1. to make a complete position analysis, describing the tasks to be accomplished in the position and the situational variables most pertinent to these tasks

2. to establish criteria for teacher behavior appropriate to the situation being considered

3. to describe the applicants accurately on a variety of factors:

    a. to interpret information from documents with relation to behavior

    b. to interpret interview information accurately with relation to teacher characteristics

    c. to translate information from documents and interview to a summary description of each applicant

    d. to group the data according to factors or dimensions of the characteristics of the applicants.

4. to predict behavior of the teacher in the situation for which the application is being made (This includes a prediction of both classroom and out-of-classroom behavior.)

5. to compare predicted behavior of each applicant with criteria, i.e., to make judgments regarding the degree to which each criterion will be satisfied

6. to make choices among applicants, i.e., to rank applicants for the position—in terms of judged suitability in comparison with all applicants

Research Needs

The eventual objective of conducting research in simulated teacher selection situations is to supply the circumstances whereby people can be taught effective decision making. It is anticipated that simulated situations which prove useful in increasing our knowledge of decision making will also prove beneficial in the instructional process. Whereas some research regarding the selection process is designed to increase knowledge of situations that exist at the present time, research in simulated situations is designed to determine what will happen if certain of the existing circumstances are changed. With this information, it is possible to control the environment so certain elements of decision theory can be tested. For example, in order to *describe* the decision-making behavior of a particular individual (or set of individuals), and to *prescribe* a manner in which a decision maker can behave more effectively, it is necessary to determine: (a) the manner in which he predicts consequences, or at least what consequences he predicts and (b) the value system he uses in the final choice. But how can the prediction of consequences be separated from the values attached to them? How is it possible to know, by observing the choice of a particular alternative, whether the choice was made on the basis of a high prediction of consequence and a low value, or the reverse, or both a high prediction of consequence and a high value? Interest in value systems has led students of decision making to devise descriptive and prescriptive decision-making models.[1] One intent of these models has been to assist people in making the consequences they predict and the values attached to them explicit, yet little work has been done to accomplish this intent.

One approach to the description of the decision-making process is to place subjects in a precisely described choice situation in which the consequences can be accurately determined and known by the subject. For example, a betting situation in which the odds are known can be used—as in coin-flipping, rolling dice, or choosing combinations from a deck of cards. Subjects can be taught the probabilities that certain consequences will occur and their value can be inferred from the alternatives chosen, i.e., the types of bets they make. However, this approach leaves much to be desired because prediction of consequences has been controlled in a sense; therefore, one can only infer that differences in behavior are due to differences in value systems rather than the way consequences are predicted. Inability to determine concomitantly the subject's manner of predicting consequences and his value system is a limitation in this case; such a limitation can elicit behavior considerably different from behavior in a less restricted decision situation.

An approach from which broader generalizations can be made is one in which the situation is described, but the decision maker must make choices on the basis of *his own* prediction of consequences and attachment of values to these consequences. An example is the simulated teacher selection situation described in the next section of this chapter. In this decision situation, subjects are not taught probabilities of consequences of choosing certain teacher applicants but must make estimates of what will occur if each teacher is hired. In addition, they must make choices among the teachers. The estimates of what will occur when a teacher is hired become the subject's explicit expression of probable consequences, and the value system of the subject is implied by this expression and his choices among teachers. Thus, it is possible through the use of simulation to provide a setting whereby descriptive and prescriptive theories of decision making can be tested.

But what types of problems can be studied in the simulated situation? An experiment described in detail in the next section of this chapter manipulated information format variables and studied the effect on time needed to make decisions, discrimination among applicants, consistency of decisions, and feelings of certainty about decisions. Additional information regarding decision making can be obtained by conducting experiments with the following objectives:

1. to acquire basic information regarding how decision makers view and process teacher selection information and how they differ among themselves and from other members of the profession with respect to certain variables which appear related to the teacher-selection process

2. to determine how certain mediating variables (e.g., nature of communities) affect decision makers in the selection of teachers and whether these variables affect other decisions to be made by administrators

3. to determine what types of variables predict the decision-making behaviors of administrators most effectively

4. to determine conditions whereby a person can be taught more consistent[2] decision making (initially in teacher-selection and eventually in other decision-making situations), including acquisition as well as analysis and evaluation of information

In general, then, simulation is peculiarly adapted to studying problems in which there is a need to manipulate certain variables to determine the effect of these variables on specified aspects of decision-making behavior.

DESCRIPTION OF AN EXAMPLE (5)

Simulation of the teacher-selection process involves three elements: a situation, a set of applicants, and a means for reacting to the applicants in relation to the situation. This description of an example covers development of (a) instructional materials for describing the hypothetical situation for which the applicants were considered, (b) audio and audiovisual materials for simulating teacher interviews, (c) written documents (transcripts, credentials, etc.) needed for describing fictitious teacher applicants, (d) materials for presenting instructions on how to process information, and (e) written materials needed to obtain responses from participants regarding applicants.

The purposes of providing a complete description of the hypothetical situation were to remove each participant from his own situation and place him in a controlled situation and to allow each participant to determine criteria he considered appropriate for selection in the given situation. The nature of the community, the school district, the elementary school, and the vacancy in the elementary school were presented via a taped audio description and 2 x 2 color slides to insure uniform presentation within a short time period. The commentary was presented continuously, and the slides were shown at appropriate intervals. A programmed text, presenting essentially the same content as the taped commentary, was devised and used for testing the participants' knowledge of the situation and for reinforcing the taped commentary.

A sound and color film was developed to display the *probing* portion of an interview with each applicant. Because of constraints, the length of each interview was limited to nine minutes, all applicants were assumed to have passed an initial screening interview, and all applicants were female between 22 and 28 years old and of acceptable appearance. These controls provided a group of relatively homogeneous applicants, a condition necessary to test the discrimination of participants' decisions. Personality characteristics (using Ryans' [43] five factors for the elementary sample) were systematically manipulated among the fictitious applicants in such a way that a different personality was "created" for each applicant. The rationale for the design of the interview was to display specific behavioral and personality factors that could be assessed by the participants. The structure of the interview was developed to control the characteristics displayed by the applicants in the interview and to retain the realism and spontaneity of the situation as far as possible.

The written documents for each applicant were developed in conjuction with the interview materials and were designed to support and elaborate on the characteristics displayed in the interview. Written documents were prepared in two formats: multiple documents, which are the type most commonly used by school districts at present, and a single summary document designed to present information equivalent to that presented in the multiple documents.

Concise instructions concerning effective, efficient information-processing techniques were given to the participants. The instructions were presented by tape recording to insure consistency of presentation and were supplemented by visual aids and a written summary of the five main points. A brief multiple-choice test was given to check the participants' comprehension. The entire process of instruction required less than ten minutes.

Response devices necessary for use in simulation include a set of instructions for estimating how each applicant would be evaluated on a Teacher Evaluation Instrument (TEI), a TEI for each applicant being considered, and a sheet for ranking the applicants. For research purposes, it was necessary to provide a way to collect information about the participants and to measure any additional dependent variables, e.g., certainty regarding the estimates of consequences or the ranking.

PROBLEMS OF SIMULATING THE TEACHER-SELECTION PROCESS

Four major problem areas exist with relation to simulating the teacher-selection process. These problems are concerned with the degree of *realism* involved in representing the process, the *scope* of activities in the simulation, the *dynamic and static aspects* of the simulation, and the provision for *feedback* to participants in the simulation.

Realism

The nature of reality has plagued scholars for centuries, and this discussion is not intended as another treatise on the subject. However, in designing materials intended to represent the realities involved in selecting teachers, one is faced with the task of abstracting a situation in such a way that it will be recognizable by participants. If teachers were selected in the same way in all school systems and if participants had similar experiences with the selection process, then the task of realistically abstracting the selection process would not be so enormous. However, such is not the case. Consequently, one is immediately faced with the decision of whether to represent the most common practices, the best practices, or the ideal practices even though they may not exist in any given district. Any one of these alternatives has liabilities, and the choice depends on specific purposes for the simulation. If one is concerned primarily with motivating a group of administration students to explore research and the literature regarding the process, a simulation that represents common practices will suffice. If one's objective is to reduce the tendency of some students to make self-protective decisions, the simulation should represent ideal practices[3] and emphasize a commitment to the specific process of selection being taught.

One potentially troublesome aspect of realism is the question of purpose of the selection process. In many school districts, this question is never raised and different people make different assumptions about the purpose of selecting teachers. Some assume that an attempt is being made to select the best set of candidates and to assign them optimally, whereas others assume that the process is designed to acquire acceptable teachers for each position (i.e., a satisficing policy is followed rather than an optimizing one[4]). The instructions in a simulation exercise should state what the purpose of the selection process is, but this purpose may appear unreal to a participant who has made different assumptions about the purpose of selection in his own district.

Conflict between the need for complexity and the need for simplicity arises from a desire for realism in the simulation. On the one hand, there should be complexity to facilitate generalizations to real situations and transference of ideas from the simulated to a real situation. In conflict with this is the simplicity needed to make total information manageable and learning a gradual progression.

The fact that participants in a simulation are provided information rather than having to search for it presents another difficulty for realism. Work by Toda (52), Lanzetta & Sieber (23) and Hickey (20) indicates that information processing in the pre-decisional stage is influential to the decision itself. In essence, search for information requires cognitive skills that are somewhat different from those needed for processing information already provided in a managable form. Although the major emphasis in simulation of the teacher-selection process is on the decision itself, considerable work is done in the pre-decisional stage to collect information about applicants and to screen out applicants who do not meet certain minimum requirements. Where this is omitted from the simulation because of the time required for information collection and screening, some participants may feel that one of the important elements has been deleted and that the simulation is, therefore, unreal.

Possibly the most serious problem of realism in simulating the teacher-selection process concerns how the interview information will be handled. If the interview is live, i.e., if each participant interviews each applicant in person, there are problems of control for comparisons and feedback. If interviews are filmed or taped, many participants feel frustrated because they are unable to determine interpersonal interactions between the applicants and themselves. Clearly specified objectives for either training or research should resolve this problem by implying which interview procedures are acceptable.

Scope

Difficulties of determining the scope of the simulation are interrelated with concerns about realism; consequently, some of the problems have already been discussed (e.g., providing information about the purpose of the selection process, conflict between complexity and simplicity, and omitting pre-decisional information search). In addition, there are questions of how exhaustive the position analysis should be, the amount of time to be spent on criteria determination, the emphasis placed on translation of information onto a summary document, the time spent on analysis of subtle communication in the interviews, and the emphasis on making predictions about behavior of each applicant.

Complete analysis of a position is a relatively complex process and goes well beyond the customary procedure of a one-page description of grade level, subject(s) to be taught, teaching load, and sketchy expectations of the community. Often these descriptions are of slight benefit to the applicant and do very little to assist a decision maker in differentiating among requirements of various positions. A more adequate position analysis would include a relatively complete description of (a) the general nature of the position, including broad goals of the system; organizational structure; and expectations in the classroom, in relationships with members of the organization, and in relationships with external groups or individuals; (b) the static and dynamic features of the position, including information about what is likely to be important at the beginning of the assignment as well as later, what is likely to change and what is likely to influence this change, how the position will be affected by other people, how the community accepts the present program, and the known and measurable characteristics of the students; (c) the teacher behaviors that are required and desired in the classroom, in relationships with members of the organization, and in relationships with external groups and individuals; and (d) the teacher characteristics sought, i.e., the factors or dimensions that may be implied by the behaviors identified in (c), including such dimensions as aptitudes, skills, social requirements, interests, and physical capacity. One can assume that participants already have (or do not need) a clear conception of the position analysis, or an orientation session or a position analysis development can be included in the simulation process. Choosing an alternative is a problem of establishing the scope of the simulation.

Determination of criteria for selection is an issue of considerable magnitude, especially where it involves designation of explicit weightings that will be placed on teacher behaviors in a given position in relation to some total utility to the organization. For certain research or training purposes, the phase of the selection process can be taught to the participant or can be assumed to vary within individuals and, therefore, can be an object of study. The way in which criteria determination is handled affects the scope of the simulation.

A recent experiment by Bolton (5) indicates that there are advantages to having written information about applicants on a single summary document, in preference to the usual multiple documents found in personnel records. The single document poses two problems for simulation: (a) since most districts do not use a summary document, participants need to be oriented to the format of the data and (b) teaching participants to translate information from a set of documents to a single document increases the scope of the simulation considerably because of the necessity to devise a single document that will accurately reflect a district's value system.

Where simulation is used for conducting an experiment, subjects are likely to be required to collect information from a single exposure to an interview. However, where simulation is used for training, the same filmed interview can be used several times with the same group in order to analyze some of the subtle aspects of the content and the non-verbal communication of the interview.

A final problem of scope is concerned with predicting behaviors of teachers. Common practice does not include the explicit prediction of detailed behavior of teachers. Consequently, the realism of common practice can be preserved without requiring participants to perform this task. However, in spite of the fact that this task enlarges the scope of the simulation, more needs to be known about the effect of explicit predictions on the reliability and discrimination of decision makers. Likewise, these predictions are necessary if participants are to be given feedback regarding the compatability of their explicit and implicit value systems.

Dynamic Aspects

It is difficult to determine how the dynamic aspects of the decision process can be displayed, examined, and taught most effectively. Static models of decision theory offer a single choice among alternatives with no responsibility or opportunity for making a second or third decision utilizing the knowledge gained from the initial decision. The dynamic model views the decision process as a sequence of decisions in which information gained from one decision is used in the next and where each decision is made with full knowledge that future decisions will depend on information obtained from prior decisions. Under these circumstances, the environment is changing and the decision maker must modify his estimates of probabilities and values of consequences according to the changes. In effect, he must attempt to maximize expected value (or satisfice) over a time period where changes occur, rather than for a single decision.

The difference between the static and the dynamic model of decision making lies in the changing environment which provides the context for the decision process. How can this be built into the simulation of the teacher-selection process? If one considers the process as consisting of two parts—(a) deciding on a rank ordering of the applicants and (b) deciding whether to offer a position to the applicant considered best or to recruit additional applicants—the first part is a static situation and the second part is dynamic. Thus the time of the year, number of applications received, number of positions offered and refused, and communication from the applicants indicating other opportunities for employment can change during the decision task. Participants can be asked to rank the applicants and make a decision to hire or not hire. If they choose not to hire at this time, i.e., to delay their decision to hire, one or more of the factors considered to be dynamic can be changed and the participant can be asked to do the task again. For example, the participant can be given letters from the two best applicants stating that they have received job offers elsewhere and need a decision from him regarding whether they will be offered positions. In addition, one new application can be received during the time lapse of one month after the initial task.

The inclusion of dynamic factors complicates the simulation. However, it adds to the realism for instructional purposes and creates a richer environment for examining how decisions are made.

Feedback

One of the problems which has plagued people devising simulated activities is how to provide realistic feedback to participants regarding the results of their decisions in the simulated situation. A later section of this chapter presents a theoretical basis for providing feedback on (a) the accuracy of estimation of teacher behaviors and (b) the congruence of implied values of the decision maker with a given value system. Providing feedback requires that assumptions be made about a particular simulated situation within which the decisions are made, viz., the relationships between the predictor variables and subsequent teacher behaviors and the relationship between teacher behaviors and the total utility to the system.

To assume that these relationships can be known is not unreasonable because they can be empirically established for known situations. Since the relationships vary from situation to situation, an assumption or specification of them for providing feedback in a simulated situation is merely one way of specifying how the components of the situation interact. These assumptions are analogous to those made by people who simulate business firms and marketing problems. They assume relationships among the variables involved in the decision process; when decisions are made which allow the variables to interact, their assumptions about relationships permit them to predict results and make these results available to the participant. Their assumptions about relationships are based on relatively well-established theories of the firm and the marketplace; consequently, their predictions of results are not as likely to be questioned as comparable predictions in education. Even if some people are hesitant because they feel there has not been enough empirical work done to justify assumptions about the relationships, one does well to consider the implications of *not* making these assumptions and *not* providing feedback on decisions. As far as learning is concerned, the participant's responses will be reinforced regardless of his decisions; and this will amount to making his assumption the correct relationship among the variables which interact. For instructional purposes, it is more desirable to assume particular relationships for a given situation than to assume that each participant will make adaquate independent assumptions about these relationships.

USE OF MATERIALS FOR SIMULATING THE TEACHER-SELECTION PROCESS

Two reasons for simulating the teacher-selection process are to conduct research and to provide an environment for learning. This section describes how simulation materials can be used for research and instruction; in addition, assistance is provided in the form of cautions and guidelines for the person who plans to use the materials.

Use for Research

The materials described earlier in this chapter were first used in an experiment conducted to determine the effects of four information-format variables on the teacher-selection process. The variables manipulated were instructions for processing information, number of documents, masking of information, and interview information. Measures used to determine the effects of these variables were consistency of decisions, fineness of discriminations made, time required to make decisions, and feeling of certainty about decisions. The design was a 2x2x3x3 factorial for which analysis of variance was used in analyzing data. The participants were 144 elementary school principals.

The results indicated that the format of information did affect decisions. The optimum format consisted of instructions about the processing of information, a single summary document, no masking of information, and interviews with audio-visual stimuli. The results of the study imply that improvements can be made in the selection of teachers by using the format found to be optimum. The improvements expected include decreased time spent in making decisions and increased discrimination, certainty, and consistency of decisions.

Recommendations made for additional research and developmental activities include studies to determine:

1. how differing value systems of individuals interact with their abilities to estimate consequences of alternatives. Because an important facet of decision making is the interaction of value systems with the estimation of consequences, this should be studied in the simulated situation—using the optimum format for presenting information.

2. how certain variables controlled in the study reported (e.g., grade level of the vacancy, sex of the applicants, age range of the applicants, racial and ethnic backgrounds of applicants) affect the decision making of administrators. It is often said that the selection of teachers should be influenced by the *situation* for which the teacher is being selected, but no empirical evidence is available to indicate that administrators actually make adjustments in their selection processes for situational variables. If they do not, they tend to select for some stereotype of a global "good teacher," whereas there is much research evidence to the effect that no uniformly good teacher exists.

3. how data processing equipment can be used for reliably transferring data from multiple documents to a single document. For the study reported here, a strategy was developed to transfer these data, but research needs to be conducted to determine how data processing equipment can be used for a variety of strategies.

Use for Instruction

The materials described earlier in this chapter are not designed to teach selection *as it is presently done;* rather, they are designed to teach a particular way of processing information to accomplish specific selection purposes. Although they have some flexibility, they also have some constraints that may not be compatible with normative behaviors of personnel directors.

Three questions must be answered by people who plan to use these simulated materials: (a) Should all of the identified objectives be sought, or only a limited number? (b) Should the situation be the one provided by the materials, the Jefferson School, a real situation, or a situation contrived by the participant-learner? (c) Should the selection process be taught as an example of the decision process? Answers to these three questions provide guidelines for use of the materials. At least two pertinent factors in answering each question are the amount of the time available for the total learning sessions and the nature of the audience for which the materials are intended.

With certain audiences it may be desirable to work with very limited objectives. For example, in working with personnel directors, it may be beneficial to spend a lot of time on translation of information from multiple to single documents and less time on the interview process. On the other hand, a complete workshop for elementary principals could be designed on the procedures for acquiring accurate information from interviews. With a graduate class, it may be profitable to use the entire set of objectives, taking the students through the whole process.

Where time is a limiting factor, the half-hour description of the hypothetical situation may have advantages over the more extended time needed to contrive a hypothetical situation. However, different objectives would be obtained, since the one task is primarily analytical whereas the other involves synthesizing. The use of a real situation would require re-examination of familiar surroundings, while the use of the Jefferson School would allow a single orientation for a variety of decision processes.

Where the selection process is to be considered as an example of the decision process, the objective will be to generalize the activities engaged in during the selection process to other situations. Several good descriptions of the decision process exist, and these can serve as bases for similarities between the selection process and other decisions (7,8). For example, all decisions involve a consideration of the state of nature and a choice among alternatives. The choice is made on the basis of predicting (attaching a probability to) the consequences of the various alternatives and then assigning a value to the consequences predicted. It is the combination of the probable occurrence of an event and the value of the event that provides a utility to an alternative. The selection materials described in this chapter include the state of nature (the description of the situation), various alternatives (the applicants), a prediction of consequences (the Teacher Evaluation Instrument), a value system (the explicit criteria for selection), and a choice (ranking of applicants).

With these component parts and with specific characteristics designed into the descriptions of the applicants, it is possible to compare the explicit criteria established by a person with the criteria implied by his choices. In addition, each phase of the process can be examined and discussed with relation to other decisions and the decision process.

Perhaps the total process can be examined best by means of a flow chart and accompanying identification of steps. The flow chart of Fig. 4-1 which follows shows how the process can be subdivided for accomplishing limited objectives.

Workshops have been conducted using all of these steps, as have workshops using only a few of them. Likewise, various portions of the materials have been used in graduate courses for limited objectives. The materials are flexible from the standpoint of scope and type of audience.

Cautions

1. Since simulation is a *representation* of reality, don't allow yourself to begin to think of it *as reality*. If you do, you may find yourself defending an inadequate representation. Use the simulation to check reality and obtain a better approximation of it. Obviously, this can be done via experimention in the simulation setting; but it can also be done by following instructional sessions with discussions and structured feedback.

2. Don't expect others to make the same assumptions that you do about reality. Remember, one of your objectives is to help others clarify their assumptions about reality and the fidelity of their beliefs about their own behavior. For example, you are likely to uncover a variety of views about control and planning. Some people believe it is unwise to attempt to control the environment within which human beings interact. They prefer to allow circumstances to shape events connected with the selection process and to depend on their ability to react to these circumstances. Others want to plan in such a

Figure 4-1

STEPS IN THE USE OF SIMULATED MATERIALS FOR TEACHER SELECTION.

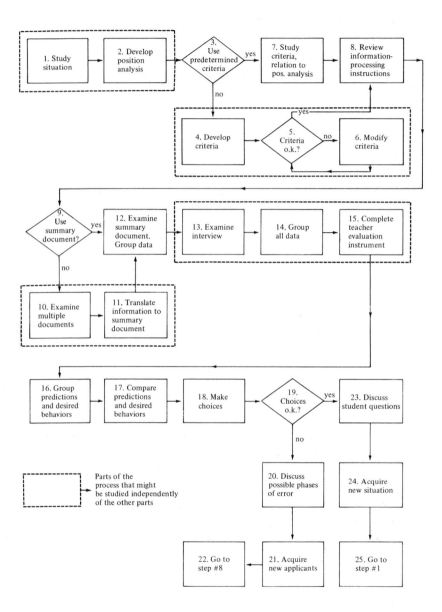

way that the circumstances which occur will be within a constricted range—thereby limiting the repetoire required for a desirable response on their part. Since a variety of assumptions can be made about reality, it is important for users of simulated materials to be well aware of their own assumptions and willing to explain them.

3. Don't expect dramatic results whether the materials are being used for research or instruction. Startling research results usually indicate a naiveté on the part of the interpreter (i.e., had he known more about the domain of the research, he would not have been so startled) or a mistake in the calculations. Likewise, quantum jumps in learning are the exception rather than the rule.

4. Don't expect all of the participants to disengage themselves immediately from their own situations and assume the hypothetical one. This is a somewhat difficult task for all and a more difficult one for the rigid, the unimaginative, and those who are easily distracted. Knowledge of the individual participants may allow an adaptation of the approach to compensate for this problem.

5. Don't try to do too much in short sessions. Remember that the participants are not as familiar with the materials or the total perspective as you are; consequently, you should establish objectives that are compatible with the time constraints. Trial sessions with colleagues and small groups will help you to make decisions on the scope of activities.

6. Don't expect all of the participants to adopt a non-threatened attitude towards the materials and the tasks required in the simulated setting. Remember, it is probably your intent to change behavior or develop new behaviors in the participants. There is a natural resistance to change, and this feeling is intensified in the less secure person; therefore, it is extremely important that you attend to the emotional atmosphere of the simulation. In this respect, it is necessary for participants to understand and accept the purposes of the simulated activities. Also, feedback should be provided to participants in a neutral fashion, i.e., without evaluative judgments, so the participants will not feel they need to defend their actions.

7. Don't conduct ad hoc experiments in simulated settings which do not fit into some plan for the development of knowledge. Experimentation is time consuming, expensive, and difficult and should not be done simply because it can be done. Unless the manipulated variables offer the promise of providing significant controls over the decision-making environment and unless the dependent variables are theoretically or practically significant, it is questionable whether enough time has been spent in planning to warrant the time and effort of conducting it.

Guidelines

The following guidelines are provided for people who have had a minimum of experience with using teacher-selection materials; they are not intended as a substitute for the experience of functioning as a participant in the simulated setting. They are further intended to assist in the use of simulated materials for research or instruction rather than in the development of new materials.

1. Consciously study the participants to obtain information for determining constraints and for modifying the materials. Their ages, experience with selection of teachers, knowledge of the decision-making process, adaptability and openness to new concepts, general emotional maturity and willingness to be introspective, views about the roles that teachers play in various situations, and attitudes toward the role of the administrator in making decisions may all affect the way you structure the situation and use of the materials.

2. Establish clear objectives. Where possible, determine the behaviors you desire the participants to exhibit following instruction. (If the simulation is for research, clarify the questions you are asking or the hypotheses to be tested.) Two approaches may be used: (a) time constraints can be considered and objectives established within the time allocated, or (b) objectives can be established and the amount of time necessary for accomplishing the objectives can be determined. The important point to remember is that objectives are not determined in terms of the portion of the simulated activities

to be completed. Rather they should be established in terms of behaviors which are desired; then the activities will be implied by the objectives.

3. Decide whether any of the materials need to be adapted; this is one reason for establishing clear objectives. The constraints of the situation may necessitate adaptation of the materials. Likewise, the materials may be designed for objectives other than the ones you have established (or not include objectives that you want to teach); consequently, they will need to be modified.

4. Develop your own background for the psychological aspects of the decision process. Unexpected questions are likely to be asked during introduction sessions, and wide reading outside educational administration literature is helpful for stimulating the discussion and referring participants to other sources. Also, such reading will stimulate ideas for research.

5. Become thoroughly familiar with the materials before using them for research or instruction. As you work with the materials, attempt to anticipate problems that may occur with relation to your specific objectives. Prior to using the materials for research or instruction, pre-test them with a small group to acquire feedback and make final adaptations.

6. In a workshop situation, work in teams of at least two people. Two benefits will accrue: (a) the logistics problems with the materials and equipment will be handled more effectively, and (b) the participants will benefit from the breadth of background which the team affords.

7. Use materials to encourage participants to validate their own selection procedures. Obviously, the use of the materials will not determine whether valid decisions are being made in a given situation; this can be determined only by research in the local situation. However, the materials can be used in such a way that there will be strong motivation to conduct such research.

As indicated previously, these cautions and guidelines do not serve as a substitute for functioning as a participant with the simulated materials. Neither do they provide the motivation to depart from more conventional research and instructional procedures in educational administration. To the person who has decided to explore and break a few boundaries, who has made some initial investigations into the materials, and who feels that his present procedures do an injustice to the complexities of the ideas and concepts he wants to teach, the cautions and guidelines will be helpful.

BACKGROUND INFORMATION AND THEORETICAL FRAMEWORK

The preceding sections of this chapter have provided some indications of the background information or theoretical framework needed to simulate the teacher-selection process. Basically, the background information can be discussed within the broad confines of decision theory, but the discussion of a special case of decision making, viz., the selection process, helps to clarify the total frame of reference. In addition, the relationship to another major personnel task, evaluation of teachers, adds perspective and significance to the selection procedure. The discussion of these three topics (decision theory, the selection process, and the relationship of selection to evaluation) is provided as background information and as a theoretical framework for the task of simulating the teacher-selection process.

Decision Theory

Since the late 1940s, there has been a growing development of decision theory and the application of mathematical models to the administrative process. This interest in decision making has permeated the literature of educational administration, (13, 16, 17), and there appears to be little disagreement about its significance to administrative behavior. Griffiths (16) was one of the first educational administrators to emphasize the importance of decision making as a theory of administration. Two of his objectives for developing decision making as a theory were to provide guides to action and to develop a framework within which researchers could find new knowledge; however, the framework has not precipitated much experimental research (19).[5]

In general, students of decison making have taken two approaches: (a) the normative, designed to tell a decision maker how he *should* make a set of decisions for which a given model is appropriate and (b) the descriptive, which has as its goal the design of a model that will simulate the behavior of the decision maker as accurately as possible (50). Mathematical statisticians, operations analysts, management scientists, and, in many cases, economists have been concerned with normative models. On the other hand, psychologists and other behavioral scientists have been more interested in descriptive models.

The distinction between these two approaches is relatively clear, in spite of the fact that the merits of the two views are in dispute. It seems evident that if one studies the descriptive models, he will be dealing with such things as the way decisions are made, the processes by which decisions are arrived at, the consequences of decisions and how they are predicted, and the sources of decision in an organization. However, the function of normative models is to study ways for improving decision making; this approach has led to the development of mathematical models of small groups and organizations and to the theory of games. Some doubt the utility of normative models because they seem to diverge from descriptions of human behavior, but Davidson and Suppes (12) indicate that even if a theory of rational decisions has little descriptive value, it still may have great interest as a normative theory. The point is well taken in that an idealized model may provide pregnant suggestions for training inefficient decision makers.

Elements of Decision Theory

Formulation of the decision problem has been described by many authors (7,8). Included as elements in the decision process are (a) the state of nature (a description of possible environmental or situational constraints which may affect goals or outcomes), (b) a list of actions or alternatives, (c) an outcome or consequence for each act, (d) a probability associated with each outcome, and (e) a value associated with each outcome. The application of a criterion determines the action that will be chosen. It is assumed that such a formulation occurs as a result of the problems being faced by individuals and organizations—problems which involve

which indicate that a participant's satisfaction with group discussions is related to whether he has had the opportunity to influence the outcome as much as he wishes. Thus satisfaction depends more on a person's felt influence than on how much he talked at the meeting (28, p.146). If these results generalize to decisions regarding selection of teachers and if it is important for principals to be satisfied with the results of selection of teachers, then it seems important to include principals in at least the planning of selection procedures if not in the actual analysis of data and choice of applicants. Although it does not appear as feasible to simulate the aspects of decision making relating to the acceptance criterion, neither does it appear to be as critical as the quality dimension in teacher selection.

Another aspect of the decision situation that needs to be considered in order to provide information for simulation is the nature of the constraints or limitations imposed on the decision maker. Limits lend reality to the description of the decision situation; without them there is very little control afforded in either the training or experimental setting. Sorensen (48) identifies five limitations to decision making in the White House: (a) permissibility (such items as law, acceptance, and whether the option is considered workable and enforceable), (b) available resources, (c) time available, (d) previous commitments, and (e) available information.

Although Griffiths (16, p.140) is concerned with entirely different content as far as decisions are concerned (assuming the unique aspect of the presidency of the United States), his listing of limits to decision making has considerable overlap with Sorensen's: (a) definition of purpose, (b) criterion of rationality, (c) conditions of employment, (d) lines of formal authority, (e) relevant information provided, and (f) time. Griffiths' list is somewhat more general and includes items which at first glance appear unrelated to some of Sorensen's items. However, rationality is related to permissibility and previous commitments; conditions of employment may be related to permissibility, available resources, and previous commitments; and definition of purpose and lines of formal authority are related to Sorensen's explanation of permissibility. Both lists give clues to information needed to provide realism for the description of a simulated situation.

Dill (13) states that the organizational environment, individuals, and groups are all limits to the rationality of decisions. Royal (42) expands this view as he places it in the context of the school principal. He indicates that a principal decides on the basis of facts and whether those above and below will approve the decision.[7] Because of the pressure to accommodate desires of those above and below, Royal proposes that sometimes principals do not fully evaluate the facts. This emphasizes that there is more than one type of consequence to decisions, and one type of consequence is the reaction that others will have to the decision. Some administrators ignore facts (pertinent to other consequences) or weight them less because of the focus on consequences related to the reactions of others to a decision. Changes in personnel, above or below the decision maker, sometimes change the value structure of the organization or of the decision maker. This change in value structure causes the decision maker to appear inconsistent; however, he may still be consistent in the sense of making decisions in terms of compatibility with those who surround him.

This concern for organizational environment is related to the decision maker's interest in the institution as a whole as compared to his regard for a certain part of it. Principals are not normally as concerned about the total system as they are about what is happening in their own buildings. The fact that a proposed action will result in progress for the institution as a whole does not guarantee its easy acceptance by teachers or principals who live within a system of rewards and penalties that uniquely influence their positions. This fact may be a source of conflict between principals and central office personnel with relation to the hiring of teachers. Principals may be more interested in maintenance of the status quo, whereas the central office may be more concerned with effecting change, or vice versa. In simulating the teacher-selection process, it is important to specify enough details about the organization to make the participant aware of any possible conflicts that exist.[8]

Some authors in the field of decision making are inclined to deviate from the formal description of the problem used by the mathematical statisticians. They prefer to think that decision making involves more than the simple choice among well-defined alternative solutions to a clearly specified problem; for them it involves the following stages: (a) agenda building, (b) goal choices or search activities, (c) commitment and allocation of resources, (d) implementation, and (e) evaluation (2,13). With relation to the relative importance of these stages, Dill expresses the view that agenda building and search activities may have greater effects on the future of an organization than the actual choice has. However, this position appears to assume that decisions regarding agenda (a choice, or series of choices) and search (which also seems to include choices) are completely unique and have no relationship to the cognitive processes of other choices. It is difficult to argue strongly for such a position; rather the case can more logically be made for agenda building (and search activities, as described by Dill) as a special case or an example of decision making.

However, it is possible to make a legitimate distinction between the process of arriving at a choice of action and the process of convincing others that this is indeed an appropriate action to take (7, p. 15). Yet, the two processes need not be completely independent. For example, an administrator may anticipate that the method by which he solves a problem (e.g., a carefully controlled correlation study or an experiment) will be partially responsible for convincing others of the efficacy of the solution. To the extent that he uses research to convince others, the two processes are not distinct; however, observation of administrators identifies many who depend more on rhetoric, deduction from the limited information available, and common practice in reputable organizations than on carefully collected and rigorously analyzed empirical data.

Also, there is a necessity to distinguish between truth and consistency in the decision situation. Truth involves reality, or empirical verification of information, whereas consistency is a logical question that does not require such verfication (7). Decision makers in education are interested in both consistency and truth in the selection of teachers. Truth is concerned with the process of validation and depends on the local definition of adequacy of the behaviors as well as the relation of these behaviors on the job to measurable indices available prior to selection, whereas consistency is concerned with the processing of data on teacher applicants. The consistent processing is a necessary condition to the validity of teacher selection, but is not sufficient. This means that any simulation designed to investigate the consistency of decision makers in selecting teachers can be accomplished without the use of real data. Such is not the case with validation because of the relationship to reality. This fact is significant in that it points to one of the limitations of simulation for the teacher-selection process, viz., the inability to check a decision maker's capability to make valid decisions. This limitation is not as severe as it may seem initially, and a discussion later in this section will help to clarify this point.

The admission of limitations (or fallibilities) of a system is not foreign to decision makers. In fact, some insist that abandoning face-saving alibis and acknowledging that incorrect predictions are not accidents—but are as much a part of the prediction system as the correct predictions themselves—will assist the decision maker by improving his perspective of the non–deterministic nature within which decisions are made (7, p. 39). In the realm of selection of teachers, this can be interpreted to mean that a decision maker should not expect all of his choices to be correct; rather, he should be seeking to improve his averages.

Within this perspective, simulation of the teacher-selection process becomes a means of improving the average of decisions made. The complexity of the simulation is dependent on the depth of the answers to be obtained and the lessons to be taught. In designing a simulation, a narrow path must be trod between the pitfalls of overcomplication and oversimplification (39, p. 67). With the elaborate theoretical framework that has been developed for decision making, it is essential to choose for the simulation only those elements which will assist either in teaching the desired concepts or in studying certain aspects of the process. It should be observed that relatively simple images of the world can serve very effectively as the basis for predictions (13, p. 206), and this fact is beneficial in the simulation process.

The concept of strategy has received much attention in the literature on decision making. Strictly speaking, a strategy is a list which specifies what move will be made for every conceivable set of moves of the particular game being played. Whereas Edwards (14, p. 406) describes strategy in game-theory terms, it is easy enough to transfer the meaning to dynamic educational situations which require a sequence of decisions. However, Edwards points out that only for the simplest games, e.g., matching pennies, does this concept of strategy have any empirical meaning.

Still if a strategy is considered to be a rule for making a decision, and limited by the information available to make predictions, then strategies are very important to decision makers. One function of strategies is to clarify relationships and preferences among conflicting organizational or individual goals. Since organizations and individuals have a variety of purposes (some of which are conflicting) the use of one method or choice of one action can result in a loss to one goal and no loss (or even a gain) for another (9, p. 258). The function of a strategy is to establish procedures for choice in such a way that the summation of predicted consequences is most beneficial to the organization. In the case of teacher selection, it is easy to see that very few choices are made on the basis that one person is clearly superior to all others on all relevant characteristics. Rather, where person "A" may be higher on measures of creativity and buoyancy, person "B" may be higher on organizational ability and empathy. The choice between the two must be determined by a strategy which specifies criteria for combining data on the individuals. Bross (7) identifies five strategies which can be used:

1. Choose the action for which the desirability of the most probable action is as large as possible. This strategy emphasizes probability and could be adopted when one probability is exceptionally high with relation to other probabilities.

2. Choose the action which can lead to the most favorable or desirable outcome, regardless of the probability of its occurrence. This is a "Pollyanna" attitude, but it can be used if the probabilities are almost equal for all actions.

3. Consider the least favorable outcome for each action and take the action associated with the most favorable one in the set. This is a pessimistic strategy, but it guards against large losses. Therefore, it has been described as a loss-control criterion.

4. Compare costs over a long period of time, subtract the costs from long-term expected gains, and choose the highest mathematically expected gain.

5. Where the probabilities have a range of some significance, choose the largest of the least favorable expectations. If each of two actions has unfavorable aspects, examine the least favorable outcome of each action; choose the action associated

with the least unfavorableness. The emphasis here is on preventing large losses.

Bross indicates that a number of other strategies can be identified, and it seems apparent that the identification of strategies is somewhat related to the content of decisions.

For example, Hilton (21) identifies decision-*avoiding* strategies (such strategies as refusal to consider alternatives, sequential strategies, and postponement) among people being counseled for career choices, as well as such decision-*making* strategies as alteration of planning horizon, alteration of requirements, and selection by elimination. As a result of his research, he raises the following pertinent questions: Can strategies be reduced to a small number of variables? Which individuals choose which strategies and why, i.e., what are the relationships between the choice of strategy and the attributes of a person? Both of these questions are pertinent to decisions made in the selection of teachers and may be investigated within a simulated situation.

The overall function of strategy is discussed by Manne (31, pp. 4-5), and he indicates that the function of an economist is to indicate clearly the extent of incompatibility among the company's individual aims. The economist must insist, for example, that the enterprise cannot simultaneously pay maximum wages and still operate at the lowest cost. In a similar manner, the educational decision maker must be aware that all characteristics are not available (in maximum amounts) in teachers, and he must assist in establishing strategies to deal with the problem.

One aspect of strategy which must be considered is whether the information presently available is sufficient for making the decision. Additional information normally costs money. Therefore, the cost of additional information plus the costs of added internal communication can be examined in relation to the probable gains resulting from the information. Thus, a calculation can be made of that point beyond which the cost of additional information is no longer justified by improved performance (26, pp. 33-34). This aspect of strategy can be considered, also, as a question of balancing the cost of information against the probable relative loss if the information is not acquired and is directly pertinent to the simulation of decisions in the selection of teachers.

Typologies

A considerable amount has been said in order to clarify aspects of decision making that are pertinent to instruction and research on teacher selection in a simulated setting. However, other perspectives regarding the conditions under which decisions are made provide additional and clarifying information.

For example, consider the conditions under which an administrator should *not* decide. Barnard (16) points out that administrators should *not* decide if the decision is not pertinent, if the decision is premature, if the decision cannot be made effective, or if others should decide. By contrast, he says that administrators *should* decide on authoritative communication from superiors, cases referred by subordinates, and actions originating in the initiative of the executive. These three conditions for deciding provide the now-familiar types of decisions known as intermediary, appellate, and creative decisions, respectively.

Luce and Raiffa (27, p. 13) provide an entirely different typology of conditions in which decisions are made: (a) certainty—where each action is known to lead to specific outcomes, (b) risk—where each action leads to one of a set of possible specific outcomes, each outcome occurring with a known probability, (c) uncertainty—where the probability of the outcomes is unknown, and (d) a combination of uncertainty and risk. More study has been done of decision making under uncertainty, and this condition is considered to be most pertinent to decision making in organizations.

To consider decision making as either static or dynamic also provides additional perspective of the complexity of the task. Although static decision-making models have been studied more than dynamic ones, simply because they are more manageable under observable conditions, static decision theories have only a limited future (14, p. 485). There future is limited because human beings learn and probabilities and values change; consequently, dynamic decision-making models offer more promise of applicability.

At least two cases of dynamic decision making that are pertinent to simulation of the teacher-selection process have been identified: (a) where the environment is unchanging but the decision maker's information changes because of successive decisions, other events, or both, and (b) where the environment changes while the decision maker is obtaining information about it. It is conceivable that simulation of the teacher-selection process might incorporate either or both of these dynamic aspects, but it is quite likely that computers will be needed in order to do so.

Two other descriptions of the decision process should be discussed at this point. First, Simon (46, p. 8) classifies decisions by using a two-dimensional grid. One dimension is concerned with programmed and nonprogrammed decisions, and the other dimension considers whether the process is traditional or modern. Thus, Simon identifies four categories: traditional programmed, modern programmed, traditional nonprogrammed, and modern nonprogrammed. The typology is useful in that it suggests long-range strategies that can be used for solving administrative problems and for training administrators. For example, it seems to be advantageous to make as many decisions as possible via such modern programmed techniques as operations research, mathematical analysis, and use of data processing equipment. In this way administrators can be relieved for the more time-consuming and difficult task of making nonprogrammed decisions. Although Simon predicts that modern nonprogrammed decisions will eventually be made by heuristic computer programs, another approach appears to be that of training administrators to make creative, nonprogrammed decisions. Certainly, one of the most promising techniques for accomplishing this task is simulation.

A second aspect of the decision process which should be considered is discussed by Cronback and Gleser (11, p. 18), who indicate that a strategy leads either to a terminal or to an investigatory decision. The terminal decision provides a choice of alternatives, whereas an investigatory decision calls for additional information—dictating what procedure will be used for acquiring the information. This investigation then leads to a further decision and the cyclical procedure continues until a terminal decision is made. This cycle of decisions is particularly pertinent to decision making in the selection of teachers where a successive-hurdles approach is used. Likewise it is related to a search function which should be included in simulating the teacher-selection process in order to train for all of the information-processing skills needed in real situations.

A basic problem for research and teaching. When an individual chooses among alternatives which involve uncertain consequences, it seems clear that there are two factors which must be given primary consideration. One is the degree to which the possible consequences are desired relative to one another, and the other is the degree to which the consequences are considered probable. The first factor is the subjective value which a decision maker places on the consequence, regardless of the value measured in some absolute terms such as dollars; and the second factor is the subjective probability associated with the consequences which occur. Since the condition is uncertain, the objective probability cannot be determined. These two factors constitute the major problem that has faced decision theorists. The difficulty lies in disentangling the roles of subjective probability and value on the basis of actual decisions (12, p. 10; 50, p. 64). Unless the two factors can be separated effectively, i.e., measures obtained of both factors, no satisfactory empirical test of the theory can be obtained.

This difficulty of disentangling the two factors is important to students and practitioners alike because it appears to be the clue to instruction as well as research. If one is limited to observing actions chosen in decision situations and is not able to infer values or subjective probabilities, then it may be quite difficult to provide assistance to decision makers in improving the choices they make. In effect, about all that can be said about a given choice is that it either matches some external criterion or it does not. But no clues can be given as to the decision maker's thought processes or factors considered in making the choice.[9] Yet, the analysis of the ingredients of the thought process appears to be essential to assisting individuals to improve their decision-making skills.

Edwards (14, p. 396) proposes that only an experimental procedure which holds one of these variables constant, or otherwise allows for it, can hope to measure the other. It seems that an attempt to design simulation materials in such a way that subjective probability and values can be separated is of prime importance. If simulated materials permit this separation, it will be possible to determine some of the effects of situational variables and prior experience on subjective probabilities and values of consequences—a problem area almost completely unexplored and of vital importance if decision theory is to be of help in the prediction of behavior (15, p. 488; 25, p. 43).

The problem of rationality. Much of decision theory has been influenced by VonNeuman and Morgenstern's *Theory of Games and Economic Behavior* (55) which is concerned substantively with economic problems. They make the following assumptions about the nature of economic man: (a) he is completely informed, (b) he is infinitely sensitive, and (c) he is rational (14, p. 381). The idea of being completely informed is intuitively comprehensible (although vulnerable as an assumption, especially if intended for a normative theory) and is necessary for developing the theory of strategies in playing games. Likewise, the infinite sensitivity to information appears intuitively understandable. However, the concept that needs elaboration is rationality. Rationality means two things. First, economic man can weakly order[10] the states into which he can get or the estimated consequences of a given alternative. Second, he makes choices among alternatives so as to maximize *something* (14, pp. 381, 403; 50; p. 51). But what is he attempting to maximize? The theory of games specifies that he attempt to maximize *expected utility* (14, pp. 391-92; 27, p. 50). Expected utility consists in its simplest form of the product of subjective probability and subjective value. This concept is assumed to be behaviorally meaningful in positing the rationale of economic man.

In contrast to economic man, and because of what are considered to be indefensible assumptions about economic man, the concept of administrative man has developed. Rather than assume that man is completely informed and infinitely sensitive, or even that he behaves rationally in the sense of attempting to maximize something, it is assumed that administrative man behaves according to a goal of *satisficing.* This term was first used by Simon (45, pp. 196-206) in his denunciation of the assumptions which he believes lead the study of decision making away from reality and application.

Administrative man simplifies the choice process because of his inability to have all information available and analyzable. The key to this simplification is replacement of the goal of *maximizing* with the goal of satisficing, which consists of finding a course of action that is "good enough" rather than maximal in some sense (50, p. 61f). In effect, it is assumed that administrative man selects the first alternative he encounters which meets some minimum level of satisfaction[11] with respect to each of the values he seeks to attain. Since he cannot acquire all information and is not infinitely sensitive (in effect, since he cannot predict consequences indefinitely into the future), he makes his choice in terms of a number of intermediate outcomes in the form of intermediate goals which he considers to be related to his long-range goals. In chess, for example, the total number of alternatives and eventual consequences of a given move early in the game is almost infinite. Yet, it is not necessary to draw a decision tree with infinite branches and develop a strategy which takes into consideration all of these potentialities. Instead, chess players attempt to simplify the choice process by working to accomplish certain intermediate goals of king safety, center control, and so forth.

Similarly, in the selection of teachers, one is not expected to predict the total effect of forty years of teaching on all children when a teacher is being considered for an initial teaching position. Rather, the choice is simplified by establishing some intermediate goals of desired teacher behavior (assummed to be related to pupil learning) during the first one or two years of teaching.

It appears obvious that the substitution of satisficing for maximizing greatly reduces the demands upon the computational capabilities of the decision maker and is closely linked to the concept of search. The essential idea is that the individual searches until he finds an alternative that is "good enough."

The significance of satisficing as a concept is that it has shifted the emphasis from normative models to descriptive models, or at least that it has increased the interest in and activity concerning descriptive models. This has probably occurred because some investigators feel that little has been done to demonstrate that the model of economic man can be fruitfully employed in dealing descriptively with decision uncertainty (50, p. 58). However, if rational behavior is more ideal than the descriptive behavior found, what can be determined via the normative models that will allow movement in the direction of rationality? Or, what substitutions for rationality are acceptable considering our descriptions of decision behavior? Simon's answer is satisficing, but other answers may be profitable to explore.

In addition to shifting the emphasis to description of decision making, satisficing points to the necessity to perform research on the perceptual processes, goal setting, and level of aspiration phenomena as they relate to administrative man's decision making in organizational settings (13, p. 210). Also, in selection of teachers, it implies using minimum cutting points for reducing search procedures.[12]

Simon suggests that administrative man should place less reliance on prediction of the future and more reliance on feedback regarding decisions (45, p. 204). With relation to teacher selection procedures, this implies (a) extension of the selection process into the employment period, (b) examination of the relationship between selection and evaluation of teachers, and (c) consideration of the interaction of selection, assignment (or placement), and supervisory treatment decisions. Both (a) and (b) are concerned with questions of validity in selection decisions and are difficult to include in simulated activities without prescribing specific local selection criteria or value systems. However, consideration of (c) can be included in the description of the situation for which the selection is to be made.

From a psychological standpoint, in terms of the theory of riskless choice which incorporates economic man, human beings are neither perfectly consistent nor perfectly sensitive (14, p. 389). Consequently, some students have become interested in problems of irrationality.

Rosenblueth (41, pp. 50-52) describes three types of irrationality: (a) real irrationality which is based on impulses that will be rejected after consideration, even though new information is not available; (b) irrationality born from ignorance where the decision maker changes the decision if fuller and better information is available; and, (c) irrationality due to a "deviation from a capitalist spirit," caused by a failure to maximize profits. It seems that this listing does not exhaust the categories of irrationality. For example, an experiment by Bolton (5, p. 3f) implies that irrationality occurs as a result of inability to process available information due to the format or organization of the data.

In addition, Schelling (44, p. 16) suggests that irrationality may result from a disorderly and inconsistent value system, faulty calculation, and inability to receive messages or to communicate efficiently. It can imply random or haphazard influences in the reaching of decisions, in the transmission of them, or in the receipt of information; and it sometimes merely reflects the collective nature of a decision by individuals who do not have identical value systems and whose organizational arrangements and communication systems do not cause them to act as a single entity. Becker and McClintock (4) echo Schelling's concern by indicating that a person's behavior may appear irrational because he assigns different (or wrong) utilities to the payoffs. Further, a person attaches different utility to a prize as his resources change.

The application of these views to selection processes via simulation is related to the need to teach a decision maker the value system which he will be using to make institutional decisions. If there is a single building in a school district and if the principal of that building has the responsibility for selecting teachers, then there is no need for reconciling his value system with that of other principals or central office personnel. However, if the district has a number of buildings and if it is desirable for the district to have a unified (in some respect) philosophy or set of goals, then it is necessary for those involved in the selection procedure to use selection procedures compatible with the organizational goals. If a principal's value system is the same as the organization's, there is no problem. Simulation of the teacher-selection process makes it possible to check whether an individual utilizes a given value system in making selections. Also, it allows a check to be made of the efficiency of instructional sessions designed to orient decision makers to the value system of a school organization.

Some authors warn, however, that verbal responses may be consistent with each other, yet inconsistent with other forms of behavior (18, pp. 132-33). This idea may lead to the conclusion that results obtained in a simulated situation will not generalize to reality since the results of an inquiry restricted to verbal responses may be different from the actual behavior in a real situation. All simulation procedures are faced with this problem, and there is a need for research in a choice situation which compares responses to paper-pencil questions, to cases, and to reality with responses in a simulated situation.

Other items may contribute to a person's consistency. Majumdar (29, p. 7-8) discusses consistency in the example of race-track betting where the little old lady who always bets on the horse with the long tail is considered to be consistent, no matter how often she is wrong, whereas the lady who sometimes bets on long tails and at other times on the color of the horse is considered to be whimiscal and inconsistent. The latter person's apparent inconsistency may be due to circumstances where the lady is indifferent to choice; therefore, the choice is made on satisfaction with what is considered to be an irrelevant factor or on a random basis. It may be that a comparable situation exists in the selection of teachers. Where a central office person is indifferent to the choice of two or more applicants, he may allow the principal to make a decision. Apparently this decision is to be made on characteristics that are differentiable and significant. Yet, in reality, the decision may be made on some rather irrelevant quality that fulfills the principal's satisfaction criterion.

Taylor (50, p. 66) points out that experimental data show that sets of choices are often intransitive and that repeated choices are sometimes inconsistent. In other words, situations exist where subjects prefer A to B, B to C, *but* C to A. Likewise, a person may choose A over B in one case, but he may choose B over A in a repetition of the choice. The reasons for such behavior are not clear, however, and research needs to be done in simulated situations to determine reasons. For example, is such behavior due to misperceptions or errors of measurement? That is, if two things are very similar and if measurement is not extremely accurate (or if the data are confused to the point that a person cannot interpret them), then it appears that intransitivity or inconsistency can be expected.

Handy and Kurtz (18, p. 133) indicate that the context of behavior may provide clues to what appears to be inconsistent behavior. A behavioral sequence in one cultural setting may reveal preferences or choices quite different from the same sequence in another cultural setting. For example, the restrictive behavior of a teacher toward a particular child on the first day of school may be interpreted differently from similar behavior at another time during the year. In effect, the context of behavior may be pertinent to deciding what a particular behavior means, and this in turn may be a clue to the nature of information provided in recommendations for teachers. There may be a distinct advantage to descriptions of teacher behavior in particular contexts over conclusions reached by the observer of the behavior. The description of behavior leaves the decision maker the choice of inferring meaning which will be pertinent to a new situation for which he is considering the applicant, where the other information requires that he assume some general behavior that is insensitive to context.

Empirical information. Although very little research has been done in educational administration to test decision theories or to deal with the psychological aspects of decision making, a number of empirical studies have been conducted in laboratories or business settings, and these are pertinent to the cognitive processes involved in making decisions. Mills and Snyder (33, pp. 458-70) have found that choices are expressed less frequently the closer the attractiveness of the alternatives. Is this closeness in attractiveness of alternatives the major reason that decision makers use a strategy of delay in the hope that a clearly superior alternative will emerge? Or is such a strategy partly due to the personality of the administrator and partly due to the closeness of the alternatives? In what way is the delay strategy related to the preceived risk in the situation? Is the delay strategy a function of the content of the decision?

Mills and Snyder report that choices are expressed more frequently when there is uncertainty about the alternative that will result if a choice is not made (i.e., if a delay strategy is used). Again, the interesting questions regarding this result revolve around the generality of the results and the way they can be applied to decision making in educational administration.

Results of some studies indicate that it is difficult to make generalizations across individuals because individuals appear to have general preferences or dislikes for risk-taking. Some people even have specific preferences among objective probabilities. For example, some prefer betting on a probability of .50 and will avoid betting on a probability of .75 (14, p. 396).

The attractiveness of a given alternative appears to be related to the accuracy and the variability of information regarding the decision. Edwards (15, pp. 485-87) discusses the propositon that the variance of a bet is as imporatnt as the subjective expected utility in determining its attractiveness, and he concludes that research which has been conducted on the question is ambiguous. However, Naylor (35, p. 43) believes that preference for an information source is related both to the accuracy of a measure and to its variability, with accuracy appearing to be the more rapidly recognized of the two. If these results generalize to decision making in the selection of teachers, it will be interesting to learn how decision makers perceive the accuracy and variability of specific information about teacher applicants. Likewise, it seems important to know how an increase in actual accuracy and decrease in actual variability of the information provided to decision makers affect their perceptions and their preferences for choices.

Roberts (40, pp. 26-37) says that subjects who have experienced experimentally produced failure on a series of problems presented just before a sequential decision task seek significantly more information than those who have experienced success. Is this related to the fact that decision makers tend to weight negative information about applicants more heavily than they do positive information? If an individual values lack of failure much more than potentially high success, is this value system generalizable across a variety of types of educational decisions? In other words, is this a general disposition to avoid failure at the risk of passing up outstanding success, or does it apply only to certain types of decisions such as the selection of teachers? In addition, can the values implied in given decision situations be modified; and if so, how does it affect the decision maker's information-search procedures?

Although information-search procedures vary, administrators generally overvalue and, at the same time, ignore most of the information they receive. They appear to use only the "key" facts, yet they are willing to pay for all of the facts, useful and useless (4, p. 253). Again, is this true for decision makers in educational administration? What is considered to be "key" information for various decisions in educational administration? Can what constitutes "key" information be taught to neophytes?

Observations made thus far concerning empirical information and how it relates to decision theory seem to imply the following:

1. The definition of the problem to be solved by a decision maker, the constraints that are pertinent to the decision, and the alternatives available can all differ due to the perception of the decision maker and the way he processes information.

2. Prediction of consequences is related to the amount of relevant information one has on hand and the amount that can be obtained. This seems to depend on the prior experience of the decision maker and his communication with sources of information. Some of this experience and familiarity with sources can be obtained through simulated activities.

3. Familiarity with institutional goals is related to prediction and interpretation of consequences. Again, experience with these goals can be obtained through simulated activities.

Conclusions regarding decision theory. As background information for simulating the teacher-selection process, decision theory is a fruitful area to study. However, much remains to be known about decision making, and three approaches have been used in seeking this knowledge.

The first approach is *introspection by those involved in decision making.* Although this procedure is time honored and respected in many circles (as evidenced by many reflective articles in administrative journals), the knowledge generated in this way is severely limited. Davidson and Suppes (12, p. 9) indicate that the essential difficulty with introspection in regard to the study of decision making is not that it is unreliable and private (although these are severe limitations to obtaining scientific knowledge) but that how to put it to use is not evident. It appears that the greatest function of introspection in scientific inquiry is hypothesis generation, or the suggestion of basic axioms and/or theorems of a theory rather than testing hypotheses or guiding conclusions. If this is true, the reflective articles based on introspection should be interpreted for what they are—preliminary hunches about the reality of the world, waiting to be tested by the systematic collection and analysis of empirical data.

The second approach is *computer modeling of cognitive processes.* The history of this procedure is very short, but the evidence collected thus far indicates that this procedure offers much opportunity for testing theories of decision making. Also, it should provide beneficial information for theories of learning and problem solving, topics which are related and important to decision making (50, p. 48).

The third approach is *the examination of actions taken in contrived settings.* Experimentation in laboratory and simulated settings has a longer history than computer modeling in most areas concerned with scientific knowledge, but the use of this procedure for studying man's decision making is very recent. Consequently, although there is a potentially great advantage in using this procedure to determine causal relationships among variables involved in the decision act, the general application to administrative behavior has not been extensive. The reasons are obvious; much of the research in laboratory situations has lacked the complexity needed for application to reality, and the use of simulated situations which incorporate more dimensions of reality has been employed primarily for training rather than for research. Consequently, although there is a potentially great advantage in using this procedure to determine causal realtionships among variables involved in the decision act, the general application to administrative behavior has not been extensive. The reasons are obvious; much of the research in laboratory situations has lacked the complexity needed for application to reality, and the use of simulated situations which incorporate more dimensions of reality has been employed primarily for training rather than for research.

If simulated situations are to be used more effectively for production of knowledge regarding decision making, work must be done on the content of decisions. Dill (13, p. 205) points out the need for examination of decision making in school settings inasmuch as school environments differ in important respects from other organizations. In discussing the content of administrative decision making, Taylor (50, p. 81) says that many management problems, including perhaps most of the important ones, are "ill-structured." He described well-structured problems as those which can be described in terms of numerical variables, where goals can be specified as an objective function, and where there are computational routines that permit solution and statement in numerical terms.[13]

With relation to structuring problems so they can be studied more effectively in contrived situations, Davidson and Suppes (12,

p. 7) indicate that the ultimate goal of decision theory is to throw light on how people make decisions in everyday life. They suggest that the decisions to be made in the contrived situation should be real in the most important sense, i.e., they should have the appropriate and expected consequences.

Much work needs to be done in educational administration if the context of significant decisions is to be structured so that decisions can be systematically studied in simulated situations and conclusions can be generalized to real situations. If significant knowledge is to be developed about decision making of educational administrators, it is important to study those problem areas and processes that can be adequately specified before tackling ill-structured problems.[14] From the study of these processes, information can be obtained for use in studying the more poorly structured problems. The selection process is more adequately described than many other educational decisions as indicated by the description which follows.

The Teacher-Selection Process

When the classifcation system specified by Cronback and Gleser (11, p. 15-17) is applied to the decision process for selecting teachers, it is evident that:

1. The person selecting teachers is involved in making an institutional decision rather than an individual one. An institutional decision is one where a common set of values is applied to a large number of comparable decisions. There is an attempt to make decisions which benefit the institution as much as possible. The applicant, however, must make an individual decision to join the organization, and this decision is made on the basis of individual values.

2. Each teacher applicant is assigned to a single treatment. A teacher cannot be assigned to a "hire" treatment and to a "not hire" treatment at the same time; neither can a teacher be assigned to a fourth-grade, self-contained classroom and also to teach art at a junior high school. At times the assignment is adapted to a teacher by modifying the specifics of the assignment to the particular abilities of the teacher. For example, a teacher may be hired for a fourth-grade assignment;

but rooms, materials or students may be changed because of the abilities of the teacher.

3. A quota is rather precisely followed. A school district has a number of vacancies to fill and only that number of teachers is hired. At times a district may hire a few extra elementary teachers with the anticipation that late registrations will occur, but seldom is this the case. When a district does hire "extras," the "extras" may be considered to be within a quota.

4. In all decisions one of the acceptable treatments is "reject." This assumes that the selection ratio, i.e., the ratio of the number selected to the number who applied, is less than 1.0. If a district is in such an unfavorable geographical location that very few applications are received, the selection ratio might indeed be 1.0. In this case, no rejections would occur. On the other hand, it is inconceivable that any district would have a policy where "reject" is not a possibility. Other administrative decisions are made under conditions where "reject" is not a possibility—for example, admission of normal students to public schools.

5. Generally the information gathered is in a multivariate form. Seldom is grade point average, or rating on personality in an interview, or recommendations regarding dependability considered separately. The total information gathered represents a variety of dimensions; it may be factor analyzed to reduce its complexity, but it still represents multiple variables.

6. The decision is commonly made at any one of various points in a sequence of information gathering, i.e., a type of sequential testing or successive hurdles is used. If cutting points are used with any of the information categories, it is not even necessary for the information to be processed in a prescribed sequence. However, all information may be collected and then a single final decision made. If this is done,[15] the data can take the form of multivariate information collected to predict various behaviors which have varying utility in relation to some institutional goal.

The tasks of the person who selects teachers include: (a) collecting reliable information, (b) using this information for predicting the consequent behaviors of the teacher, and (c) relating these behaviors to the operation of the organization so that some measure of the total utility of the individual to the organization can be made. These tasks are necessary to determine the relative merit of each applicant for a specific assignment. In addition, of course, the decision maker must determine how many (if any) of the applicants should be hired at a particular time. This decision depends on the quota to be filled, the quality of the applicants being considered, the probability that additional people will apply, and the probable quality of such additional applicants. The number of additional applicants and their quality are related to the time of the year.

We can ignore temporarily the problem of deciding whether or not to hire and concentrate on ranking the available applicants on the basis of overall contribution to the major goals of the organization. Let us assume that we can collect information about a group of teachers who are already members of the school system and that we can collect information about applicants for this school system. It can be arranged in tabular form as in Table 4-1.[16]

Table 4-1

RELATION OF INFORMATION, CONSEQUENT BEHAVIOR AND
TOTAL UTILITY IN THE SELECTION OF TEACHERS

	Person	Information Categories (Y) 1 2 ......m	Consequent Behaviors (C) 1 .... p	Total Utility (U)
Members of the School System	1 2 . . . N	I	II	III
Applicants	N+1 N+2 . . .	IV	V	VI

The *Information Categories* (Y) represent biographical entires on an application blank or credential form, test scores, grades, ratings by people who have knowledge of specific or overall behavior of the individual, or interview ratings. The *Consequent Behaviors* (C) are the behaviors exhibited by teachers in job-related activities. Examples of such behavior include warmth and friendliness or verbal facility. These behaviors can be specified by a district and reliably noted by trained observers. They may take the form of scaled descriptions of factors such as those identified by Ryans (43, p. 388) in his Teacher Characteristcs Study. The *Total Utility* (U) is a measure of the value of the individual to the operation of the system. This measure can be in the form of a scaled value, a ranking, or a clustering of people into groupings or categories.

It is assumed that the consequent behaviors and the utility are *situationally determined* (e.g., no combination of Ys will yield Cs of a particular nature regardless of situational factors; likewise, the value or utility of a given set of Cs is determined in situational context, rather than being uniform across situations). For example, a teacher may exhibit much more verbal facility with a group of senior honors students than with an average group of sophomores. Likewise, a rural district may value verbal facility differently from a suburban district.

The task is to decide which applicants are likely to make the most valuable overall contribution to the major goals of the organization. This decision is made by predicting consequent behaviors (C) and attaching values to these behaviors. The prediction of consequent behaviors is made on the basis of information collected (Y), and the attachment of values is based on institutional goals.

Some of the elements which must be considered in teaching a person to make these decisions about which of several teachers to select include the following: (a) knowledge of relationships between various Y and C categories in the present members of the system (or in the treatment category for which selection is to made); (b) knowledge of the relationships between various C categories and U in the present members of the system; (c) practice is using the relational knowledge on applicant groups to predict C and determine U; (d) feedback regarding the effectiveness of the decisions made.

To provide these elements for learning to make selection decisions, materials for simulating a teacher-selection process have been devised (see pages 93-94 for a description). In the simulated situation, the decision maker performs the following tasks: (a) he predicts what kind of behavior will be exhibited by the applicants during the last three months of the first year on the job, and (b) he ranks the applicants in terms of suitability for the position.

As indicated previously, prediction of consequent behaviors and attachment of values to these behaviors is situationally determined. Consequently, it is necessary to provide feedback in relation to a specific situation, i.e., in regard to a specific treatment if an individual is to learn to make selection decisions for that situation.

How can this be done? Consider Table 4-1 and its six parts. Provide the student with information, Parts I,II, III, and IV. (Parts V and VI are a section of the student's task.) In a real situation, Parts I-IV are available from measurement of member and applicant teachers. In a simulated situation, the data can be acquired from a real situation or created as hypothetical data. The creation of hypothetical data merely *operationally defined* a part of the situational context.

Also, provide the student with the weights $W(C:Y)$ necessary to predict C when given Y, and the weights $W(U:C)$ necessary to predict U given C. In a real situation, $W(C:Y)$ can be obtained via multiple regression techniques from the Y and C data provided in Parts I and II. This allows the prediction of each C separately, but it does not allow a decision to be made regarding the selection of an applicant—where all Cs contribute to total success but in varying amounts. In this real situation, some relative weighting needs to be developed for each C. The weightings, $W(U:C)$, can be developed by either an explicit or an implicit method.

1. *Explicit method.* Ask those who are responsible for evaluating and supervising the work of the personnel selected to rate each C on a scale in terms of the contribution the behavior makes to the overall successful behavior of individuals. (Consideration can even be given to varying amounts of the behavior, and the relative value of these amounts. In effect, this is a determinaiton of curvilinear relationship between the behavior and utility.)

2. *Implicit method.* Acquire a measure of overall utility of each teacher in the member group. If the unit of measure is continuous, multiple regression techniques can be used to establish the weightings on the various Cs to predict U. If the measurement is ordinal (i.e., if teachers are simply grouped into ordered descriptive categories), then a discriminant function analysis can be used to determine the weightings.

Again, a hypothetical determination of W(C:Y) and W(U:C) is simply a way of operationally defining a part of the simulated situation.

The student now has information about (parts I - IV, W(C:Y), and W(U:C) for a hypothetical situation. Have the student predict Parts V and VI in any way he chooses, attempting to satisfy the school system from which the information was obtained. Give him feedback regarding how *his* prediction of consequences and *his* value system compare with the school system's.

At least two possibilities exist at this point as far as instruction is concerned. First, it is possible to give the student new sets of applicants asking him to predict Parts V and VI until his predictions agree with those of the school system. When this occurs, it is relatively certain that he has learned how people are likely to behave when placed in the situation required by the school system and what value the school system has attached to these behaviors. Second, when the student is provided feedback, he can be asked to examine his predictions and value system in relation to the feedback. Then, he can choose between learning to be consistent with the school system's values, with his own predictions and values, or with a modification of either of them. At any rate, a new W(C:Y) and W(U:C) can be established at this point (or stabilized over a few trials) and the student has the task of learning to be consistent over a series of sets of applicants. If it is desirable for a student to learn to be consistent with various situations the Cs, W(C:Y) and W(U:C) can be modified for use with the same set of applicants.

This description of the selection process has not emphasized common practices used in public school systems; rather, an assumption has been made that improvements in common practice are more likely to occur if attention is paid to some of the actuarial aspects of the process. This does not mean that clinical judgments are not to be made or that they are not important. However, judgments made in the selection process are subject to examination within a framework that permits control and evaluation. The framework emphasizes the multidimensionality of predictor variables, and this emphasis is commonly accepted in the literature on selection. More importantly, it provides a way for the multidimensional behaviors exhibited in a particular teaching situation to be related to both the predictor variables and overall organizational goal. In addition, there is an emphasis throughout that selection occurs within a particular situation and that relationships among the predictors, consequent behaviors, and total utility may change when situations change. There has been an attempt to describe the process in a way that clarifies the complexities. It is hoped that the abstractions of reality have focused attention on those aspects of the process which should be attended to and studied.

Relationship to Evaluation Procedures

Traditionally, administrative processes have been concerned with control devices. However, recent authors have been interested in the applications of cybernetic cycles which include feedback and self-correcting mechanisms. Horst (22, p. 244) points to the necessity for the evaluation of proficiency to provide feedback to the selection and classification subsystem. He argues that evaluations must be readily and freely available to the selection subsystem if the (selection) model is to include self-correcting mechanisms. Evaluation of teachers, then, provides the means whereby validation of the selection process can occur; without reliable evaluation information which differentiates, selection practices will continue to rely on the untested abilities and insights of those individuals involved in the process. Yet few school systems take time to relate their evaluation and selection procedures so that they can determine where and under what circumstances mistakes are made (37, p. 7).

The relationship of the evaluation of teachers to the teacher-selection process can be seen by examination of the model presented in the previous section (see Fig. 4-1). The consequent behaviors which are related to the predictor variables are the focus of attention during the evaluation process. These behaviors are exhibited in classrooms as well as out of classrooms, and the value of each behavior (i.e., its evaluation) is determined by its relationship to the major goals of the school system. The accuracy of the measurement of behaviors and determination of the relationship to the goals (or total utility) is crucial if the evaluation process is to provide feedback to the selection process.

Some selection personnel seem to believe that making both their evaluation and selection procedures somewhat less formal solves the criterion problem.[17] A moment's reflection will surely indicate that such is not the case; it is more likely that the problem has been repressed rather than solved.

If necessary and desirable teacher behaviors are identified, care should be taken to insure that these behaviors represent the types of behavior that can be and have been observed in specific situations. They should not represent general after-the-fact impressions of some event that occured, because these observations are notoriously untrustworthy and are likely to establish criteria that are biased in favor of factors such as general appearance, manner, and personal likeableness.[18] Although these factors may be more important in teaching than in some other professions, they are likely to affect first impressions more than long-term effectiveness.

Mandell (30) indicates that a distinction should be made between the qualifications required for entrance to the job and those that can be obtained after entrance to the job. Where the cost of search for rare skills is relatively high in comparison to the training of those skills on the job, it makes more sense to enlarge the applicant pool by reducing the required qualifications and to depend on the employee's learning the requirements after being selected. If, however, there are requirements that are not likely to be learned on the job, more care than usual should be taken in measuring the predictors of these behaviors.

Further, Mandell says that any qualification requirement that substantially decreases the number of applicants for a position for which the number of applications is few to begin with can be justified only on the ground that a person cannot perform the job unless he has this qualification before entrance. Therefore, people selecting teachers should re-examine their job specifications in terms of those that are desired and those that are necessary *prior to entrance.*

Any measure, including criterion variables, has the problem of reliability. Where reliability is low, the correlation with predictor variables is reduced. If it is impossible to obtain the reliability of a criterion measure, it is extremely difficult to interpret correlations that are low and lacking predictive power (51). This lack of predictive power of correlations in teacher effectiveness studies is partially accounted for by the lack of reliability of the criterion measure in that many of the criterion measures have been ratings by principals who have had very little training in specific observation techniques and minimum supervision regarding these processes. Where the criterion variable is unreliable, nothing is likely to be found that will correlate with it. When a correlation does show up occasionally, it is likely to be spurious and unreplicable.

The implications of this discussion regarding the development of criteria are that the criteria should be multiple and specific; they should be situationally determined; and they should distinguish between requirements before entrance and those which can be acquired on the job. An inherent danger in situationally determined criteria (49) is that a firm may perpetuate a particular kind of employee and thus constrict the spectrum of personalities within the firm. This may be a problem where criteria have been established in terms of past experience rather than future needs. In the selection of teachers it need not be a problem if such factors as creativity (especially divergent thinking ability) and adaptability are included in the criteria for selection.

This points to the necessity of relating the behaviors exhibited on the job to the purposes of the system. Horst (22, pp. 243-44) emphasizes that a selection program can be no better or more effective than the evaluation program within the system. This statement is plausible only if evaluation is considered to include a measurement system that is reliable (or accurate), adequately differentiates, and is valid. It is possible to have an evaluation program that accurately measures factors which are largely irrelevant to system objectives. If behaviors are classified according to the two dimensions of relevance (or validity) and differentiation and if these two dimensions are dichotomized into high and low categories, then four conditions emerge:

	relevance	*differentiation*
1.	high	high
2.	low	high
3.	low	low
4.	high	low

Condition No. 1 is desirable in that it indicates relevant behaviors on which teachers can be measured as different. Where this relationship exists, the behaviors identified are suitable for validating a selection procedure. Condition No. 2, however, is meaningless for validating a selection procedure. For example, the method of erasing a chalkboard might differentiate among teachers, but it is irrelevant to system goals. Obviously, behaviors identified by condition No. 3 are to be rejected, also. Behaviors represented by condition No. 4 are less easily disposed of. For example, kindergarten teachers' empathy for children might be considered very relevant to the job, yet a group of kindergarten teachers and applicants for kindergarten positions may vary only slightly on this characteristic. Therefore, this factor becomes useless for validating the selection process. In effect, the evaluation of all kindergarten teachers on this variable would yield such similar results that the relationship between this factor and overall success would be low.

Some people believe that the work of individual teachers cannot be evaluated and that the school should be considered a social system and evaluated in terms of its contribution to individual students (24, p. 35). However, this evades the problem of measuring and evaluating the contribution of each individual member of the system to the overall effect. If such a position is taken, no information about the behavior of individual teachers is available for improving the system through either supervisory or selection procedures. Without information on the contribution of teachers to the school as a social system, one might just as well select teachers and choose supervisory practices via random procedures. Although this might please some people, it would represent an unpredictable professional world in which to work.

Considerable controversy has occurred with relation to the necessity to evaluate teachers in terms of locally determined goals. Although some argue that the definition of teacher efficiency should be socially justifiable in terms of *what should be* (6, p. 33) and that mediocrity is perpetuated if the definition is based on *what is* or even the best of common practices, the domain of the definition is not altogether clear. For example, some might desire to include the goals of a school system within *what should be.* Others believe in basing the evaluation of teaching on the psychological conception of what is learned (i.e., the mode or strategy of teaching) rather than what is socially acceptable in a given community (47, p. 70). If this approach is used, evaluation entails determination of whether a certain person using particular methods achieves predetermined and accepted goals. Under these conditions, evaluation becomes a technical, scientific judgment that is essentially value-free (32, p. 187). In effect, it becomes the expression of a relationship among the consequent behaviors and the total utility in Table 4-1.

In expressing a relationship of this kind, care must be taken to develop objectivity and inter-rater consistency. Otherwise, an anxious evaluator is likely to judge as valuable those behaviors which promote his immediate or delayed anxiety reduction (1, pp. 74-95). thus judgments are more likely to represent needs of the evaluators than to express the goals of the organization.

Turner (54) emphasizes the need to look at interrelationships among behaviors that can be modified and those which need to be selected. If, in accord with a local value, "permissiveness" in a classroom is desirable, thought should be given to whether or not teacher applicants have developed the problem-solving skills which are prerequisite to succeeding in this atmosphere.[20] If not, perhaps they either should not be selected, or they should not be encouraged to attempt to accomplish some of the goals for which a permissive atmosphere is necessary. This idea is not incompatible with either the idea of situationally determined goals or Smith's view that there is a need to determine the dependability of diagnoses and treatments independently of who is performing them. Rather, it illustrates the necessity of relating locally desired outcomes to teacher behaviors during the evaluation process and of developing some knowledge of what types of predictor variables are related to the desired behavior in the local situation.

The relationship of the selection process to evaluation procedures is clear even though specific procedures for collecting, analyzing, and interpreting data on teacher behaviors for evaluation purposes have not been presented. Whereas evaluation of teachers may be performed for several purposes within a school system, its function with relation to selection is singular. It provides information necessary to validate the selection process. In effect, it provides feedback which is needed to make corrections if errors are being made. Selection procedures are uninterpretable when information from the evaluation process is ambiguous.

SUMMARY

The general purpose of this chapter was to provide detailed information about simulation of the teacher-selection process. The discussion included the following topics: the need for simulation, an example of the simulation of teacher-selection, some problems involved, the use of materials for simulating the teacher-selection process, and a theoretical framework for developing materials.

An example of simulation of the teacher-selection process was provided in this chapter by describing how materials were developed and how they can be used for research and instruction. The simulation situation is designed so that research can be conducted to increase knowledge of the decision-making process. The teacher-selection process provides the specific example whereby variables can be manipulated to determine their effect on specified aspects of decision-making behavior.

The potential advantages of simulation for teaching the selection process include sufficient realism to develop interest and ego involvement of learners, non-threatening experiences, feedback to the learner and the instructor, and flexibility with relation to setting and time factors. In simulating the teacher-selection process, four major problems exist. They are the realism of the simulation, scope of the activities, dynamic and static aspects of the situation, and feedback to the participants.

In using the materials one should be cautious about allowing himself to think of the simulation as reality, expecting others to make the same assumptions about reality as he does, expecting dramatic results, expecting participants to disengage rapidly from their own situations and to assume the hypothetical one, doing too much in short sessions, expecting participants to adopt non-threatening attitudes toward the materials, and conducting experiments that do not fit into some overall plan.

Three topics (decision theory, the selection process, and the relationship of selection to evaluation) provided backgound information and a theoretical framework for the task of simulating the teacher-selection process. Although introspection by decision makers and computer modeling of cognitive processes offer some promise for contributing to knowledge of the decision process, examination of actions taken in contrived settings also offers a beneficial approach.

NOTES

[1] A much more detailed discussion of decision making is included in the Backgound Information section of this chapter.

[2] Consistent selection decisions are not necessarily valid decisions. Consistency is a necessary condition for validity, but it is not sufficient.

[3] At least, the simulation will need to be sensitive enough to reveal the student's bias, which will mean that his implicit value system will need to be measured and compared with some pre-established value system.

[4] See page 122-23 for a description of *satisficing* and how it differs from a strategy for *optimizing*.

[5] This was a relational study that determined factors of performance of elementary principals and then related these factors to certain attributes of the principals studied. There was no attempt to manipulate variables to determine causes of performance.

[6] He may or may not perceive it as a problem. Likewise, his action may be to do nothing about it.

[7] This introduces the criterion of *satisfaction* to decisions (as different from *quality*). See the discussion in Maier (28) .

[8] Providing such information in the simulated situation violates certain aspects of realism since a person in an administrative position is not furnished this information in similar form. In fact, certain problems confront him in a real situation as far as determination of the state of the world is concerned. For example, when new in a position, many administrators are quite careful to study the situation in great detail. However, after being in a position for some time, they are reluctant to study the situation; consequently, they no longer have current information on which to make decisions. Another real problem faced by administrators in this regard is deciding whether to depend on the natural input of information or to seek other information. Even if a decision is made to seek additional information, he must decide whether to use the informal collection procedures or more rigorous procedures, such as research and experimentation. Normally, the simulation of decision tasks does not require data about the situation; rather, the administrator is required

to interpret information provided and make inferences regarding the pertinence of the information to the decision task.

[9] In effect, the situation would be analogous to a baseball coach who was only able to provide information to a batter that he either missed a pitch or hit it—without being able to analyze what motions of the batter were adequate or inadequate.

[10] Stable preferences or ranking are required, but no other quantitative measures are required.

[11] Here the term, *satisfaction,* is used with relation to standard of quality rather than in the manner previously referred to by Maier.

[12] Coombs and Kao (10) suggest the use of a conjunctive composition model in which successful performance on a task requires a certain minimum in each of the relevant dimensions. For example, suppose a person is taking a history examination in French. It is impossible to answer the history questions unless he is able to read French adequately. However, excellent French reading skills will not compensate for lack of history knowledge. The concept is basic to the statement that one cannot be a good teacher without being a good scholar. Under this model, if an individual has too little in any one component, he lacks the complex aptitude; but having more than enough on one component is not sufficient condition for possession of the complex aptitude. The relationship to satisficing seems apparent.

[13] Oskar Morgenstern (34) makes a similar point when he argues for the use of mathematics and logic as a basis for decision making in the Department of State. At another point he states that complex problems should be handled as much as possible by mathematical means, leaving to intuition and art only those parts which cannot be handled by such mathematical means. The implication is that an attempt should be made to structure educational administration problems in the way suggested by Taylor so that mathematical procedures can be used.

[14] Simon's (46) description of problem solving is compatible with the strategy suggested here. One starts by erecting goals and detecting differences between the present situation and the goals. If one's memory does not provide relevant information about how these differences can be reduced, search tools are applied. If the problem is too large to be handled in this way, each problem will generate sub-problems until a sub-problem that can be solved is found, i.e., until memory or search processes can deal with differences between goals and the situation. By successive solution of sub-problems, the overall goal is accomplished or one gives up.

[15] This is the more general case (in the sense of encompassing the sequential testing case), and any investigatory decision is a special case with the availability of an additional treatment, viz., collect additional information of a specific nature.

[16] Paul Horst (22) gives an explanation of relationships between predictor and criterion attributes that uses a four-cell model.

[17] Others attempt to solve the criterion problem by allowing goal setting to be determined entirely on an individual basis by teachers; see George Redfern, *How to Appraise Teaching Performance* (Columbus, Ohio: School Management Institute, Inc., 1963). This method has some merits for the promotion of teacher growth, but the growth may have very little relevance to the system's goals unless leadership is exerted by the principal who plans with the teacher. Such leadership implies a clear establishment of criteria for the behavior of teachers.

[18] Robert L. Thorndike (51) gives an example of a relationship between likeableness rating and overall rating of effectiveness in the U.S. Air Force. Although likeableness was explicitly rated low in importance, it correlated very high with overall rating—indicating an implicit importance to the raters. This implicit importance was probably obtained because no formal strategy required pooling of the ratings in a specified manner that would prevent the overall impression from unduly influencing the specific observations.

[19] This assumes, of course, that such a factor is not *sufficient* for success and that kindergarten teachers are not uniformly successful.

[20] Roger E. Wilk and William H. Edson (56) have found that students who have the greatest command of their first two years of college work (as exhibited by a high GPA) and who have an attitudinal disposition that enables them to relate easily to groups of pupils (high MTAI scores) turn out to be teachers who allow more freedom of action in their classrooms.

BIBLIOGRAPHY

1. Anderson, C. C. & Hunka, S. M. "Teacher Evaluation: Some Problems and a Proposal." *Harvard Educational Review* 33(1963), pp. 74-95.

2. Anshen, Melvin. "The Manager and the Black Box." *Harvard Business Review* 38, 6(1960): 85-92.

3. Bates, James. "A Model for the Science of Decision." *Philosophy of Science* 21(1954), pp. 326-39.

4. Becker, Gordon M. & McClintock, Charles G. "Value: Behavioral Decision Theory." *Annual Review of Psychology* 18(1967), pp. 239-86.

5. Bolton, Dale L. *Variables Affecting Decision Making in the Selection of Teachers.* Final Report, Project No. 6-1349, U. S. Office of Education, 1968.

6. Bradley, Ruth; Kallenbach, Warren; Kinney, Lucien; Owen, Viola; & Washington, Eva. "A Design for Teacher Evaluation." *The National Elementary Principal* XLIII, 2(1963): 32-37.

7. Bross, Irwin D. *Design for Decision.* New York: The Macmillan Company, 1953.

8. Chernoff, Herman & Moses, Lincoln E. *Elementary Decision Theory.* New York: John Wiley & Sons, Inc., 1959.

9. Churchman, C. West. *Theory of Experimental Inference.* New York: The Macmillan Company, 1948.

10. Coombs, C. H. & Kao, R. C. "Nonmetric Factor Analysis." *Engineering Research Bulletin;* No. 38. Engineering Research Institute, University of Michigan, 1955, p. 63.

11. Cronbach, Lee J. & Gleser, Goldine C. *Psychological Test and Personnel Decisions.* Urbana: University of Illinois Press, 1965.

12. Davidson, Donald & Suppes, Patrick. *Decision Making: An Experimental Approach.* Stanford, California: Stanford University Press, 1957.

13. Dill, William R. "Decision-Making" in Daniel E. Griffiths, ed., *Behavioral Science and Educational Administration.* Chicago: National Society for the Study of Education, 1964, pp. 199-222.

14. Edwards, Ward. "The Theory of Decision Making." *Psychological Bulletin* 51, 4(1954): 380-417.

15. Edwards, Ward. "Behavioral Decision Theory." *Annual Review of Psychology* 12 (1961), pp. 473-98

16. Griffiths, Daniel E. "Administration as Decision-Making" in Andrew W. Halpin, ed., *Administrative Theory in Education.* Chicago: Midwest Administration Center, 1958, pp. 119-49.

17. Griffiths, Daniel E. *Administrative Theory.* New York: Appleton-Century-Crofts, 1959.

18. Handy, Rollo & Kurtz, Paul. *A Current Appraisal of the Behavioral Sciences.* Great Barrington, Mass.: Behavioral Research Council, 1964.

19. Hemphill, John K.; Griffiths, Daniel E.; & Fredericksen, Norman. *Administrative Performance and Personality.* New York: Columbia University Teachers College, Bureau of Publications, 1962.

20. Hickey, Michael E. "Pre-decisional Information Processes in Teacher Selection." Unpublished doctoral dissertation, University of Washington, Seattle, Washington, 1969.

21. Hilton, Thomas L. "Decision-Making Strategies in Career Development." A paper read at the American Educational Research Association meeting, Chicago, 1963.

22. Horst, Paul. "The Logic of Personnel Selection and Classification," in Robert M. Gagne, ed., *Psychologial Principles in System Development.* New York: Holt, Rinehart & Winston, 1962, pp. 231-71.

23. Lanzetta, John T. & Sieber, Joan. "Predecisional Information Processes: Some Determinants of Information Acquisition Prior to Decision Making," in *Predecisional Processes in Decision Making: Proceedings of a Symposium,* Report No. AMRL-TDR-64-77, Aerospace Medical Research Laboratories, Wright-Patterson AFB, Ohio, 1964.

24. Laurits, James. "Thought on the Evaluation of Teaching," in *The Evaluation of Teaching,* Pi Lambda Theta, pp. 32-42, 1967.

25. Lindman, Harold Robert. *The Simultaneous Measurement of Utilities and Subjective Probabilities.* Ann Arbor: University of Michigan Press, 1965.

26. Lindsay, Franklin A. *New Techniques for Management Decision Making.* New York: McGraw-Hill Book Company, Inc., 1958.

27. Luce, R. Duncan & Raiffa, Howard. *Games and Decisions: Introduction and Critical Survey.* New York: John Wiley & Sons, Inc., 1957.

28. Maier, Norman R. F. *Problem-Solving Discussions and Conferences: Leadership Methods and Skills.* New York: McGraw-Hill Book Company, Inc., 1963.

29. Majumdar, Tapas. *The Measurement of Utility.* London: MacMillan & Co., Ltd., 1958.

30. Mandell, Milton M. "Some Hypotheses for Research in Executive Selection," in R. Tagiuri, ed., *Research Needs in Executive Selection.* Boston: Harvard University Press, 1961.

31. Manne, Alan S. *Economic Analysis for Business Decisions.* New York: McGraw-Hill Book Co., Inc., 1961.

32. McGuire, Christine. "A proposed Model for the Evaluation of Teaching." Pi Lambda Theta, 1967, pp. 85-108.

33. Mills, J. & Snyder, R. "Avoidance of Commitment, Need for Closure, and the Expression of Choices." *Journal of Personnel,* 30 (1962), pp. 458-470.

34. Morgenstern, Oskar. *The Question of National Defense.* New York: Random House, Inc., 1959.

35. Naylor, James C. "Accurancy and Variability of Information Sources as Determiners of Performance and Source Preference of Decision Makers." *Journal of Applied Psychology,* 48, 1(1964): 43-49.

36. Peres, S.H. & Garcia, J.R. "Validity and Dimensions of Descriptive Adjectives Used in Reference Letters for Engineering Applicants." *Personnel Psychology* 16 (1962), pp. 279-86.

37. Redefer, Frederick L. "Recruiting and Selection of Teachers," American School Board Journal 145 (1962) pp. 7-8.

38. Redfern, George. *How to Appraise Teaching Performance.* Columbus, Ohio: School Management Institute, Inc., 1963.

39. Ricciardi, Franc M., Craft, Clifford J.; Malcom, Donald G.; Bellman, Richard; Clark, Charles; Kibbee, Joel M.; & Rowdon, Richard H.. *Top Management Decision Simulation.* New York: American Management Assoication, 1957.

40. Roberts, J. S., Jr. "Information Seeking in Sequential Decision Making as Dependent upon Test Anxiety and upon Prior Success or Failure in Problem Solving," in D. W. Talyor, ed., *Experiments on Decision Making and Other Studies.* Technical Report 6, Contract Number

609(20). New Haven: Yale University, Department of Industrial Administration and Psychology, 1960, pp. 26-37.

41. Rosenblueth, K. W. "The Meaning of Rationality, a Note on Professor Lange's Article." *Review of Economic Studies* 14 (1946), pp. 50-52.

42. Royal, R. E. "Decision Making in the Middle Echelons of Public Education." *NASSP Bulletin* 45 (1961), pp. 85-87.

43. Ryans, David G. *Characteristics of Teachers, Their Description, Comparison and Appraisal.* Washington, D. C.: American Council of Education, 1960.

44. Schelling, Thomas C. *The Strategy of Conflict.* Cambridge, Mass.: Harvard University Press, 1960.

45. Simon, Herbert A. "Rationality and Administrative Decision Making," in *Models of Man, Social and Rational.* New York: John Wiley & Sons, Inc., 1957, pp. 196-206.

46. Simon, Herbert A. *The New Science of Management Decision.* New York: Harper & Row, 1960.

47. Smith, B. Othanel. "Teaching: Conditions of its Evaluation," in *The Evaluation of Teaching,* Pi Lambda Theta, 1967, pp. 65-84.

48. Sorensen, Theodore C. *Decision-Making in the White House.* Columbia Paperback Series, No. 50, 1963.

49. Tagiuri, Renato. *Research Needs in Executive Selection.* Boston: Harvard University Press, 1961.

50. Taylor, Donald W. "Decision Making and Problem Solving," in James G. March, ed., *Handbook of Organizations.* Chicago: Rand McNally, & Co. 1965, pp. 48-86.

51. Thorndike, Robert L. *Personnel Selection, Test and Measurement Techniques.* New York: John Wiley & Sons, Inc., 1949.

52. Toda, Masanao. "Pre- and Postdecisional Processes of the 'Fungus-eater,' " in *Predicisional Processes in Decision Making: Proceedings of a Symposium,* Report No. AMRL-EDR-64-77, Aerospace Medical Research Laboratories, Aerospace Medical Division, Wright-Patterson AFB, Ohio, 1964, pp. 81-92.

53. Tupes, Ernest C. & Cristal, Raymond E. *Recurrent Personality Factors Based on Trait Ratings.* Technical Report ASD-TR-61-97, Personnel Laboratory, Aeronautical Systems Division, Air Force Systems Command, Lackland AFB, Texas, 1961.

54. Turner, Richard L. "Task Performance and Teaching Skill in the Intermediate Grades," The Journal of Teacher Education XIV, 3(1963): 299-307.

55. Von Neuman, John & Morgenstern, Oskar. *Theory of Games and Economic Behavior.* Princeton: Princeton University Press, 1944.

56. Wilk, Roger E. & Edson, William H. "Predictions and Performance: An Experimental Study of Student Teachers," *The Journal of Teacher Education* XIV, 3(1963): 308-317.

5

Simulating the Process for Selection of Administrators

Kenneth E. McIntyre

The prediction of human behavior is perhaps the most uncertain of all tasks confronting the administrator. This uncertainty makes the selection of personnel a gamble in which the predicted behavior of two or more candidates is compared, and a decision is made—a decision that is usually difficult to reverse should the results prove disappointing.

Since the author of this chapter has witten extensively on this subject in other available publications, no attempt will be made here to survey the literature *in toto.*[1] In general, however, the research in educational administration as well as in other fields, some of which will be cited in subsequent sections of this chapter, tends to support the following statements:

1. Although we have become disenchanted with the trait approach to the study of administrative behavior, we know that part of the variability in such behavior resides in factors within the individual administrator. One of the contributions of simulations such as the Madison School in-baskets is the opportunity they

provide to study different individuals' behavior in a given situation. Although we do not know nearly enough about what makes people different or how to measure or predict those differences, we can quite confidently assert that there is something about the personal need dispositions of people that causes them to behave in unique ways.

2. Administrative behavior is a product of environmental influences as well as personal need dispositions. In the past, we tended to ignore the environmental factors. There have been a few recent studies of the impact of situational variables on administrative behavior, revealing that there seem to be some predictable differences in such behavior in different kinds of school environments, but we know very little about those differences or their causes.

3. Assessment problems have been enormous. We cannot precisely measure many of the personal and situational variables that we think might be important predictors. This, together with our halting efforts toward developing satisfactory ways of *describing* administrative behavior—much less *valuing* it—has handicapped our research severely. Only recently have we been making progress along these lines.

4. We have a great deal of evidence to convince us that the tools we use in administrator selection are considerably less trustworthy than most practitioners realize. We can state without equivocation that such devices as letters of recommendation, rating scales, and interviews are of extremely limited value as used in most situations. However, we can much less confidently point the practitioner toward practical alternatives.

Simulation provides an ideal means of teaching important generalizations concerning the selection of administrators. Through simulation, actual case histories can be utilized, challenging the learner with the task of making predictions which can be appraised with solid criteria of the actual histories. The effectiveness of prediction variables can be tested and demonstrated by supplying data selectively to different predictors. In short, the simulation of the selection process is a "natural"; it is in some respects better than the reality it simulates, in that it gives the learner immediate feedback on his predictions, whereas in the "real" world he usually has to wait for years to discover his mistakes—if he ever does.

One of the earlier systematic attempts to simulate the tasks of school administration, including the selection of personnel, was the Development of Criteria of Success (DCS) Project (3). Although that project was conducted largely for research purposes, one of the concomitant payoffs was the enthusiastic response of the participants. As a result, simulation was launched as a major component of training programs for school administrators throughout the United States. The DCS Project simulation included an exercise dealing with the selection of personnel, and even though the selection exercise did not produce the excitement that the in-baskets did, the total experience helped to bring about a new era in preparation programs.

EXAMPLES

To illustrate the use of simulation in the selection process, three examples will be described here in some detail. All were developed for use with in-service groups of administrators, but they have been used many times with pre-service trainees as well. Each one could easily require a three-hour session for adequate treatment of the topic, although limited objectives could be met in two hours or even less. On the surface, one is more complex than the other two, although this depends on how the exercises are used. All three have been employed primarily for teaching purposes, although their potential for research and theory development is considerable.

Example #1: The Effectiveness of Letters of Recommendation in Distinguishing Promising from Unpromising Personnel. Although the research on letters of recommendation borders on the non-existent, the little solid evidence that we have suggests that selectors of personnel should be extremely wary about placing much confidence in such letters. In one of the few systematic attempts to relate the content of letters of recommendation to measurable attributes of the people about whom the letters were written, Bozarth found a correlation of .00 between statements concerning intelligence, as categorized and weighted by a jury, and combined scores on the *Miller Analogies* and the *Watson-Glaser Critical Thinking Appraisal.* Similar correlations were found (.15

and -.08) when statements concerning social acceptability were compared with standings on a peer acceptance inventory for two different groups (1). It is small wonder that we learn so little about people in the letters written about them, when one considers that the letters are usually written upon invitation of the person being recommended, by people who probably have little relevant data on which to base a recommendation, for positions that are usually either ill-defined or unknown to the writer. In addition, it is conceivable that writers' motives could contribute to the confusion, as when a letter is seen as an opportunity to do a good turn for a friend or, conversely, to unload an unproductive employee on somebody else. Whatever the reasons, letters of recommendation are undoubtedly among the least dependable of all selection tools, and yet they are almost universally used.

The primary purpose of the exercise immediately following is to convince those who select personnel, particularly school administrators or trainees for school administration, that letters of recommendation are not to be trusted as much as is usually the case. Once the participants in the exercise are convinced of this, they are presumably more open to a serious consideration of other alternatives.

Ten former students of educational administration at the University of Texas were chosen as the subjects of this exercise—five who had been outstanding students and who had subsequently attained unusual degrees of "success" by every known criterion, and five who were least-likely-to-succeed types as students and who later became conspicuously unsuccessful as school administrators. All forty-seven letters in the ten ex-students' files were reproduced—25 from the files of the "unpromising" group and 22 from the "promising" group. All of the letters were written to a University of Texas faculty member who was in charge of recruiting students for a special training program in school administration; therefore, they pertained to *potential* for high-quality performance in administration rather than fitness for any specific position or situation. Names and other identifying information were, of course, disguised; only the positions of the writers were stated.

The resulting training exercise consists simply in each participant's reading the forty-seven letters and categorizing each of them as either "promising" or "unpromising," with regard to the person about whom the letter was written. In addition, the participant indicates *why* he made each decision, that is, which cues influenced him. One further variable that is often included in the exercise is the grouping of the letters for half of the participants so that the effect of "bunching" several letters written about a candidate can be compared with evaluating them one at a time.

For teaching purposes, certain hypotheses can be formulated, either by the group leader or by the group itself, while the responses are being scored. For example, the following might be stated (both of which will probably be supported by the data produced):

1. The average number of correct responses will not be significantly greater than chance.

2. The participants for whom the several letters on each candidate are grouped will make a higher average percentage of correct choices than will those who must make their decisions on individual letters.

In addition to testing such hypotheses as these, the group can discuss and compare the cues that influenced them. Results produced by other groups can be presented and compared.

Where more time is available, certain other research and teaching objectives can be met in this exercise. For example, studies can be made to determine whether certain categories of letter writers (professors, school principals, school superintendents, etc.) produce more correct choices than others; the scores of various categories of participants in the training group can also be compared; and studies can be made to determine whether such factors as length of letter or the use of certain words or phrases bear any relationship to the promise or lack of promise of the person about whom the letters were written.

This exercise is reliable, in that the results are quite predictable, even if the participating group is small. The data of Table 5-1 were produced in typical groups of various sizes:

Table 5-1

ACCURACY OF JUDGMENTS REGARDING ADMINISTRATOR
APPLICANTS, USING LETTERS OF RECOMMENDATION

		Ungrouped Letters (highest possible score: 47)		
Participants	*N*	*Mean*	*Median*	*Accuracy (of Mean)**
Superintendents	18	27.1	27	58%
Principals	5	28.4	29	60%
Beginning Graduate Students	9	26.2	26	56%
Professors of Educational Administration	23	27.1	28	58%
Advanced Graduate Students	5	28.6	30	61%
School Board Members	7	26.6	27	57%

		Grouped Letters (highest possible score: 10)		
Participants	*N*	*Mean*	*Median*	*Accuracy (of Mean)*
Superintendents	19	7.1	8	71%
Principals	4	5.0	5	50%
Beginning Graduate Students	9	7.4	8	74%
Professors of Educational Administration	24	7.0	8	70%
Advanced Graduate Students	4	7.5	8	75%

*Since these were all dichotomous choices, a score of 50% could be attributed to chance.

In most teaching situations time constraints will not permit elaborate statistical treatment of the data, nor is such treatment necessary in most cases. Immediate feedback of individual and group performances can usually be accomplished, and this is the important concern of the instructor. With exercises such as the one reported here, a simple eye-balling of the data is enough to reveal that none of the groups' average scores was significantly greater than chance. On the other hand, the percentages of correct choices made by the participants for whom the letters were grouped were slightly higher than for those who had to deal with each letter individually, with only one exception, so the two hypotheses were supported in almost every instance. The big point in the exercise, then, is the revelation that at least *these* forty-seven letters would not have been very useful to most readers for the purpose of discriminating between high-potential and low-potential future school administrators.

This exercise, in its simplest form, requires approximately sixty to ninety minutes for the participants to read and categorize the letters, for the group leader to score them and report the results, and for the group to discuss the implications. If a study of other variables is included—cues, writers of the letters, and categories of participants—then several hours will be required, after the choices are made, before the results can be reported. If possible, it is usually advisable to assign the task of categorizing to be done as homework so that the group's time can be devoted to analysis, interpretation, and discussion of the results.

Example#2: The Effects of Several Predictor Variables on Accuracy. This training exercise was developed to serve several purposes: (a) to demonstrate that certain important aspects of the careers of school administrators are not predictable beyond the chance level with the usual selection tools; (b) to demonstrate that the accuracy of such predictions (as stated above) is increased as the predictors consider additional increments of information concerning the candidates, but that certain types of information account for most of the increase in accuracy; (c) to provide a basis for discussing the selection of personnel with the participating group and for planning further study of selection problems; and (d) to generate hypotheses for further testing, both in the laboratory setting and in the field.

Eight former graduate students of educational administration at the University of Texas comprised the subjects of this exercise. Files for all eight included biographical data, letters of recommendation, transcripts, and scores on several psychological tests and inventories, together with ratings of various kinds, all acquired *before* the eight individuals entered positions in school administration. All data were retained, although names and other identifying information were disguised. All eight subjects had been in the administrator preparation program several years prior to the development of this laboratory exercise, so that the answers to the following questions were a matter of record:

Within the next 5 to 10 years, will he (the subject):

1. Earn a doctor's degree?
2. Leave the profession of education and work for a private corporation?
3. Be principal of a school that, during his tenure as principal, will achieve a reputation that draws visitors from many states?
4. Be fired from a principalship?
5. Become superintendent or assistant superintendent of a large school system?
6. Be ranked by professors in the Department of School Administration, at the end of the first twelve semester hours of his preparation, as being among the top twenty percent of his training group in overall promise?

For each of the six questions, there are some "yes" and some "no" answers. The task of the predictors in the exercise is to study the information pertaining to each of the eight subjects and to make as many correct predictions as possible. Since predictions are made from actual data, and are evaluated with actual case histories, the criteria are unassailable if one accepts their meaningfulness.[2] Predictions can be made by teams of two or three people or by individuals, but henceforth in this discussion the term *teams* will be used.

By dividing the participants entirely at random into six (or perhaps nine, twelve, or fifteen) prediction teams and by rotating the information inputs among the teams, the effects of the various inputs can be revealed. For example, if all of the prediction teams make their initial forty-eight predictions (six questions concerning eight people) based on letters, test scores, or transcripts—plus the biographical data that all teams possess—the effectiveness of each of the three types of information can be compared with the other two. Then, by requiring eaching team to make two other sets of predictions, each time with additional information, the additive effects can be compared. Table 5-2 shows how the information can be rotated among teams in a six-team exercise, and it also shows the scores that one group of six teams achieved on each of three successive sets of predictions.

Table 5-2

ACCURACY OF PREDICTION
USING DIFFERENT TYPES OF INFORMATION

	First Prediction	*Second Prediction*	*Third Prediction*
Team A	Letters Score: 25	Transcripts Score: 32	Tests Score: 38
Team B	Letters Score: 29	Tests Score: 31	Transcripts Score: 33
Team C	Transcripts Score: 34	Letters Score: 35	Tests Score: 37
Team D	Transcripts Score: 19	Tests Score: 20	Letters Score: 13
Team E	Tests Score: 30	Letters Score: 29	Transcripts Score: 26
Team F	Tests Score: 33	Transcripts Score: 31	Letters Score: 31
	Average: 28.3	Average: 29.7	Average: 29.7

Comments: In general, the six teams in this group did slightly better in their second prediction than in their first one but no better on the third than on the second. Considering first-prediction scores only, the two teams that had letters averaged 27.0, compared with 26.5 for transcripts and 31.5 for test scores. Considering the additive effects of each type of data, letters produced an average *loss* of 1.75 points, compared with an average *gain* of 1.00 point for transcripts and an average *gain* of 2.75 points for test scores.

After the last set of predictions, the predictors are requested to rank the eight subjects in terms of overall promise. This permits the teams to compare rankings with each other and with a criterion ranking made by faculty members who know the subjects well.

Certain hypotheses can be tested with this exercise in a teaching situation. For example, the following are feasible for testing in a three-hour session, and in most cases each one will be sustained:

1. The more information a predictor has at his disposal, the more accurate his predictions tend to be.

2. Of the three categories of initial prediction data, test scores are the most useful, followed by transcripts and letters. In other words, when predictors have only biographical data and one other type of information, test scores yield the greatest number of correct predictions, followed by transcripts and letters, in that order.

3. When each of the three categories of data is added to other data, test scores tend to be most useful, followed by transcripts and letters, in that order.

4. Rankings of the eight subjects on "overall promise" tend to vary greatly, but to coincide more at the extremes than in the middle rankings.

Research hypotheses, which can be tested if more time is available, include those pertaining to influential cues and differential predictability as a function of selected characteristics of the

Table 5-3

ACCURACY OF PREDICTION
USING SINGLE TYPE OF INFORMATION

Composition of Groups	Average Number of Correct Responses (highest possible score: 48)		
	Transcripts	Letters	Test Scores
School Principals	29.7	29.3	33.3
	31.0	30.0	33.5
	31.3	28.0	31.0
	33.5	23.0	32.5
	26.5	27.0	31.5
Graduate Students in Educ. Admin.	26.0	28.0	31.5
	27.0	29.5	37.0
	31.5	26.0	31.5
	30.5	28.0	38.5
	29.7	29.3	33.3

predictors. Also, each of the six questions can be studied separately to determine whether certain kinds of data are more effective with certain questions than with others.

To illustrate the results that might be expected from the use of this exercise, the following data are presented, with scores representing the average number of correct responses out of forty-eight (and a score of twenty-four being attributed to chance), when the predictors had only one type of data.

Table 5-3 reveals that test scores were the most useful single type of information in seven out of the ten groups; transcripts were most useful in two groups, and two types of information tied in one group. Letters were never most useful; in fact, they were least useful in seven out of ten groups.

Another way of analyzing the scores is to compare the additive effects of various kinds of information on the number of correct responses previously achieved. For example, if a prediction team makes a score of 29 with only transcripts at its disposal and makes a score of 31 when test scores are added to the team's information, then the test scores are credited with a gain of two points. Table 5-4 shows the additive effects of the various types of information for the same ten groups included in Table 5-3.

Table 5-4

ADDITIVE EFFECTS OF DIFFERENT TYPES OF INFORMATION

Composition of Groups	Average Number of Points Gained or Lost		
	Transcripts	Letters	Test Scores
School Principals	-1.3	.2	2.2
	-2.3	-1.3	3.6
	2.3	-.5	2.3
	-.3	-2.5	2.5
	1.0	-1.8	2.8
Graduate Students in Educ. Admin.	2.3	1.0	4.0
	-.5	-.3	4.8
	2.3	.8	3.0
	.6	-4.5	3.6
	-1.3	.2	2.2

From Table 5-4 we can see that test scores were the only type of information that consistently improved the accuracy of predictions when added to other types of information. Transcripts increased prediction accuracy five times out of ten but decreased accuracy in the other five groups. Letters decreased prediction accuracy six times out of ten and produced only small gains in the other four.

If time is a major problem, certain limited objectives can be met in a session lasting only two hours or slightly less. Instead of rotating the prediction data and requiring each team to make three sets of predicitons all of the data can be distributed at one time to each team. This, of course, eliminates some of the most important and interesting uses of the exercise.

Example #3: Expectations for Principalships in Different Situations. We have known for some time that leader behavior is influenced by the situation in which the leader serves. Stogdill surveyed the literature and reported, in 1948, certain conclusions "supported by uniformly positive evidence from fifteen or more of the studies surveyed." One such conclusion stated, "The qualities, characteristics, and skills required in a leader are determined to a large extent by the demands of the situation in which he is to function as a leader" (16).

The studies surveyed by Stogdill dealt with leader behavior in a variety of organizational contexts. Recently several studies have focused on the situational aspects of administrator behavior in schools. Nicholas, Virjo, & Wattenberg found some rather striking differences in school principals' behavior in attendance areas serving people of high as compared with low socio-economic status (14). Laidig found the same tendencies in a later study (5), as did Cross & Bennet (2).

Two investigations (Sexton, 15, and Herriott & St. John, 4) suggest that lower-class schools are discriminated against in the assignment of staff members, at least insofar as teaching experience and tenure in the current school are concerned. Although there is little evidence concerning the characteristics of principals assigned to different types of schools, one might reasonably hypothesize that such assignments are not made on a completely random basis—nor should they be. The point here is that we have good evidence to support the contention that principals in different school environments do behave differently, although we do not yet have the research to show us how much of the difference in behavior is due to situational influences and how much to selective placement.

The simulation which follows was developed to test some hypotheses concerning *expectations* for principals' behavior and traits in schools serving people of low and high socio-economic status. One purpose of this learning exercise is to reveal differences in expectations for the two types of situation, with respect to twelve characteristics. Some of the characteristics are of the trait genre (e.g., intelligence, physical size, and breadth of interests) and some are behavioral, in the sense that they would have to manifest themselves in a job situation (e.g., control of pupil discipline, tendency to back teachers, and style of supervision of teachers). Finally, the exercise is designed to reveal how important each of the twelve characteristics is considered to be and whether there is any relationship between perceived importance and socio-economic status of the schools.

Forms H and L are distributed randomly to the participants. Form H describes a junior high school situation in a high socio-economic area, and Form L describes a junior high school situation in a low socio-economic area. Each form is attached to the twelve-item checklist which follows

CHARACTERISTICS DESIRED IN POMROY
JUNIOR HIGH SCHOOL PRINCIPAL

First you are to rate each of the following twelve characteristics in terms of their importance to the principalship in Pomroy Junior High. For *each* of the twelve characteristics, *circle* the number that best represents your estimate of its importance in this particular situation, keeping in mind that a rating of *3* represents the average for all junior high school principals.

_____Intelligence	1 low	2	3 average	4	5 high
_____Physical size	1 small	2	3 average	4	5 large
_____Breadth of interests	1 narrow	2	3 average	4	5 wide

_____*Control of pupil discipline*	1 lax	2	3 average	4	5 strict
_____*Grade-point average*	1 low	2	3 average	4	5 high
_____*Tendency to back teachers*	1 weak	2	3 average	4	5 strong
_____*Appearance*	1 unimpressive	2	3 average	4	5 impressive
_____*Political stance*	1 liberal	2	3 average	4	5 conservative
_____*Orientation to change*	1 resistant	2	3 average	4	5 innovative
_____*Love of Children*	1 unloving	2	3 average	4	5 loving
_____*Longe-range planning capability*	1 low	2	3 average	4	5 high
_____*Style of supervision of teachers*	1 low control	2	3 average	4	5 high control

Now go back and rank the twelve characteristics by placing numbers from 1 through 12 in the blanks in the column at the left. Place a *1* at the left of the characteristic that seems most important for the Pomroy principalship, a *2* in the blank for the second most important characteristic, and so on through *12*.

Each participant is asked to assume the role of superintendent of schools in the district and is instructed to rate each of the twelve characteristics in terms of its desirability in the person to be selected for the principalship in the school described. In addition to rating each characteristic on a five-point scale, the participant is instructed to rank the twelve characteristics as to their importance for the specific position.

Table 5-5 presents the mean ratings for the twelve characteristics as assigned by participants in the five groups in which the exercise has been used.

Although the differences in average ratings assigned by the H and L sub-groups on most trait or behavior categories are not statistically significant, the differences are consistently in the predicted direction for most of the characteristics. In fact, the differences are in the predicted direction in all five groups for six of the twelve characteristics, and in four of the five groups for an additional four characteristics. Only for "long-range planning capability" and "tendency to back teachers" does there seem to be no predictable pattern at all. Based on experience with this

Table 5-5

JUDGED IMPORTANCE OF 12 CHARACTERISTICS FOR HIGH AND LOW SOCIO-ECONOMIC ATTENDANCE AREAS

Rating Categories	Texas School Principals N=29		Ed. Admin. Graduate Students N=16		Ed. Admin. Graduate Students N=14		Colorado School Prin.&Sup. N=31		Idaho School Admin. N=18	
	H*	L	H	L	H	L	H	L	H	L
Intelligence	4.7	4.1	4.7	4.3	4.1	4.0	4.3	3.6	4.3	3.7
Physical size	2.9	3.3	2.9	3.6	2.9	3.0	3.2	3.5	3.1	3.9
Breadth of interests	4.7	4.4	4.4	3.9	4.7	4.6	4.6	4.4	4.8	4.3
Control of discipline	3.8	3.9	3.2	4.6	3.4	3.7	3.5	3.7	3.0	3.8
Grade-point average	4.1	3.1	4.0	3.0	3.0	3.4	3.7	3.2	3.9	3.1
Tendency to back teachers	4.4	4.3	4.7	4.7	3.4	3.9	4.4	3.9	4.2	4.2
Appearance	4.4	3.6	4.1	3.7	3.6	3.6	4.1	3.5	4.2	3.7
Political stance	3.7	2.6	3.1	2.3	2.9	2.4	3.1	2.5	2.7	2.9
Orientation to change	4.3	4.1	4.4	4.3	4.6	4.7	4.6	4.0	4.8	4.4
Love for children	3.9	4.8	4.0	4.6	3.9	4.4	4.3	4.5	3.8	4.3
Planning capability	4.6	4.8	4.4	4.7	4.7	4.7	4.4	4.1	4.9	4.5
Style of supervision	3.5	4.2	2.8	3.0	3.0	3.6	3.8	3.6	3.0	3.8

*H indicates high socio-economic area, L indicates low socio-economic area, scores are mean ratings.

exercise, then, one might hypothesize that school leaders tend to regard intelligence, breadth of interests, grade-point average, appearance, conservative political stance, and innovativeness to be more important for principals in schools serving areas of high socio-economic status. Conversely, we might hypothesize that school leaders tend to regard large physical size, strict discipline, liberal political stance, love for children, and high controlling supervision of teachers to be more important for principals in low socio-economic areas.

The relative *ranks* assigned to the twelve characteristics generally confirm the findings presented above, with intelligence and breadth of interests consistently ranking high for the high socio-economic areas and love for children ranking high for the low socio-economic areas.

One strength of this exercise is that it requires only a few minutes of the participants' time for responses and it is simple to tabulate. This leaves the remainder of the available time for discussion of the findings. The data produced in a group of fifteen or more participants will undoubtedly show that we do tend to place predictably different values on the characteristics expected of principals in different situations. The reasons for these findings should constitute an interesting basis for discussion.[3]

Three examples of the use of simulation in teaching about the selection of school administrators have been presented in considerable detail. These exercises have a relatively long history of successful use in both pre-service and in-service training programs, and each one can be employed with confidence. Occasionally some part of the data will not turn out as expected, but the overall reliability of each exercise is quite high. We now turn to another example of simulation in the selection of administrators.

Example #4: Policy Capturing. Although the policy-capturing model described here has been used largely for research purposes, there is no reason why it could not be used partly or entirely for teaching purposes, provided that time, equipment, and group-leader competency are adequate. Simply stated, policy capturing is a technique whereby the personnel selection policies of individuals or groups are revealed in the variables associated with the choices that they make. Following is an example of the use of policy capturing in a research study.

A least-squares weighted linear regression model was used to capture the faculty selection policy of presidents, deans, and chairmen of mathematics departments from nine selected Texas public junior colleges. Twenty-five individual characteristics were identified as potential policy predictors, and a pre-test was applied to reduce this number to twelve. The twelve variables were incorporated into profiles representing fifty hypothetical applicants for a position as mathematics instructor in a junior college. The twenty-eight judges from the junior colleges in the sample were asked to rate the profiles according to the acceptability for employment of the applicant represented by each profile. The policy-capturing model was used to obtain a regression equation for each judge. The equation was assumed to represent the faculty selection policy of that judge. A cross-validation technique was employed and served to verify the validity of the previous assumption. The *Individual Characteristics-Perception Question-naire* was administered to each subject in order to classify the judges according to their professional orientation and also to determine their perceptions regarding the distribution of influence among persons engaged in the faculty-selection process. The policy-capturing model was found to be very effective. At least eighty percent of the time, for every judge, the actual ratings of the hypothetical applicants were within one unit (on a five-point rating scale) of the values predicted by his regression equation. Other results were contrary to the hypothesized results. Policies of subjects classified as locals were not found to differ significantly from the policies of cosmopolitans. Policies of administrators of the same school were not found to be more similar to each other than to policies of subjects from other schools. No significant difference was found between schools having a written statement regarding faculty selection and those not having such a statement, with respect to similarities among policies of the subjects from the respective schools. The policies of presidents and deans of specific junior colleges were not found to be more similar to each other and different from those of department heads. Some evidence was found that the policies of presidents and deans, as a group, were similar, and that they were different from the policies of depart-ment chairmen, as a group. The evidence was inconclusive, however. Three ancillary questions were considered. The first dealt with the characteristics having the greatest and least overall influences upon the policies of the subjects. Of the twelve variables considered in the study, quality of recommendations, religion, and mathematics grade-point average had the greatest overall influence. Extra-curricular activities and honors in college, membership in professional organizations, and two categories of junior college philosophy were found to have the least influence. The next two questions dealt with the subjects' perceptions of the distribution of influence over faculty selection (6).

It is obvious that procedures such as this can be useful both in the selection of personnel and in the training of people for the selection task. Even such an elaborate study as the one described above can be accomplished in a laboratory type of setting if the training group is together long enough—three days should be adequate—for the data to be gathered, processed by computer, analyzed, and discussed. Although the writer has not seen an example of a simpler model that could be used in a half-day training session without a computer, such a session seems to be quite feasible. Certainly it would be worth a few hours of a training group's time to discover and ponder the implications of findings such as those emerging from the study cited above which revealed that the junior college administrators involved in making the selections were most strongly influenced by such questionable variables as letters of recommendation and the religion of the applicants.

OTHER SOURCES FOR EXAMPLES

Several of the other chapters in this book deal with simulation techniques that have been used in connection with the selection of school administrators. No attempt will be made here to treat the topics of those chapters exhaustively; rather, an example of each will be mentioned briefly, with the suggestion that the reader refer to the cited chapters for further elucidation.

In Chapter 2, the use of cases is discussed. Several of the published cases contain issues pertaining to, or related to, the selection of school personnel. In-basket techniques (Chapter 3) are also useful for teaching about selection, and a related technique has been developed for the training of school board members, in the form of a simulated agenda which includes as one item the appraisal of three sets of credentials of candidates for the superintendency.

Some important learning pertaining to interviewing as a selection technique can be achieved by way of human interaction laboratory exercises. Interviews are sometimes role played, in order to illustrate something about the process, and they are sometimes staged "for real" with unknown interviewees, with the observers instructed to make observations or ratings which are later compared or evaluated against relevant data.

Although the writer is not aware of a selection-of-administrators game (Chapter 6), some of the elements of gaming are present in the exercises described in detail earlier in this chapter. The use of computers (Chapter 8) has been mentioned earlier, in connection with policy capturing as a type of simulation. Many other uses of computers can be envisioned for treating data generated in laboratory or real-life simulations of the selection process.

EVALUATION OF SIMULATION FOR
SELECTION OF ADMINISTRATORS

We are not entirely in the dark as to the way in which learners evaluate training sessions such as those described in this chapter. Evaluation data from the writer's several years of experience in using simulation techniques for both pre-service and in-service training of school administrators have been quite reassuring. In-service training groups have consistently, year after year, rated simulation far above other techniques in the School Administration Research Project conducted by the University of Texas. Similarly, prospective school administrators enrolled in the University of Texas' block-of-time program consistently rank the simulations at the very top of the list of activities in which they engage. As for the training exercises dealing specifically with the selection of administrators, those sessions always rank high on the list of valuable learning activities, as seen by the learners.

The writer's bias in favor of simulation in training programs as well as in research is undoubtedly obvious. That bias, however, is supported by a growing body of evidence. It is becoming increasingly clear that in teaching school administrators to avoid the quackery commonly associated with the selection of personnel, nothing is quite as impressive as proving it to them by comparing their predictions with unquestionable criteria, or showing them how certain kinds of data will help them to improve their predictions whereas other kinds will not, or capturing their selection policies for them to examine. In effect, on-the-spot research is thereby used as a vehicle for teaching, or for improving the practice of, administration. In addition to this, the theory-building possibilities of simulation are great; some of the laboratory-type uses of in-baskets have generated some hypotheses concerning situational influences on administrative behavior that have been tested and confirmed in field studies.

There are limitations, of course, in the use of simulation. One is not always able to develop a group activity that will generate the supporting data or produce the type of experience desired within the time ordinarily available for a training session. The time required to construct simulations is considerable, as is the time usually required to use them, and we should always ask ourselves if the benefits are likely to justify the costs. Then too, one is never completely sure that he is not taking too many liberties in generalizing from the simulated situation to the real situation, and some of our studies suggest that we should be careful in this regard. These caveats are not unique with simulation, however; they should be considered in the selection of *any* teaching or research device.

In this chapter we have presented what was intended to be a convincing case for the use of simulation in the selection of school administrators. Several examples of simulations were presented, and the results of evaluations of such exercises were summarized, together with some of their inherent limitations. We hope that our undisguised enthusiasm for the selective use of simulation as discussed in this chapter will encourage the reader to give it a try.

NOTES

[1] For further elaboration of the research and theory supporting this chapter, see the following by Kenneth E. McIntyre: *Recruiting and Selecting Leaders for Education* (Austin, Texas: Southwest School Administration Center, The University of Texas, 1956), pp. 18-38; (with Roy M. Hall) "The Student Personnel Program," in *Administrative Behavior in Education,* Roald F. Campbell and Russell T. Gregg, eds. (New York: Harper and Brothers, 1957), Chap. 11; *Selection and On-the-Job Training of School Principals* (Austin, Texas: Bureau of Laboratory Schools, the University of Texas, 1960), pp. 9-25; *Selection and Recruitment in Fields Other Than Educational Administration* (Austin, Texas: Department of Educational Administration, The University of Texas, 1965); "The Selection of Elementary School Principals," *The National Elementary Principal* XLIV, 5 (1965), 42-46; *Selection of Educational Administrators* (Austin, Texas: The University of Texas and the University Council for Educational Administration, 1966); and "Six Studies on the Prediction of Administrative Behavior," *Educational Administration Quarterly* IV, 1 (1968), 45-54.

[2] On the other hand, even the most knowledgeable and sophisticated predictors will make a few incorrect choices. Sometimes a "good" prediction (in the sense that any reasonable person would predict the same way if given the same information) will turn out to be wrong simply because the subject's career didn't (or did) happen to take a particular turn.

[3] For example, the writer has enjoyed listening to various groups' attempts to explain why the slippery and practically meaningless term *love for children* always rates so high as a characteristic of principals in low socio-economic areas. Is this phenomenon a genuine sub-conscious attempt to provide affection for children, many of whom presumably suffer from a lack of it, or is it an attempt to compensate with an empty phrase for the fact that we have endowed the principal of the school in the high socio-economic area with more of the culturally valued characteristics?

BIBLIOGRAPHY

1. Bozarth, Henry C. "A Study of the Validity of Letters of Recommendation in Screening Applicants for Foundations in Educational Administration at the University of Texas." Unpublished Master's thesis, University of Texas, 1956, pp. 30-31.

2. Cross, Ray & Bennett, Vernon S. "Problem Situations Encountered by School Principals in Different Socioeconomic Settings." Mimeographed. University of Minnesota, 1969.

3. Hemphill, John K; Griffiths, Daniel E.; and Fredericksen, Norman. *Administrative Performance and Personality.* New York: Bureau of Publications, Teachers College, Columbia University, 1962.

4. Heiriott, Robert E. & St. John, Nancy H. *Social Class and the Urban School.* New York: John Wiley & Sons, Inc., 1966, pp. 57-58.

5. Laidig, Eldon L. "The Influence of Situational Factors on the Behavior of Selected Elementary School Principals." Unpublished Ph.D. dissertation, University of Texas, 1967.

6. McBride, Galen Frederick. "A Policy-Capturing Model Relating to Faculty Selection in Nine Junior Colleges." Abstract of an unpublished Ph.D. dissertation, University of Texas, 1968.

7. McIntyre, Kenneth E. *Selection and On-the-Job Training of School Principals.* Austin, Texas: Bureau of Laboratory Schools, University of Texas, 1960, pp. 9-25.

8. McIntyre, Kenneth E. *Selection and Recruitment in Fields Other Than Educational Administration.* Austin, Texas: Department of Educational Administration, University of Texas, 1965.

9. McIntyre, Kenneth E. *Selection of Educational Administrators.* Austin, Texas: University of Texas, University Council For Educational Administration, 1966.

10. McIntyre, Kenneth E. "Selection of Elementary School Principals." *The National Elementary Principal* XLIV, no. 5 (1965), pp. 42-46.

11. McIntyre, Kenneth E. "Six Studies on the Prediction of Administrative Behavior." *Educational Administration Quarterly* IV, no. 1 (1968), pp. 45-54.

12. McIntyre, Kenneth E. "The Student Personnel Program." In Roald F. Campbell & Russell T. Gegg, eds., *Administrative Behavior in Education.* New York: Harper and Brothers, 1957, Chap. 11.

13. McIntyre, Kenneth E. with Hall, Roy M. *Recruiting and Selecting Leaders for Education.* Austin, Texas: Southwest School Administration Center, University of Texas, 1956, pp. 18-38.

14. Nicholas, Lynn N.; Virjo, Helen E.; and Wattenburg, William W. *Effects of Socioeconomic Setting and Organizational Climate on Problems Brought to Elementary School Offices.* Cooperative Research Project Number 2394. Detroit: College of Education, Wayne State University, 1965.

15. Sexton, Patricia C. *Education and Income.* New York: The Viking Press, Inc., 1961, pp. 201-02.

16. Stogdill, Ralph M. "Personal Factors Associated with Leadership: A Survey of the Literature." *The Journal of Psychology,* January 1948, pp. 35-71.

6

Some Applications
of Game Theory to
Administrative Behavior

Robert E. Ohm

The use of simulations in management training has become the status technique among the newer training tools. Though the use of simulation as a training device dates at least as far back as 1789 with the introduction of *Kriegspiel* (war games) in Prussian military training, the Top Management Decision Simulation, introduced by the American Management Association in 1956 and billed by its creators as "a major breakthrough in management education," signaled the start of the current flood of training games and other simulations (17). Management games have led the way in numbers, complexity, and sophistication and have become a widely used method in management education programs. Currently this leadership is being challenged by the rapid development of academic games for use in classrooms in elementary and secondary schools. It seems clear that training and educational games are becoming increasingly popular tools in the armamentarium of devices offered in the hope of inducing behavioral change.

Generating game formats of educational administration simulations has proved to be an extremely difficult task. The major simulations in the field continue to rely on such devices as the one-shot in-basket technique and role playing. The Madison Townships Simulation, developed under the auspices of the University Council on Educational Administration (22) and based on the in-basket format, continues to be the most comprehensive simulation available for training purposes. The purpose of this chapter will be to examine the theory and structure of games as applied to simulations in educational administration in the hope of furthering the development of an array of training games in the field.

The omnibus nature of the word *simulation* suggests the need for a definition of terms:

1. *Simulation* is a method of structuring a learning experience based on a model requiring some form of decision activity.
2. A *model* is a theoretical, analytical, and/or simplified representation of a system, or subsystem.
3. *Games* are a class of simulations characterized by a conflict of interest, interdependence, rules, and a set of preferred outcomes. They may have, in addition, imperfect information, the element of chance, and forms of cooperative competition.

GAMES AND GAME THEORY

Game theory approaches to the study of conflict-of-interest situations have had extensive treatment in the literature. In this section, only those components of games that apply most readily to simulations in educational administration have been selected. The treatment is selective rather than exhaustive, giving major emphasis to the concepts of game rationality, conflict, and game structure.

Games

Games as models of social behavior have had wide applicability. Complex institutions such as the stock market, interactions such as international relations, and even the deadly serious business of war have been treated as having some of the characteristics of games. The game-like economic competition inherent in business is attested to by participants in such phrases as "the oil game" or "the insurance game." Strategy, teamwork, moves, rules, wins and losses, and other game terms are commonly used by managers and subordinates as they discuss a deal or plan a take-over. It may be said that organizational behavior in general is open to analysis through the application of game models of social interaction.

Similarly, individual behavior in social interaction has been examined from the perspective of games. Bernes' *Games People Play* (1) is probably the most widely known example of using game structure to gain a new understanding of individual behavior and to use this understanding to improve individual functioning. A fellow psychiatrist, Thomas Szasz, has suggested that the game model of behavior unites elements of the sign-using and rule-following characteristics of behavior into a coherent pattern and considers the game analysis approach to be especially fitting for an integration of ethical, socio-political, and economic considerations with the more traditional concerns of the psychiatrist (19). Not to be outdone, a number of psychologists are using games to study individual behavior under conditions which require or permit cooperation, use of strategies, and comparisons of actual versus purely rational choices. The study of individual as well as organizational behavior from a game perspective suggests the potential of games as models of behavior in organizations.

A further example of the usefulness of the game model is the relation of play and games to the development of culture. According to Huizinga (9), play is a necessity, a starting point from which culture evolves. His thesis is that civilization continues to develop in play forms. In his analysis of the play element in contemporary civilization, he points out that sports and athletics have become systematized, regimented, and professionalized to such a degree that the play quality is lost and, therefore, its ability to contribute to the culture is also lost. His suggestion, that in one respect the play element in culture has moved into the arena of management competition, is somewhat staggering in the light of much of the contemporary reaction to administration and administrators. Though the notion that civilization may be advanced through management as a form of play and games may be stretching a point, it does suggest the fundamental nature of game structure in all forms of social interaction.

Game Theory

Games remained a generally unanalyzed phenomenon until the advent of Von Neuman & Morgenstern's *Theory of Games and Economic Behavior* (13). Though the mathematical theory of games of strategy is a static theory difficult to apply to the dynamic analysis involved in such conflict activities as bargaining and negotiation, the theory generated extensive activity through the plausible correspondence of its concepts with those of social organizations. The original terminology and concepts, concerned primarily with two-person, zero-sum games with a minimax solution, have had extensive development and application to the more dynamic forms of conflict faced by administrators.

As Schelling (18) has pointed out, though zero-sum game theory has yielded important insights and advice on the strategy of pure conflict, it has not yielded comparable help on the strategy of action where conflict is mixed with mutual dependence, e.g., the non-zero-sum games involved in wars, strikes, bargaining, or bureaucratic maneuvering. Schelling then goes on to provide a rationale for analyzing those games in which mutual dependence is a part of the logical structure of conflict, which demands some kind of collaboration or mutual accommodation either tacit or explicit, as a part of the strategy involved in making choices or decisions. A further extension of game rationality in collaborative conflict is Harsanyi's set of postulates for non-zero-sum conflict situations (7). These postulates permit a definition of what a purely rational person would do in mixed conflict-of-interest situations and provide a base for comparing purely rational with real behavior under conditions of dynamic rather than static conflict. Though extensions of game rationality continue to be developed, a caveat is essential at this point.

A common error in the use of game theory to examine social interactions is the assumption that the rationality postulates of game theory are prescriptive and, therefore, can be used as a course of action in any given conflict situation. It is this notion of game theory as a form of higher rationality capable of solving conflicts through the application of mathematically or logically derived "laws" of behavior that constitutes its most serious misapplication or misunderstanding. The propositions of game theory do not necessarily predict how real people and organizations behave in conflict situations. In this sense it is a normative theory of rational conflict. And, as in all rational theories, it has limitations in dealing with real strategies involving complex human variables and interactions. As Rapaport (14) has pointed out, purely rational decision theory confronts special cases which lead to "absurd" conclusions—conclusions incompatible with common sense. These paradoxes have forced the abandonment of a strictly rational approach and opened the real system and models of it to empirical questions and other definitions of rationality. Rapaport goes on to say that:

> The greatest lesson to be derived from "higher" game theory, that is the theory of games beyond that of the two-person, zero sum game, is that purely strategic considerations are not sufficient for a basis of "rational decision," indeed the very concept of rational decision becomes diffuse in most real life conflict situations (15).

If game theory is neither prescriptive nor descriptive, what is it? Again Rapaport has provided the most succinct answer.

> Game theory is essentially a structural theory. It answers the *logical structure* of a great variety of conflict situations and describes this structure in mathematical terms. Sometimes the logical structure of a conflict situation admits rational decisions, sometimes it does not. The discovery of logical structures of conflict situations allows a content free classification of conflicts (15, p. 196).

It is this logical structure of conflict that constitutes the most important contribution of game theory to the study of administrative problems involving conflicts of interest. In administrative games, the fact that normative game theory is not a sufficient base for action and, in some situations, may be irrational, requires a shift from rigorously developed normative theory to an experimentally conceived descriptive theory.

Application of Game Theory

The exposition that follows relates selected terms and concepts of game theory to the analysis of an administrative conflict situation for the purpose of clarifying game theory and demonstrating its usefulness in understanding conflict.

Administrative situations may or may not involve conflict. A first step in an analysis is separation of conflict and non-conflict situations within an administrative context. Figure 6-1 is a flow chart of the criteria leading to a classification of a conflict-of-interest situation. A non-conflict situation is one for which a non-discretionary rule exists for administrative handling of a problem or situation. In accepting the situation as within his responsibility, the administrator initiates a search of the rule or programmed decision-making framework of the organization at such levels as the faculty handbook, personnel policies, board policies and minutes, the school code, and perhaps a search of the rulings of the attorney general for an existing decision applicable to the situation.

According to the strictly rational view of organization, if a ruling is found, it must be applied. Continuous application of this strict rationality, of course, leads to such bureaucratic dysfunctions as goal displacement or actions which make the rule more important than the client. However, in terms of game theory in an administrative context, rather than to define to make an exception, the rule is applied until action is taken to change it.

The search-find-apply process keeps an event which may have an internal conflict structure from becoming an administrative conflict event. Direct involvement is avoided through such statements as, "I don't make the rules . . . . " The administrator, however, can be and generally is held accountable for knowing the rule system.

The training objective for dealing with a non-game class of events is the development of a knowledge of the rule system and skill in the search process. Simulations have been devised which provide opportunities for developing search skills and a knowledge of the system, but they lack the dynamics which permit them to be put into a game format requiring risk taking, discretionary decision making, mediating behavior or other forms of administrative action requiring the exercise of judgment.

Figure 6-1

CLASSIFICATION CHART FOR AN ADMINISTRATIVE SITUATION

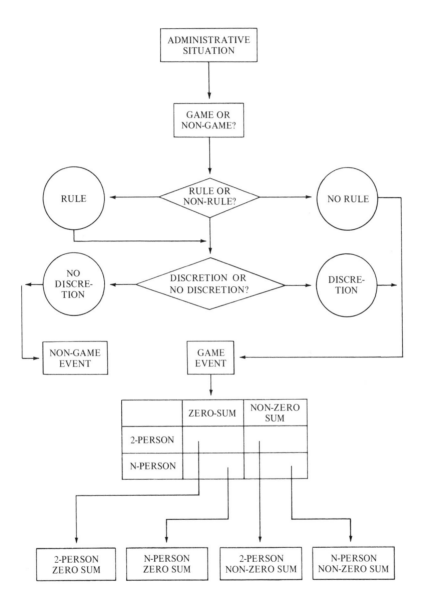

If the administrative event is shown to be one for which no decision rule exists and/or discretionary decision is required within the framework of a general policy and involves a conflict of interest on the part of one or more participants in the event, game theory may be applied to the further classification of the event. Such events may have one or more of the characteristics of games; namely, opposing sets of interests, a choice set of strategies, interdependence, chance factors, imperfect information, and a preferred ordering of outcomes.

Once classified as a game event, a further classification of type of game can be made based on the number of opposing sets of interest and form of pay-off as charted in Figure 6-1. The two dimensions form a grid with four cells giving a four-way game typology. The two-person, zero-sum game is defined as (a) two opposing sets of interests of players, and (b) a pay-off in which the sum of the gains and losses of the two players in the game equals zero, i.e., the gains of player X equal the losses of player Y. It should be noted that the "two-person" distinction refers to opposing sets of interests and not to the number of persons involved. Any number of individuals could be involved in a two-person game providing that no more than two sets of interests are in conflict, a point particularly applicable to the analysis of bargaining or negotiation situations.

Administration conflict situations in which the administrator is one of two players in a zero-sum game are infrequent and extremely difficult to fit within the constraints of the two-person, zero-sum model due to the difficulty of specifying the utilities of each strategy option to form a pay-off matrix. Even in what may appear to be a showdown event, such as a situation in which a faculty member confronts an administrator with the ultimatum of staying if he gets a raise and leaving if he does not, it may be cast as either zero-sum or non-zero-sum depending on the strategies considered appropriate to the problem and·the utilities assigned to the choices of each of the players.

In dealing with conflict situations, an administrator generally faces a decision to be either one of two contending parties in a two-person game or a third party in a game involving conflict between individuals or between an individual and the organization. Direct application of quantitative game theory to conflict events in educational organizations is likely to lead to limited analysis and understanding. However, the present level of theoretical development does permit limited application to conflict events classified as n-person, non-zero-sum in form. The n-person, non-zero-sum conflict characterizes most, if not all, administrative conflicts, a finding supported by a review of all in-basket items for all roles in the *Madison Township Simulation* (22). In any given sample of twenty in-basket items considered to represent a typical array of events for administrative handling, no more than two or three can be classified as game events, and all of the game events fall into the n-person, non-zero-sum category. Therefore, our treatment will concentrate on the logical structure of n-person, non-zero-sum conflict situation within an organizational context.

The non-zero-sum distinction refers to a pay-off in which the sum of the gains and losses of the players does not equal zero, several outcome preferences are equally admissible, or the utilities of the available strategies cannot be specified simultaneously for the players. The logical structure of a non-zero-sum administrative conflict situation includes the notion of mixed-motive, cooperative conflict, partly indeterminate situations with several pay-offs equally plausible, and/or a set of chance or unknown factors identified as a part of the conflict subsystem. The cooperative-competitive situation is one in which the interests of the players are partly coordinated and partly conflicted. Each player has the power of preventing an outcome or of choosing a strategy in which both lose all. Consequently they must in some way collaborate to make choices which payoff in benefits to both, though one may benefit more than the other and though neither one may get the maximum benefit available.

Since game theory by itself has only partial applicability to the analysis of administrative conflict, it needs to be incorporated into an administrative theory of conflict resolution before a conflict event can be analyzed fully.

A Conflict Theory

Discontinuities, such as role conflicts, are characteristic of organizations in pursuit of goals. They stem from such limitations as the difficulty of individuals and groups to agree on goals, to communicate, to change, or to behave rationally. The flow of organizational conflict converges on the administrator. Administrators work within a conflict milieu. A part of an administrator's job is that of maintaining or arranging working relations among at best antagonistically cooperative individuals and groups. Balancing, mediating, or relating individual needs and organizational demands or rationalizing conflicted organizational structures are critical administrative tasks. In conflict situations the administrative role is typically a mediating or third-person role. In game theory terminology, rather than accepting a role in a two-person, zero-sum game, the administrator in a conflict event can choose a strategy defining a three- or n-person, non-zero-sum game. Each of the other players rationally tries to form a coalition with the administrator. If a coalition is formed, the game becomes a two-person game, with a zero-sum pay-off, i.e., forming a coalition is a decision move that wins for one player and loses for the other. Therefore, the administrator in a conflict situation faces constant pressure to form coalitions so that one of the contending parties may win.

Administrative strategy for maintaining a three-person, non-zero-sum game is to engage in a series of moves leading to what Schelling has defined as convergence. In a situation in which the outcome is determined by the expectations that each player forms of how the other will play (behave), where each of them knows that their expectations are substantially reciprocal, the players must jointly discover and mutually acquiesce in an outcome or mode of play that makes the outcome determinate. Together they must find the "rules of the game" or together suffer the consequences. This process is one of communicating intentions, as much through the decision moves one makes as through direct verbalization. Moves can in some way alter the game by incurring manifest costs, risks, or a reduced range of subsequent choice. Moves have an information content or evidence content of a different character from that of speech.

Intentions or expectations communicated through moves or words lead to a convergence point that the parties involved finally come to consider inevitable, the point at which no further concessions can be expected to be made or further gains expected to be achieved. Schelling argues that what brings expectations to convergence is the "intrinsic magnetism" of particular outcomes, especially those that enforce prominence, uniqueness, simplicity, precedent, or some rationale that makes them qualitatively differentiable from the continuum of possible alternatives. For indeterminate situations in which the logical structure of the game provides no rationale for the convergence of expectations anywhere, any mutually perceived analogue may exercise a power of suggestion that can focus expectations. And this analogue may simply be an alternative game of determinate form. For example, the conflict situation exemplified by student occupation of an administrator's office cross-cuts a number of subsystem boundaries with little indication of the boundary appropriate to a resolution or even containment of the situation. However, as the occupation tactic spread to a number of institutions of higher education, a convergence toward the legal subsystem emerged as the most prominent "rational" subsystem for dealing with the conflict.

Administratively, the moves toward convergence are moves to determine boundaries, i.e., finding the relevant boundaries of a conflict situation, or deciding what boundaries are relevant. The base for this assertion is the concept of the school as a system, subsystem arrangement with boundaries that serve to identify or separate one subsystem from another in which the boundary defining elements may range from physical to legal, role, work, group relation, or cognitive elements.

In a boundary-determining process, *determining* is used in two general meanings of the word. Determining behavior may refer to (1) the process of *ascertaining or fixing* the position of or giving a direction to a decision, or (2) *limiting* by adding differentiating characteristics. In short, boundary determination is a rationally perceived sequence of moves in a game strategy leading to convergence on a boundary for conflict of interest situations having an n-person, non-zero-sum, indeterminate matrix structure.

Administrative strategy for dealing with a three-person conflict-of-interest situation may be flow charted as a sequence of decision sets representing arrays of possible decisions and the game rational responses to these decisions. The flow chart in Figure 6-2 begins with a situation that has been identified as a game event involving a conflict of interest between two contending parties that has been moved to an administrator's desk.

The first decision point in dealing with an item is to decide whether or not to engage in an information search. In general, information search moves for this class of events are of three kinds: rule search, conferences, and authority checks. In a simulation exercise involving a conflict with the logical structure of a game, appropriate feedback to the information search moves would indicate that no rule or policy exists, that the two persons in conflict are set on winning (getting administrative support for their position), and that a decision of some sort is necessary (Feedback Set #1, Figure 6-2).

For all conflict events with a game logic structure the actual decision made can be categorized as one of the four types diagrammed in Figure 6-2: (1) no decision, (2) a decision as if a rule or policy exists, (3) a decision to form a coalition with one or the other protagonist, or (4) a decision to maintain the situation as a three-person game through some form of mediating or boundary-determining behavior.

The rational consequence of each type of decision is given in Feedback Set #2. The decision to make no decision leads to a second complaint. Treating the conflict situation as a non-game event would bring a response confirming that no prior rule existed to cover the situation. Forming a coalition with one or the other of the parties in conflict would bring a more vigorous, negative response from the party excluded. Maintaining a three-person game through action to determine the boundaries of the conflict could be rationally expected to lead to a desirable solution which would be perceived as at least a partial win by both parties in conflict.

Decision Set #2 and Feedback Set #3 in the flow chart carry the sequence one additional step. The consequences of decisions that do not bound the conflict lead to feedback which would document or describe actions which extended the conflict. Decision Set #3 holds five alternatives. One typical move in the face of continued or extended conflict is a more detailed information search in the hope of uncovering some rule that can be made to apply. Such a move, particularly if the rule is not directly related to the problem, is likely to be perceived as an authority move or

Figure 6-2

FEEDBACK FLOW CHART FOR 3-PERSON, NON-ZERO-SUM CONFLICT SITUATION

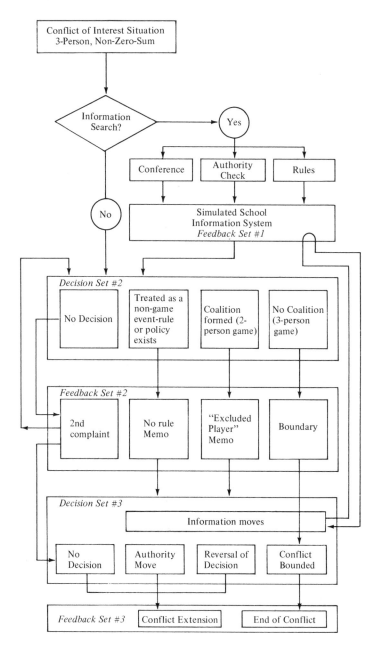

lack of decision. Appropriate feedback, as indicated in Feedback Set #3, is a continuation or extension of the conflict.

A second typical decision move is to rely on the authority ascribed to administrative positions. The consequence of the exercise of authority not only activates the consequences of coalition formation but is likely to intensify the "losing player" response so that the conflict spreads. Similarly, the reversal of a decision, no matter how well rationalized, will intensify the response of "loser." Further charting of decision sets and feedback requires a specific organizational context. The boundary determining process is context dependent and a function of the convergence process. The specific charting of these actions is a function of the specific situation and the organizational context, formal and informal, in which it occurs.

It should be emphasized that the general flow chart of a strategy for a class of conflicts is independent of the roles, personalities, and content of the conflict. For example, the conflict structure of a teacher-devepartment chairman confrontation is similar to a conflict between principal and assistant superintendent that has been appealed to the superintendent.

An Application of Game-Administrative Conflict Theory

A further understanding of the rationale can be gained by describing an application to a real conflict situation and the responses of practicing administrators to a game-type simulation requiring them to respond to the conflict and the feedback to the decisions made. Groups of administrators were asked to respond to a set of conflict items presented as memoranda, letters, or situations requiring some action to be taken. A brief and almost stereotypical verbal description of the school and school system was provided to introduce the simulation and suggest a context. Information questions were solicited and answered until all requests for information were satisfied. Individuals were asked to respond in writing to the situations. Appropriate feedback was given. The group and instructor *then* analyzed responses according to the game rationale. The following letter to Principal MacDuff is an example of a conflict situation to which individual responses were made for subsequent analysis.

Dear Mr. MacDuff:

I came by your office yesterday and you were out. A matter disturbs me so much, however, that I will outline the situation to you in writing.

Mr. Ley has gone way beyond the limits of a department chairman. He has visited my classes and insists that I follow the departmental syllabus more closely. To me the inquiry approach is far superior to the coverage of subject matter. The situation has reached a point where I need your help in getting him to respect the rights of teachers. He is also complaining about my high grades. I hope you will take action as soon as possible.

Hal Wilson

Figure 6-3 is a flow chart of the decision sets and feedback appropriate to each decision. The first decision set is a decision to search for more information or decide to make a decision based on the information made available or on past experience with similar problems. The decision to call for a conference with either of the contending individuals or with both is treated as a form of information search. The game-event question is to ask the participant in the simulation, acting in the role of principal, to describe what he wants or expects from the conference. The responses to this question fall into three categories: personality information, extent of commitment to position on the part of each of the antagonists, and various expressions and the general expectation that a discussion convened and monitored by a superior will resolve most conflict situations. The information responses to each of the response categories follow.

1. The effort to assess relative personality strengths and weaknesses of each of the contending parties is responded to by statements that describe each protagonist as stable and well adjusted. The teacher involved is an above-average teacher, well liked by fellow teachers and by students and respected in the community. The department chairman does not have an authoritarian personality, is liked by his colleagues, and has performed well in his role. The information provided is designed to eliminate

Feedback 6-3

FEEDBACK FLOW CHART FOR 3-PERSON, NON-ZERO-SUM ITEM

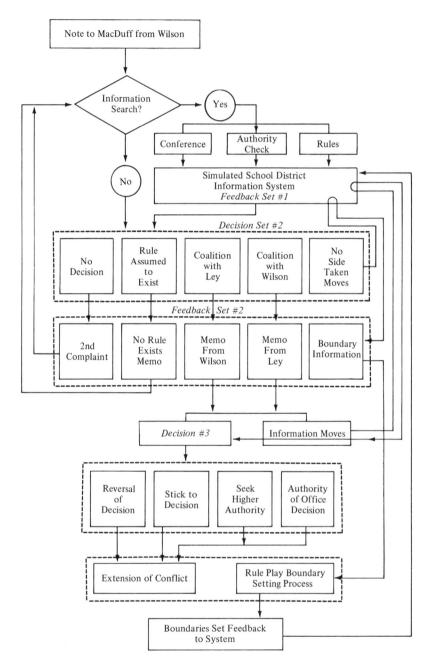

186

any cues that would identify the "good" guy from the "bad" guy. In this respect, the appropriate post simulation discussion question to ask is whether it is ethical for an administrator to make a decision in favor of one or the other of the protagonists on the basis of a personality or character weakness.

2. The question of, the extent to which the protagonists are committed to their positions is answered on the basis of game rationality postulates. Each player is committed to win and is willing to expand the conflict if necessary. Each argues for the support of the principal. The department chairman leans on the principle that an administrator should support his subordinates. The teacher raises the issues of academic freedom and interference in classroom teaching. Both feel that the only appropriate action on the part of the principal is a coalition against the other which in effect wins the game for the one who is successful in achieving this support.

3. The rational position of each player makes some sort of administered compromise through conferences improbable. The conference approach leads to a reaffirmation of the conflice and requires the administrator to move into the next decision set.

Decision Set #2 encompasses four choices. The decision not to make a decision or take an action leads to a second, more vigorous note from Wilson questioning the delay and urging immediate action. The decision to form a coalition with Wilson, usually taken on the basis of the need to support the freedom of the teacher to teach, wins the game for Wilson and brings a strong reaction from Ley about lack of administrative support and the need to appeal as well as a possible resignation. The point to be made about coalitions is that they move a three-person game with the potential for a non-zero-sum solution to a two-person, zero-sum game in which both the organization and the individual may lose. Consequently the fourth decision, to maintain a three-person game and take a sequence of actions that will provide some gain for each of the players through some form of boundary-setting action, is the preferred game solution. Boundary determining moves are designed to limit the conflict. The specific solution may be found by forming the simulation players into teams and asking each team to role-play to a point where they have arrived at a satisfactory solution. For example, one team may take the role of a faculty council, another the role of a faculty in a departmental meeting, and a third an appointed *ad hoc* committee. Proposed solutions can then be discussed for their conformity to a non-zero-sum solution and characteristics of the relevant boundary for limiting the conflict.

Feedback for Decision Set #2 moves the game to one of three alternatives for each player. No decision or an action taken on the assumption that a rule exists receives feedback that returns the player to the initiating information search question. Logically this is an iterative loop. A coalition with subsequent feedback from the losing member of the initial triad moves the sequence to Decision Set #3. The decision to maintain the triad with subsequent moves involving the acquisition or identification of boundary information leads to the formation of a boundary-setting process.

Decision Set #3 includes typical administrative decision moves in the face of continued or expanded conflict. The reversal of a decision under pressure or holding to a coalition decision continues the conflict. Bucking the conflict to a higher authority at any point in the decision sequence elicits either a request for a recommended decision or a note suggesting that the problem should be handled at the building principal's level. Further moves in the game could be programmed. However, playing the game to Decision Set #3 establishes a decision sequence to a point where there is sufficient behavioral information for profitable post-game discussion.

THE LABORATORY FUNCTION OF GAMES

Training simulations in educational administration are relatively simple and unsophisticated in comparison with other management simulations. However, the usefulness of simulation as a training technique is more a function of the behavior generated in the simulation and the level of the theoretical analysis of the behavior during post-session or post-game discussions, than of the complexity of the simulation itself. Simulation is a form of social laboratory, a way of structuring experience and producing data for subsequent analyses. Games are a class of simulations with characteristics that shape individual and group behavior in specific ways. The training problem is also a design problem in which simulation variables, dimensions, or structural characteristics are put together to achieve desired outcomes.

Simulation outcomes can be classified as intrinsic and extrinsic in form. Intrinsic learning outcomes are those occurring directly from the process of participating in a simulation or playing game. Extrinsic learning outcomes result from the post-participation discussion or analysis of the behavior of the players exhibited during the game.

Current management simulation users rely almost entirely on the learning intrinsic to the simulation. Designers and users of simulations have made extensive claims about the superiority of simulation exercises over other training techniques. The development of intellectual initiative, conceptual understanding, decision-making ability, and social and negotiating skills have been thought to occur in measurable quantities. Such generalized skills as analytical problem solving, probabilistic decision strategies, and system concepts or organizations are assumed to occur in forms that transfer to real life management problems. The more enthusiastic proponents of management games see no limits to the possible outcomes. However, supporting evidence is hard to find.

McKenney's (12) own research and his review of the literature on the training results of gamed simulations led him to conclude that there is little evidence to support the superiority of learning through games over such conventional techniques as case studies, role playing, lectures, and discussions. The acquisition of knowledge is not necessarily greater through experience in a management game. A similar review by Cherryholmes of the results of six studies of acquired experience in educational simulations led him to conclude that "simulation does produce more student motivation and interest but there are no consistent or significant differences in learning, retention, critical thinking, or attitude change" (4).

When simulations are compared with other techniques, the equivocal findings are consistent with the findings of method comparison studies in general; i.e., little or no significant or consistent differences among methods. The traditional method comparison approach, however, may be an inappropriate and unproductive response to the problem when the problem is defined as the design of a laboratory experience to achieve specified outcomes. Assuming that simulation is a way of structuring experience differently than other, more conventional teaching methods, the appropriate question is, "In what ways are design variables related to the shaping of what experiences?"

Some Design Variables

Considerable support exists for a wide array of learnings and behaviors considered to occur during participation in a well-designed simulation. Games, in particular, generate a high level of involvement and motivation. Game users report that the excitement of play is the most obvious difference between gamed simulations and other techniques. And since motivation for learning continues to be probably the most critical and unpredictable variable in the instruction process, a technique with a structure that can be formed to produce high involvement must be given serious consideration.

The motivational structures of a game are complex. One source of motivation may be attributed to the fact that a game requires actions to be taken that are "public" and therefore "real". Subsequent analysis of actions or decisions is a reality-testing process. The individual has a stake in the process since he has made visible his personal or professional view of reality for testing against the reality of the group (consensual validation) or against some externally defined "reality" criterion as the final outcome or score of the game. If the individual, professional view deviates significantly from a consensus norm, the player or discussant confronts the threat of having to defend or reconstruct the rationale or assumptions on which his actions were based. The process may involve deep layers of self-concept, examination of basic values or the process of maintaining "professional face". A prior knowledge of or intuition about the degree and kind of self that may be involved through playing a game that purports to test one's ability to make effective administrative decisions, solve problems, or engage in leadership acts is not only motivating in the traditional sense but also may tap the motivation of anxiety.

A second structural characteristic that has motivational as well as learning outputs is the cooperative-competitive structure of a non-zero-sum game. In such games, the interests of the participants are partly coordinate and partly conflicted. Each player has the power of preventing an outcome so that neither achieves a positive pay-off. Consequently, players must concert their actions in order to achieve a positive benefit, though the structure may be set so that the winner receives a higher pay-off than the other, though both win something and either has the power to act so that both lose.

The cooperative-competitive dimension can be varied to increase the amount of competitiveness or the amount of cooperation or interdependence; to increase or decrease the opportunity and temptation to take unfair advantage; or to vary the form of competition from competition against an environment to competition between two or more individuals or groups. Differences in cooperative-competitive structure may lead to differences in intrinsic outcomes as well as differences in behavior produced for subsequent analysis. For example, a highly competitive game structured to suggest a test of the player's leadership ability might be used to develop the ability of an administrator to deal with conflict while greater emphases on cooperation might test the player's predilection for cooperation rather than winning.

In summary, those learnings intrinsic to playing the game which have been claimed to be the most significant outcomes in the use of the technique are generalized in the following list.

1. An understanding of complex concepts, complex systems and system models can be acquired in greater depth through participation in a role, task or interaction sequence. The player acquires a feel for complexity and learns to function as a part of a complex system.

2. Practice in decision making under conditions of uncertainty, incomplete knowledge, and consequences in the form of probabilities is a major characteristic of most management games. Players have an opportunity to learn that decisions are affected by past decisions or states of the system and affect the alternatives in subsequent states of the system. Immediate feedback of the consequences of decisions should lead to more effective decision making skills.

3. The understanding of risk taking in decision making. Kogan and Walach use risk taking in decision making in a fundamental reanalysis of the problem of how man thinks (11). Their findings suggest that the concepts of "motivation," "personality," "attitudes," and "thinking" may be more productively viewed from the perspective of risk and conservatism in decision making. Management games can be designed to focus on risk taking behavior.

4. The development of the ability to deal with stress. Bower (2) discusses the utilization of games as a means of building immunity to stress. The conflict in some forms of games or simulations, requiring the player to respond to and deal with conflicts, may be an important instructional characteristic of the technique.

5. Though the acquisition of facts about a system, organization, or subject seems to be no more effective through game playing than through other techniques, such acquisition should not be downgraded, particularly if factual learning occurs in conjunction with other learnings.

The enthusiastic claims of the wide variety of intrinsic learnings that may be expected to occur ignore the limitations of the technique and the assumptions about learning unsupported by evidence.

The modeling of a real system, by definition, omits many essential parts of the real world. Model development usually requires the acceptance of assumptions which are only partly true or deliberately speculative. Actions taken within the constraints of the system model may not be directly transferable to the real world. Students may develop a false sense of competence based on successful decisions made within a simulated system constructed on unvalidated assumptions. It is important, therefore, to engage in a critical analysis of the game or simulation with participants or players so that the learnings that have occurred are checked against reality.

A second limitation on learning through games is that the game is based on a closed system. Feedback in closed systems is likely to discourage originality and imagination in solving game problems. A radical action or solution may be outside the rules and boundaries of the game so that the parameters and relations among variables exceed design units. The radical solution may cause a computer-based game to come to a grinding halt.

The closed-system problem is particularly serious in administrative games in which rule and policy tend to determine the decisions made, with error as the feedback constant. The opportunity for the creative solution or a change in rule or policy is almost impossible to design into a game with feedback loops and an end point which defines success or failure. Consequently, users of games in administrative training must accommodate to the limitations in the state-of-the-art.

RESEARCH POTENTIAL

The research potential of games and simulations has had relatively little exploration. The early study by Hemphill et al. continues to be the most comprehensive in educational administration (8). Using the *Whitman School* simulation and the in-basket technique, in-basket items reflecting an array of administrative problems, were presented to a total of 232 elementary school principals, each of whom assumed the role of the principal of the *Whitman School*. Responses to memos, letters, telephone messages, reports, and the task items were collected and analyzed. Personality test scores and effectiveness ratings were also collected.

The analysis of responses required a set of 68 categories which were factor analyzed to produce two major and eight sub-factors. Major factor X was defined as "preparation for decisions versus taking final action." Major factor Y was identified as "amount of work done in handling items." The sub-factors described in greater detail what the principal did in handling items. Significant differences were found in the amount of work done and the amount of preparation made prior to a decision. Principals rated as most effective had a higher work output and engaged in a larger amount of preparation before making a decision. In a further analysis, eight administrative styles were identified and related to personality variables. As a whole, the study was an excellent demonstration of the use of a standardized simulation for the production of behavior for research purposes.

The obvious potential of games and simulations as standardized laboratory structures for the generation of behavior for research purposes has not been exploited in research on administrator behavior. Considerable use, however, has been made of game theory and game structure in the study of individual behavior. The research design typically uses a simple game structure such as "prisoner's dilemma." Subjects are brought in to "play" for some reward. Game variables such as the pay-off matrix, the cooperative-competitive relations, imperfect information, number of players, and form of communication are varied and subject responses are compared to theoretical predictions. One central research problem of interest to administrators has been the question of why subject behavior does not correspond to rationally predicted behavior, particularly in non-zero-sum situations in which cooperative choice would provide higher pay-offs for both players than would the other choices (16). The search for answers to this question continues amid tentative and sometimes conflicting evidence.

More directly related to the field of administration is the set of studies concerned with personality differences between high-risk- and low-risk-takers. Administrative games can be designed to elicit risk-taking behaviors, which in turn might be related to job performance, thus opening up research territory more or less inaccessible to direct empirical investigation.

Another research-oriented, game-related area of social interaction is the modern development of the study of coalitions. N-person games provide an unusual opportunity to study coalition formation in organizations. Fortunately, a well-developed theory of coalitions in triads has been formulated which can provide the necessary theoretical base for further research (3).

FUTURE TRENDS IN GAME DEVELOPMENT AND USE

The development and expanded use of games in preparation and in-service training programs is likely to be a long-term prospect. The central problem is the difficulty of constructing complex system models capable of supporting a game structure and decision moves of interest to educational administrators. One alternative, therefore, is to utilize existing management with appropriate modifications.

A number of urban land use planning games have been devised for use in training programs in urban ecology and government. *The Cornell Land Use Game* was designed for a course in urban ecology for the purpose of teaching some of the basic principles of community growth and development (6). An understanding of the complexities of community development and the basic economic forces affecting such development would seem appropriate material for preparation programs in school administration. The game technique and discussion of the results of play may be a way of foreshortening learning time. Rather than a one-semester class with lectures, discussions and a long and diverse reading list, it may be possible to acquire a minimum knowledge of urban ecology and urban growth within a week of play and discussion. Other land use games such as those developed by Duke (5) and Taylor (20) involve some game specific as well as generalizable principles, thus providing the opportunity to select a game for specific learning outcomes.

The "University Administrators' Decision Laboratory—360 Version," a computer-based management game utilizing a systems model of a university, reflects the rapidly developing area of administration in higher education (10). Though fun to play, the model is restrictive and the game has been used primarily to demonstrate the nature of computer-based gaming rather than as a training game for administrative decision making. However, the game could be modified to give greater emphasis to the system concept of administrative decision making with a consequent increase in its usefulness in training programs.

Numerous other potentially adaptable and useful games exist and new ones are being created almost daily. Unfortunately, information about management games is scattered and unorganized. Perhaps the best available source of information at present is the annotated bibliography of instructional simulations edited by Twelker (21).

A second direction for the future lies in the application of the gaming technique to administrative and training problems identified by groups or teams of on-the-job administrators. The application may be made in two ways.

The first method is through an administrators' workshop in which a group plays one or more games and, in subsequent discussions, is led through the structure and development of the game to a point where the group has understanding of the gaming technique sufficient to develop simple training or problem-solving games of their own. At that point an administrative problem, identified as common to the schools represented, is used to construct a training or problem solving game for eventual use by each administrator in his home situation. A follow-up of each test use of the game would provide feedback for further refinement and generalization.

A second method is the use of a consulting team working with the administrative staff of a school system. The consulting team would help the staff to model their system to the point where it can be used as the base for a game or simulation. At that point, a set of administrative problems may be identified and cast in game form. The staff and consultant team would engage in one or more runs of the simulation or game and the results would be analyzed for application to the real problems of the system. Player behavior in the game would be discussed in relation to the solution of the problem. Thus, through the use of the simulation technique, a set of immediate and system specific problems may be examined and solutions tested prior to making an actual decision. It is in this last application, that the full potential of the gaming technique in educational administration is most likely to be realized in the next decade.

BIBLIOGRAPHY

1. Berne, Eric. *Games People Play.* New York: Grove Press, Inc., 1965.

2. Power, Eli M. "The Modification, Mediation, and Utilization of Stress During School Years." Paper presented to the Orthopsychiatric Society. March 1963.

3. Caplow, Theodore. *Two Against One.* Englewood Cliffs, New Jersey: Prentice-Hall, Inc., 1968

4. Cherryholmes, Cleo H. "Some Current Research on Effectiveness of Educational Simulations: Implications for Alternative Strategies." *American Behavioral Scientist* 10 (October 1966), pp. 4-7.

5. Duke, Richard D. *Gaming Simulation in Urban Research.* East Lansing, Michigan: Institute for Community Development and Services, Michigan State University, 1964.

6. Feldt, Allen G., *Operational Gaming in Planning Education.* Ithaca, New York: Division of Urban Studies, Cornell University, Article 16, reprint, 1966.

7. Harsanyi, John C. "Rationality Postulates for Bargaining Solutions in Cooperative and Non-Cooperative Games." *Management Science* 9 (October 1962), pp. 1-141-53.

8. Hemphill, John T.; Griffiths, Daniel E.; and Ferdericksen, Norman. *Administrative Performance and Personality.* New York: Bureau of Publications, Teachers College, Columbia University, 1962.

9. Huizinga, John. *Homo Ludens.* Boston: Becon Press, 1955.

10. Klaproth, W. W. *University Administrators' Decision Laboratory–360 Version.* Springfield, Illinois: IBM Corporation, 1170 South Lex Street, 62705.

11. Kogan, Nathan & Wallach, M. A. *Risk Taking.* New York: Holt, Rinehart & Winston, Inc., 1964.

12. McKenney, J. C. "An Evaluation of a Business Game in a MBA Curriculum." *The Journal of Business* XXXV (July 1962). pp. 278-86.

13. Newman, John von & Morgenstern, C. *Theory of Games and Economic Behavior.* Princeton, New Jersey: Princeton University Press, 1955.

14. Rapoport, Anatol. *Two-Person Game Theory.* Ann Arbor, Michigan: University of Michigan Press, 1966.

15. Rapoport, Anatol. "Game Theory and Human Conflict." In Elton B. McNeil (ed.), The Nature of Human Conflict. Englewood Cliffs, New Jersey: Prentice-Hall, Inc., 1965, p. 225.

16. Rapoport, Anatol. "Experimental Games: A Review." *Behavioral Science* 7, 1 (January 1962), 1-37.

17. Ricciardi, Frank M., et al. In *Top Management Decision Simulations: The AMA Approach,* ed. Elizabeth Marting. New York: American Management Association, 1957.

18. Schelling, Thomas C. "The Strategy of Conflict: Prospectus for a Reorientation of Game Theory." *The Journal of Conflict Resolution* II (September 1958), pp. 203-64.

19. Szasz, Thomas. *The Myth of Mental Illness.* New York: Hoeber-Harper, Inc., 1961.

20. Taylor, John L. "6 Synoptic Views of Urban Phenomena." Draft copy of a paper. Sheffield, England: Department of Town and Regional Planning, University of Sheffield, January 1967.

21. Twelker, Paul A., ed. *Instructional Simulation Systems.* Annotated bibliography. Corvallis: Oregon State University, 1969.

22. University Council for Educational Administration. *The Madison Township School District Simulation.* Columbus, Ohio: UCEA, 29 W. Woodruff Ave.

7

Simulation of
Collective Negotiations

John J. Horvat

Nearly all members of the profession of educational administration agree that the need for training in, and understanding of, the processes of collective negotiation[1] in education is urgent. Negotiation, along with school finance and integration problems, ranks as one of the top three concerns of local, regional, and national administrator groups in their various conferences, workshops, and other meetings. This concern extends from practicing administrators at the elemenatry school level through superintendents and board members to the university level where professors of educational administration are searching for methods of instruction, materials, and techniques which can provide training for students in the area of collective negotiation.

There is good reason for this concern. The nation's teachers are on a rampage of activism and/or militancy. It has become almost *"the* professional imperative" for teachers (and other public employees as well) to engage in negotiations with their employers. Laws have been enacted in a number of states which either permit or mandate negotiation between public employees and their employers. These laws have served to accelerate the spread of negotiation activity wherever they have been enacted. One professor of educational administration may have said it all with respect to the global aspects of the negotiation situation when he commented, "Indeed, negotiation is like an avalanche that is sweeping the country. I see no restraining walls that can stop it"(2).

However the fact that an avalanche of negotiating activity is occurring is only one major element of the total problem. The other major problem is that administrators, boards of education, and professors of educational administration have been (and in most cases, still are) totally unprepared to face and deal with this avalanche. It must be remembered that prior to 1964 very few individuals in education were concerned with the matter of collective negotiation—even as an academic problem. Virtually no one in educational administration, or in all of professional education, anticipated the revolution that was to take place in teacher-administrator-board of education relationships. This, perhaps understandable, lack of foresight helps to explain why the profession as a whole has found it difficult to make adequate praxiological and training responses to the phenomenon of negotiation.

Administrators have begun to accept, albeit reluctantly in many cases, the point of view that negotiation is here to stay. They typically feel quite uncomfortable with the break with past practice and tradition in teacher-administrator-board relationships brought about by the advent of collective negotiations, but they are beginning to recognize that arguing about the legitimacy of negotiations is probably a pointless activity. Administrators, including professors of educational administration, are beginning to look for ways to *survive* in school situations in which negotiation is (or will be) a way of life, and they are now trying to *discover* ways in which the processes of negotiation can be used as constructive, positive forces in education rather than as the destructive, negative forces of the recent past.

"Survive" and "discover" are key words or elements of the problem of training administrators to function in the milieu of collective negotiation. Practitioners are particularly concerned with the matter of survival in negotiations. Their concern is immediate and short-range, and their questions are typically of the "what to do" or "how to do it" type. Educational administrators who are not immediately and directly involved in negotiation activities are not as much concerned with survival as with understanding. This latter group is searching for answers with respect to the long-range ramifications of the educational establishment's widespread involvement in negotiation activity. They are concerned with matters of theory, attitudes, objectives, and methods of behavior which will, through the process of negotiations, lead to the general improvement of education and to the improvement of the relationships among the concerned parties. Professors of educational administration are in a unique position. On the one hand, many of their advanced graduate students and former students appeal to them for help with questions of immediate survival in negotiations. On the other hand, other students and the profession in general turn to them for advice, ideas, and guidance relevant to the long-range approaches which educational administration should take with respect to the entire phenomenon of collective negotiation. Of course, all individuals in educational administration should be concerned with both the immediate survival problems and the long-range, good-of-the-profession problems. But the professional and ethical responsibility which accrues with the professorial role makes this dual concern one of utmost importance for the professor of educational administration.

It is an unfortunate fact that efforts to deal with the immediate problems of survival and success in negotiation (however "survival" and "success" may be defined) are not always compatible with the development of understanding of the total negotiation phenomenon and the ultimate improvement of education. Quite simply, training for survival in an emergency situation (e.g., negotiations) will often lead to behaviors and actions which are inimical to the long-range "togetherness" and compatability of the parties involved in the emergency situation. Time and situational constraints often preclude giving attention to both training needs. The individual who would provide training and/or advice to others in the area of collective negotiation should recognize that circumstances and the audience may require the emphasis of training for survival to the neglect of training for long-range understanding. If such is the case, the trainer should recognize what he is doing, and he should be able to justify his actions at least to himself. This caveat is given at this point simply because the simulation device,[2] the essential subject of the remainder of this chapter, provides a means by which training for survival, training for long-range understanding, or both can be (at least partially) provided.

There are certain assumptions upon which the simulation materials described in this chapter were built and upon which the notion of providing training for administrators in the area of negotiation rests. Not everyone in educational administration will be in agreement with these assumptions, but the reader should be aware of them so that he can interpret that which follows. The assumptions are:

1. *That educational administrators will continue to be personally involved in negotiation processes.* This involvement may or may not be at the face-to-face negotiating level; but at the very least administrators will be involved (a) in setting the directions and tenor of face-to-face negotiation behaviors and of the total negotiations relationship, (b) in advising face-to-face negotiators, (c) in both long- and short-range planning for negotiations, and (d) in the day-to-day administration of negotiated agreements and arrangements.

2. *That participation in negotiation at any level is a serious and potentially critical activity which should not be entrusted to untrained individuals.* The impact and consequences which may result from negotiation are too important and far-reaching to allow the task to be assigned to amateurs.

3. *That on-the-job training[3] in the processes of negotiation can be very expensive.* On-the-job training can (and often does) result in needlessly high reductions in budgetary flexibility, in heavy loss of administrator-board prerogatives, in great loss of face, and reduced ability to work with professional staff. Methods to supplement on-the-job training of negotiators must be found.

THE SIMULATION DEVICE

In this section the Negotiation Game (6) will be described in both general and specific detail. The various forms or versions of the Game will be discussed. The purposes and outcomes which can be expected from the utilization of the Game as a training device will be considered. The section will conclude with a short discussion of formal as opposed to informal gaming.

General Description of the Game

The Negotiation Game and its related materials are designed to assist in the training of students and/or practitioners in the theory and practice of collective negotiation with particular emphasis on the face-to-face, across-the-table aspects of negotiating. The Game provides:

1. methods and materials for selecting and placing trainees on teams for the purpose of engaging in simulated negotiations
2. background materials which set the context of the simulation and which serve to prepare the trainees to engage in simulated negotiations
3. substantive issues to be negotiated in simulation, and negotiating guidelines for the negotiators (trainees)
4. materials and methods for use in the analysis of the outcomes of the simulated negotiation sessions—so that feedback on negotiating behaviors and outcomes can be provided to the trainees

Stated very simply, the Game provides (a) a means by which a trainer may set up one or more teams of trainees to engage in simulated face-to-face negotiation sessions, (b) materials for the simulation itself, and (c) materials for use in the analysis of the simulated negotiation sessions.

The Game materials are available in three versions or "forms" which will be described in some detail. The forms are adaptable for use in various instructional time periods. The "Short Form"(6) is recommended for use in training settings in which the total time available for instruction is on the order of twelve to twenty hours. The "Intermediate Form" (6) is designed to be used in training settings which allow twenty to forty hours for instruction. The "Long Form"(6) is adaptable for use in situations where more than forty instructional or "class" hours are available, e.g., a two-week summer workshop. Any of the three forms can be used in regular college-course settings so long as the time requirements suggested above can be met. Typically, the "Short" or the "Intermediate" form of the Game is used in quarter or semester university courses, particularly if the courses are not focused exclusively on the area of collective negotiation. There is reasonable flexibility in the time requirements for utilization of the

Game. With the addition of enrichment materials and activities, more time will be required. By deleting certain portions of the basic Game materials, the time required for use is reduced. Any use of the Game in periods of less than twelve hours has been, in the writer's experience, rather unproductive.

Detailed Description of the Game Materials

The essential difference among the three versions of the Game is in the amount of material presented to the trainees. The simulation techniques, feedback techniques, and purposes remain the same for the three forms. In the detailed outline description of the Game materials to follow, the "Short Form" will be described and additional materials of the other two forms will be noted. This detailed description will be presented in three parts, i.e., *pre-simulation* materials, *simulation* materials, and *analysis and feedback* materials.[4]

Pre-simulation Materials

A. The introductory section of the Game materials provides the following information for the *trainer*: (a) prefatory remarks, (b) general description of the Game, (c) suggestions for use of the Game, (d) details of possible post-negotiation-session activities, (e) comments on the role of the superintendent in negotiations, (f) suggestions with regard to the number of negotiators per team in simulated negotiations, (g) description of the three forms of the Game, (h) a description of, and scoring instruction for, "The Labor-Management Attitude Questionnaire" (a device which may be used by the trainer in setting up negotiating teams and groups).

*B. The "Labor-Management Attitude Questionnaire" is a forty-item opinionnaire device which attempts to measure the pro-labor or pro-management leanings of the respondee. It can be used for the purpose of manipulating the composition of membership of negotiating teams as described below.

C. The essence of the simulation involves setting up role-playing negotiating groups. A "group" in this context refers to two negotiating teams of two or three players each. One team of the group represents the board-administration in the simulated negotiations, while the other team represents the teachers' organization. Obviously, the most realistic or true-to-life simulation situation is one in which the trainees who assume the role of board-administration negotiators are, in fact, practicing teachers. In the typical instructional situation, however, the trainees are usually a rather homogeneous group, e.g., all practicing administrators or students of educational administration. In such situations the trainer has a number of options with respect to the placement of trainees on negotiating teams and groups. This section of the materials suggests a number of ways in which the Labor-Management Attitude Questionnaire, or trainer prompting of trainees, can be used to structure groups and teams so that they represent varying degrees and polarities of pro-labor or pro-management orientation. Such manipulation of group and team composition provides opportunities for making enlightening comparisons of the "attitudinal-behavioral" relationships among the negotiating groups and also provides opportunity to conduct on-the-spot action research studies of behaviors as part of the simulation.

Simulation Materials

*A. A notice of appointment to a negotiating team is provided to each of the trainees, i.e., a letter of appointment to the Board of Education Negotiating Team for trainees who will play this role and a letter of appointment to the Teachers' Organization Bargaining Team for trainees who play the role of teacher representatives in the simulated negotiations.

*B. Twelve pages of detailed background materials relative to the simulated school district are provided for trainees using the "Short" and "Intermediate" forms of the Game. Forty additional and highly detailed pages of background material are provided for trainees using the "Long" form of the Game. Background information of the "Short" and "Intermediate" forms of the Game includes:

1. Data on the simulated city in which the negotiators live

and work, including social, business, income, political, educational level, and other demographic information.

2. Data relative to the simulated school district describing:
   a. The Board of Education
   b. The three-track curriculum system
   c. General financial data, e.g., assessed valuation, tax rates, and bonded indebtedness
   d. History of the growth of the teachers' organization and results of the "representation election"
   e. The number and enrollments of the school units of the system
   f. The number, assignments, and educational levels of the systems's professional staff
   g. Teacher-turnover information, male-female composition of professional staff, and years of experience of professional staff
   h. Teacher salary schedule
   i. Other miscellaneous data

3. A summary of practices, salary schedules, etc. of other school districts of comparable size in the state.

4. Laws of the state relative to negotiation.

A wealth of additional and different kinds of data are provided in the background section of the "Long" form of the game.

C. This section provides instructions which should be given by the trainer to the trainee negotiators immediately prior to the start of simulated face-to-face negotiations. The section also includes hints for the physical arrangements of the simulation situation and suggestions on timing of activities.

*D. The various issues to be negotiated and resolved are presented in this section. Each issue (i.e., item to be negotiated) is presented according to the following format (See example, "Issue for Negotiations #14):

1. The teachers' demand is given.
2. The Board's pre-negotiation reaction is given.
3. A statement of past practice in the district is given.
4. The dollar cost of yielding on the issue is given.

Issue for Negotiation #14 (6)
Statement of Positions

Credit for Prior Service

Teachers: demand that all teachers currently employed and those entering the system for the first time be given full credit, for salary purposes, for *all* teaching service rendered both in the system and/or elsewhere before entrance into the system. Proof of service must be provided by the teacher and service must have occurred under a bona fide teaching certificate for this credit to be given.

Board: rejects this demand outright.

Past Practice: credit on the salary schedule is given for prior service in other systems, but the maximum credit allowed is five years.

Dollar value: indeterminate

E. Twenty issues to be negotiated are provided in the "Long" form of the Game. The "Intermediate" form presents eleven and the "Short" form seven issues for negotiation. These issues are:

1. Recognition of Teacher Organization (All forms)
2. Dues Check Off (All forms)
3. Salary Increase (All forms)
4. Hospital and Medical Plan (All forms)
5. Duty-Free Lunch Periods (All forms)
6. Preparation Periods (All forms)
7. Class Size Limitation (All forms)
8. Extra Pay for Extra Duties (Intermediate and Long forms)
9. Revision of Salary Schedule (Intermediate and Long forms)
10. Transfer Policy (Intermediate and Long forms)
11. Sabbatical Leaves (Intermediate and Long forms)
12. Grievance Procedure (Long form only)
13. Sick Leave Policy (Long form only)
14. Credit for Prior Service (Long form only)
15. Preliminary Disciplinary or Discharge Procedures (Long form only)
16. In-Service Education Policy (Long form only)
17. Level of Professional Preparation Policy (Long form only)

18. Teachers' Organization Meetings (Long form only)
19. Consultation with the Superintendent (Long form only)
20. Teacher Evaluation (Long form only)

Suggestions are also provided in this section for the addition or deletion of issues by the trainer.

*F. A memorandum of instructions for the guidance of the negotiators is provided to the trainees. Of course, a different set of instructions is given to the board-administration negotiators than is given to the teachers' organization negotiators. These memoranda provide statements of the position of the respective sides on all of the issues and, in addition, suggest guidelines to the negotiators for good-faith negotiating.

*G. A set of "Final Terms of the Agreement" forms (see below) is provided to the trainees. These forms are used by the trainees to indicate the nature of the agreements produced on each of the negotiated issues.

Post-Simulation Materials

*A. A "Post-session Questionnaire" is provided with the materials to be administered to each trainee upon the conclusion of simulated negotiation sessions. The purpose of the "Post-session Questionnaire" is to ascertain the following:

1. The general satisfaction felt by the trainee-negotiator with respect to the negotiation situation(s) in which he has just participated.
2. The realism of the simulation as perceived by the trainee.
3. The trainee's satisfaction with the substantive outcomes of the negotiations.
4. The trainee's satisfaction with the procedural (interpersonal) outcomes of the negotiations.
5. The degree of residual disagreement held by the trainee-negotiator.

Final Terms of the Agreement (6)

ISSUE #14—Credit for Prior Service

   a. ( ) Credit allowed for all prior service.

b. ( ) Credit allowed for a maximum of 5
    years prior service.
c. ( ) Other.   Describe_____

_____

Initials of Negotiators:

    Board #1_____   Board #2_____
    RTO #1 _____   RTO #2 _____

Dollar Value: Indeterminate

B. Suggestions and methods are provided in the materials for
    rating the substantive outcomes of the negotiation sessions.
    Participants in a gaming situation are nearly always concerned
    with the question of "who won?" Winning is, of course, a
    subjective concept in collective negotiations, and this is
    particularly the case in simulated collective negotiations. The
    materials of this section do not attempt to define a winner,
    but rather attempt to provide means for ascertaining the
    relative "goodness" or "fairness" of particular negotiated
    agreements produced by the trainees.

C. An extensive section of the post-simulation materials is
    devoted to the provision of methods for the analysis of
    behaviors within the simulated negotiation sessions. Part of
    the procedure of using the Negotiations Game involves record-
    ing, on audio tape, the interactions of the negotiating teams.
    These tapes are then analyzed by the trainees, using a
    modification of the Bales (1) interaction system, so that
    feedback information can be supplied to trainees relative to
    their own, and their team's, behaviors in the small group
    interaction of negotiations. This method for the analysis of
    behavior requires, in effect, that the trainee confront his own
    behaviors so that he may understand the effect of this
    behavior on others and on the processes of negotiation in
    general.

  This lengthy, but actually not highly detailed, outline description of basic Negotiation Game simulation materials should
provide the reader with the background information needed to
understand what follows in this chapter. Essentially, the Negotia-

tion Game provides materials and suggestions for the simulation of real world, face-to-face, collective negotiations situations, and it provides materials and suggestions for the detailed analysis of substantive and behavioral outcomes of the simulated negotiations.

A word should be said at this point about the terminology used in this chapter. The terms *game* and *simulation* are used synonymously throughout the chapter. This is probably a misuse of the word "game." The Negotiation Game *is not* a formal game in which mathematical projections and breakdowns of behaviors and outcomes can be made. A formal or "classic" game is a device in which all possible behavioral commutations, permutations, and parameters are foreknown—typically the formal game is easily computerized. Obviously, the Negotiation Game is not such a formal game. For the purist, it should be referred to as a "game-like simulation" in which inputs, behavioral parameters, and pay-offs are largely unknown and are indeed affected by the moment-by-moment behaviors of the participants in the simulation.

Intended Purposes of and Expected Outcomes from Utilization of the Game

The Negotiations Game was designed with a professorial audience in mind. It was thought that the materials would be most useful to professors of educational administration who wished to conduct a course or workshop in collective negotiations, or who wished to add consideration of collective negotiations to already established courses covering staff personnel administration.

The objectives to be attained through the use of the Game were seen to be the following:

1. To provide general information to trainees relative to the total area and processes of collective negotiation in education, i.e., to provide information and training *about* collective negotiation.

2. To provide general experiences in the processes of preparing for and engaging in face-to-face negotiations, i.e., to provide *"how-to-do-it"* experiences.

3. To provide a situational base, and a methodology for the analysis of that situational base, which aids trainees in under-

standing the effect of individual behaviors and group interactions within face-to-face negotiation contexts, i.e., to force a self-confrontation of behavior on the part of trainees.

The materials have been used by the writer in over fifty different instructional-training situations. In all of these situations, objectives (1) and (2) above have met with average to high success. Objective (3) above has been met only when the instructional situation permitted the analysis of behaviors to occur, i.e., when time was available to engage in analysis and provide feedback.

While the Negotiation Game was intended for use at the university level, it has found application at the in-service training level as well. The Game has been used extensively by administrator and board groups in the process of preparing for their initial (or early) contact with a teachers' organization for the purpose of formal negotiations.[6]

It should be noted that participation in the activities of the Negotiation Game will not enable the participant to function as a skilled negotiator. It will, however, help him understand the context and processes of negotiation; it will help him understand much of what is required to become a skilled negotiator; it will provide a beginning understanding of the strategies and tactics of face-to-face negotiation; and, if analysis of simulated negotiations is used effectively, it will provide insights relative to the impact of his behavior as a negotiator.

TECHNIQUES OF THE SIMULATION

In this section the various procedures which have been found to be helpful in the utilization of the Negotiations Game will be described and some of the problems which may occur as the Game is used will be indicated.

General Methods and Procedures of the Simulation

The trainer or instructor who would use the Negotiation Game needs to be concerned with the following five major procedural elements:

1. Trainee preparation for simulated negotiations
2. Selection-composition of negotiating teams and groups
3. Starting and maintaining the simulation
4. Physical arrangements for the simulation
5. Providing feedback to trainees with respect to the simulation activities

Trainee Preparation for the Simulated Negotiations. Preparation for the simulation, in the sense used here, refers to preparing *trainees* to engage in simulated negotiations. The nature of the trainee group largely determines the amount of effort which is necessary to ready the trainees for the simulation.

Some trainees may be totally naive about the entire phenomenon of collective negotiations in education while other groups may be highly knowledgeable about the phenomenon, if not about the processes. Typically, the college class in educational administration will contain a number of students who possess little knowledge or understanding of collective negotiations in either the public or the private sector. This is particularly true with groups of trainees who have had little or no administrative experience, or with groups of lower-echelon administrators, e.g., supervisors and elementary principals. Such groups require fairly extensive preparation, such as reading assignments,[7] lectures, and seminar discussions, simply to understand the "nature of the territory" to be simulated.

College course groups which have as members higher-level administrators, who typically have both recent and relatively extensive experience, are fairly well informed with respect to the general negotiations phenomenon. Workshop trainee groups are also fairly well informed in a general sense about this phenomenon—a possible exception in this instance may be workshops which include members of boards of education. Board members can and do run the entire spectrum of sophistication in the area of negotiations. Some board members barely understand what the term "negotiation" means, while others have served as prime spokesman for a management negotiating team in industry. In any event, the trainer must take into account the level of sophistication of his trainee group, and where sophistication about the general negotiations phenomenon is lacking, it must be developed.

With reasonably well-informed trainee groups, one to two-hour lecture-discussion is usually sufficient to prepare the group to engage in simulated negotiations with useful and positive results. Such lecture-discussions should contain the latest or best information on (a) the spread and impact of negotiations locally, regionally, and nationally, (b) the apparent, presumed, or hypothetical precipitating causes for teacher militancy and/or activism, (c) the goals which teachers and teachers' organizations seem to be striving for, and attaining, through negotiation processes, (d) the rules and niceties of negotiating in good faith as legally construed, (e) examples of recent laws, court decisions, and labor relations board rulings which exemplify the "gains" which organized teachers have made, (f) the latest information on state laws pertaining to negotiations in the state in which the training is being conducted, and (g) a general indication of, or emphasis on, the apparent fact that "negotiation is here to stay" and that one should not be unprepared if he intends to participate.

Of course, a second phase of the preparation of trainees for participation in the simulation requires that they become familiar with the background materials of the particular form of the Negotiation Game that is to be used. This task is relatively easy to accomplish simply by giving the trainees the background materials (after they have been placed on negotiating teams) and providing time for the materials to be studied, for discussion to take place, and for questions regarding the background to be asked and answered.

Selection-Composition of Negotiating Teams and Groups. The placement of trainees on particular negotiating teams and groups can range from a simple and straightforward to a rather complex process. The effort required at this point will depend upon the trainer's wishes for the outputs of the simulation. If he simply wants the trainees to become involved in simulated negotiation sessions, negotiation teams can be selected arbitrarily, e.g., with a trainee group of twenty-four individuals, twelve of them represent teachers' organization negotiators and the other twelve represent board-administration negotiators. These twelve-man camps are then broken down into four to six negotiating teams[8] of two or three men each. A two- or three-man[9] teachers' organization team can then be paired with a similar board-administration team to form a negotiating group. Of course, if a trainee group contains an odd number of individuals, those left can be spotted on teams at random, i.e., a three-man teachers' team can negotiate with a two-man or a four-man board-administration team.

There are two reasons why a trainer may not wish to use the arbitrary assignment method in placing trainees on negotiating teams. First, he may wish to increase the *realism* of the simulation. Second, he may wish to structure negotiating groups so that behavioral and output *comparisons*, based on input attitudes, can be made among the groups.

The realism of the simulation can be increased by increasing the teams' polarization of the attitude orientations toward each other. The most realistic simulation situation, as has been suggested earlier, probably involves having teachers' organization negotiating teams which are comprised of real-life, highly militant teachers who oppose board-administration teams comprised of real-life administrators and/or board members. When the trainer does not have real-life teachers at hand, he may wish to try to rig the composition of the negotiating teams so that the highest possible polarization of attitude orientation exists. This can be done through use of the Labor-Management Attitude Questionnaire (6) to match, for example, teachers' negotiating teams holding highly pro-labor attitude orientations with board-administration negotiating teams holding highly pro-management attitude orientations.[10]

Another means by which a degree of "natural" polarization of attitude orientations may be gained is simply through the expedient of prompting team members, prior to the simulation, to assume high, moderate, or low pro-labor or pro-management attitudes and behaviors in the negotiation sessions. However, prompting a trainee-negotiator to take a "hard-nosed," highly pro-managment attitude, for example, may require the trainee to assume a role which is antithetical to his temperament. The use of the Labor-Management Attitude Questionnaire can help the trainer discover trainees who are "naturals" for the hard-nosed and other roles.

The second reason for manipulating the composition of the negotiating teams is so that comparisons may be made among variously structured groups after the simulated negotiations have been concluded. Interesting comparisons can be made, for example, between the behavioral and substantive outputs from a group containing highly polarized negotiators and from a group in which the attitudes of the negotiators were not so highly polarized. The combinations of team and group compositions, and the comparisons which can be made upon the basis of differing group compositions are nearly endless. Further discussion of the kinds of comparisons which can be made and the utility of such comparisons will be deferred until the "research applications" section of this chapter.

Thus, the trainer may wish to structure his negotiating teams and groups on a convenience basis, on a realism basis, or on a potential-for-making-comparisons basis. All of these options are possible and suggestions are provided with the Negotiation Game for utilization of each option.

Starting and Maintaining the Simulation. Once the stage has been set to engage in simulated negotiations (i.e., the teams and groups have been defined, the preparatory activities completed, and the trainees have studied the simulation background materials and planned strategy with their negotiating partners), the initiation of the simulation itself is relatively easy. The trainee-negotiators are brought together and the ground rules for simulated negotiations are presented to them. Suggested ground rules are presented as a part of the Negotiation Game materials, but there is much flexibility for variation of ground rules on the part of the trainer. For example, trainees may be told that they should attempt to come to some agreement on all issues for negotiation, or they may be told to agree only when they actually feel that agreement is realistic and justified. The trainees may be told that they must make every attempt to negotiate in good faith or they may be given freedom to bargain as they choose.

The following ground-rule statements have been used extensively by the author and they have worked well in practice.

1. Negotiators should assume a role position, e.g., superintendent, board member, president of the teachers' organization, etc., and they should maintain this role position throughout the negotiations.

2. The background provided in the Negotiation Game materials is not total information—one never has total information.

Where you lack information needed to negotiate you may seek it or you may contrive it. The background information is to be accepted as fact, but any other information which may be presented at the table can be questioned.

3. You have been given guidelines for the negotiations from the particular organizations which you represent at the table. These guidelines are to be taken as "the best of all possible worlds" from your organization's point of view. You should try to operate from the basis of these guidelines, but you need not adhere to them throughout the negotiations. You have complete freedom to negotiate what you will and to deviate from the guidelines. Your agreements are, of course, subject to ratification—by the teachers in the case of the teacher negotiators and by the full board in the case of the board-administration negotiators.

4. You need not feel compelled to agree on any issue. The purpose of negotiating is, of course, to reach agreement, but you do not have to agree. You should, however, attempt to abide by the rules of good faith negotiating.

5. You need not deal with the issues in any particular order. The order in which issues are considered is itself a negotiable issue.

6. You may take a short break for a caucus with your partner(s) at any time.[11]

7. Any person at the table may fill in the "Final Terms of Agreement Form" but all negotiators must initial it.

8. You will engage in free negotiations. That is, anyone may talk at any time. The single-spokesman procedure should not be used.[12]

Other instructions or ground rules may be given as the trainer desires. Often instructions are given separately to each of the sides to the negotiations. For example, the trainer may (if he wants the sessions to be fairly bitter and acrimonious) advise the teacher-negotiators that they "need not feel that the anti-strike law precludes the use of a strike threat in the negotiations" or he may advise the board-administration negotiators that they "should not give the teachers a thing, make them earn it because time is on their side anyhow."

After the ground rules are presented, the trainees are given information about the number and duration of negotiation sessions in which they will engage. They are assigned to particular negotiating rooms and/or tables. They are given a short time for last-minute planning. When they arrive at their positions, they are told to introduce themselves and to begin negotiating. Typically, if the trainer leaves the room after giving these instructions, the negotiations begin immediately.[13] Once all the negotiating groups are underway, the trainer is free to move from group to group for purposes of observation.

The initial simulation sessions will easily sustain themselves for three to four hours. Usually only one or two issues will have been resolved in this time period, unless the negotiators have been strongly urged to reach agreement. Depending upon the total time available for training, there are several options open to the trainer after the initial simulation sessions are concluded. He can, for example, (a) begin immediately to provide feedback on the just concluded negotiation sessions, (b) provide additional information and input and send the trainees back to the table, (c) provide time for trainees to study, plan strategy, and otherwise prepare for the next sessions, or (d) provide formal instruction on negotiations and so on.

The total time available for training will determine, in large part, how the trainer will proceed after the initial session. If the total training time available is on the order of one-and-one-half days (12 hours), the first half-day will be spent with the preparations for the simulation, the second half-day block will be taken up with the simulation, and the final half-day will be filled with discussion and feedback activity. In such short training periods, one, or at the most two, simulation sessions can be accommodated with profit. For longer training periods, two, three, and more simulation sessions can be planned. Strategy sessions, information gathering, study, lectures, etc. can be interspersed between the negotiation sessions. It should be noted that three to four hours of continuous negotiation is about all that the trainees can tolerate. After this length of time in session they need time to rest, think, plan, converse with other trainees, etc.

Other than serving as a roving observer during the simulation sessions, about all the trainer needs to do during this activity is serve as a referee. He should not interfere with the activities of a negotiating group unless a complete impasse occurs and the group is unable to proceed without outside help. In such impasse situations the trainer should serve as an arbitrator, help the negotiators resolve the impasse, and get the group back to the table. The methods by which the trainer resolves impasses are totally at his discretion. Typically, the key elements of the impasse can be discovered by talking with the negotiators, and a more or less arbitrary ruling by the trainer will serve to allow the simulation to continue.

Physical Arrangements for the Simulation. The equipment and facilities required to conduct the simulation are relatively simple. Of course, a (bargaining) table and sufficient chairs are needed for each negotiating group. The table should be large enough to accommodate the four to eight trainees in each group and should provide space for papers, water, ash trays, and a tape recorder. The tape recorder is used to record all interactions at the table and to provide important inputs to the feedback activities which are an essential element of the Negotiation Game.[14]

The ideal physical arrangements for the simulation include the provision of a separate room for each of the negotiating groups. With separate accommodations for each of the groups, one group does not disturb the other, the noise level is lower, the tape recordings are easier to understand, and the setting seems more realistic to the trainees. However, it is often impossible for the trainer to provide a separate room for each negotiating group, particularly if eight or ten groups (32 to 80 individuals) are simulating negotiations simultaneously. When separate rooms are not available, the trainer should attempt to get as much room as possible. The critical need is simply that of spatial separation of groups so that intergroup interference is avoided. A large room which allows wide physical separation of groups is usually a workable arrangement for four to six negotiating groups (16 to 60 individuals).

Other than the tables and chairs, space, tape recorders, and trainees, little else is required in terms of physical facilities for the simulation.

Providing Feedback to Trainees with Respect to The Simulation Activities. While preparation for and participation in simulated negotiations are useful activities which accrue some learning for trainees, the most enlightening activity is probably the analysis of behavioral and substantive outcomes of the various negotiation sessions. Feedback to the trainees, trainee confrontation of behaviors, and comparison of behaviors and outcomes among the various negotiation groups form the heart of the learning process in this, or in any other, simulation.

There are four varieties or modes of feedback which can be provided to the trainees. They include:

1. Group discussion feedback
2. Feedback on issue settlements and dollar costs
3. Feedback on the post-session feelings and attitudes of the negotiators
4. Feedback on the behaviors and interactions of the negotiators

Group discussion can be used as a means of providing feedback to trainees. Incidents which occurred in various sessions can be related and discussed, strategies and tactics revealed, blunders which were committed can be examined, and so on. Opponents at the table can discuss the telling points which were made by the other side. Strengths and weaknesses of various negotiators, negotiating teams, arguments, and negotiating strategies can be illustrated. If observers have been used during the course of the simulation, they will be able to provide data on key events of the simulation which should be considered and discussed. The advantage of the group discussion as a means of providing feedback is its simplicity. This method requires relatively little time or effort in preparation. In fact, if the total training period is short (e.g., two days or less), the group discussion method along with feedback on the actual settlements made is probably the only approach which should be assayed—the other forms of feedback simply require too much time to prepare. The disadvantage of the discussion feedback methodology is that it lacks high-level analytical focus.

Feedback can be provided relative to the *actual settlements* and dollars costs of the settlements. Information for this feedback mode is easily gained through the analysis of the "Final Terms of the Agreement Forms"(6) of each of the negotiation groups. Comparisons of the agreements attained by each of the groups can be made in term of items yielded, powers yielded, and dollars yielded. A particularly interesting comparison can usually be made between the negotiating group which "got the most" from the teachers' point of view and the group that "gave the least" to the teachers. Discussion of the various strategies used within these two groups is often quite enlightening to the trainees.

Feedback on the *feelings* and *attitudes* which the negotiator-trainees hold immediately at the conclusion of the negotiation sessions is often a helpful input to the trainees. The feelings that negotiators take with them from the table are of inherent importance in real world negotiations. Ill-feeling generated at the bargaining table can, and often does, result in failure to gain ratification of agreements, bitterness which pervades the relationship and makes administration of the agreement difficult, and an evolutionary growth of rancor and animosity which builds up over the years and ultimately leads to a form of open warfare between the parties. Thus, it is important that fledgling negotiators give some consideration to the question of negotiator feelings. Analysis and discussion of the trainee responses to the "Post-Session Questionnaire" (6) is the means by which feedback data on feelings and attitudes of the negotiators can be provided.

Feedback on the *behaviors* and *interactions* of the trainees which occurred during the simulation is perhaps the most useful of all feedback. One means of providing this kind of feedback is to have each of the negotiating groups listen to the tape recordings of its sessions. Each trainee can listen and take notes on his own behavior and on that of the group as a whole. Inter- and intra-group discussion on these elements of behavior can take place either with or without the trainer's leadership. By this means the trainees are forced to confront and consider their own negotiating behaviors.

In-depth analysis of behaviors can be accomplished through the use of the Bales (1) interaction analysis methods and materials which are provided with the Negotiation Game. If this analytical tool is used to provide feedback, the individual, team, and group behaviors of the trainees can be examined in terms of:
1. Social-emotional positive behaviors exhibited
2. Social-emotional negative behaviors exhibited
3. Task-oriented questioning behaviors exhibited
4. Task-oriented answering-information providing behaviors exhibited

5. Problems of communication exhibited
6. Problems of evaluation exhibited
7. Problems of control exhibited
8. Problems of decision exhibited
9. Problems of tension reduction exhibited
10. Problems of reintegration exhibited

The depth of analysis of behaviors that is possible through the use of the Bales system is virtually unlimited. The wealth of analytical data that is available by means of the analysis of the negotiation session tapes is perhaps the major drawback to the use of this feedback methodology. Use of the system is a complex and time-consuming task. Obviously, it requires at least as much time to analyze one tape (no matter what analytical technique is used) as it did to record the tape in the first place. Even though the trainees handle the analysis of the tape recordings, the time required to coordinate and present the accrued data is fairly great. For these reasons, the use of this form of feedback is recommended only when a large block of time is available for training purposes. In the author's experience a minimum of forty training hours has been needed for the Bales methodology to be feasible and productive.

Problems Encountered in Using the Game

The major problems involved in the use of the simulation are time and timing. There is almost never enough time available for the trainer to accomplish all that he would like. There is probably no remedy for this problem other than experience with the simulation so that individual trainer priority activities and outcomes can be identified and served.

Timing becomes a problem in the use of the materials simply because some negotiating groups progress more rapidly than do others. It is useful, from the trainer's point of view, to keep the groups fairly close together in terms of the number of issues resolved so that meaningful comparisons can be made among groups after the negotiations have been terminated. Unless flexible scheduling can be used to allow the slower negotiators to catch up, it is virtually impossible to maintain homogeneity of substantive outcomes.

Another problem which occurs frequently is the strong tendency of many trainees to become so caught up in the simulation that they transfer their personal background, e.g., costs, enrollments, and other data from their school district, to the simulated negotiations. Such negotiators tend to forget or ignore the background of the simulation; and this, of course, tends to confuse and disrupt the other negotiators in the group—including even the culprit's own negotiating partners.

A problem which merits mention is that of intransigence of one or more negotiators in a group. Intransigence when used cunningly is a quite suitable negotiation tactic. A problem occurs only when a negotiator refuses to budge from his position for reasons of pure obstinacy. In actual negotiations, such behavior typically leads to a breakdown in the negotiations, a show of force by the other side, a work stoppage or strike, and the need for outside intervention to break the impasse. In simulated negotiations the usual techniques for overcoming intransigence cannot be applied simply because time does not permit their use, nor are the pressures which can be applied in the simulation situation very powerful. If the negotiations of a group are stymied by intransigent behavior, the trainer must either allow the group to adjourn or he must take action to change the behavior. Usually, a short talk with the individual responsible for the breakdown in negotiations (during a group caucus, if possible) is sufficient to get the process of negotiations moving once again.

Finally, there is the problem of realism in the simulation. If the materials are used skillfully they provide a realistic facsimile of actual negotiation situations. However, the penalties imposed by the real world for mistakes and imprudent behavior in negotiating cannot be simulated. The board-administration group which yields $2,000,000 in concessions to its teachers in simulation does not have to begin seeking $2,000,000 in new revenue the next morning, or any morning. The teachers' negotiating team in simulation which fails to get a salary increase for the teachers does not have to face the wrath of the membership. Fortunately, the limited realism of penalties does not destroy the usefulness of the simulation. This is fortunate simply because there appears to be no method for overcoming this particular problem. Money penalties, reduced grades, and extra assignments for so-called losing negotiating teams have been suggested. But such procedures do not seem to be feasible or realistic substitutes for real world penalties.

ASSESSMENT OF THE UTILITY OF THE SIMULATION

The main purposes for which the Negotiation Game materials were created are training and instruction. However, the simulation device can also be utilized as an effective research tool. An assessment of both training and research applications of the simulation will be presented in this section as will the findings of two external reports on the utility of the simulation materials.

Training and Instructional Applications

As has been mentioned earlier, the simulation materials have been used with apparent success for training purposes with a number of diverse groups including (a) both master's and doctoral level students of educational administration, (b) educational practitioners including elementary and secondary school principals and superintendents at various levels, (c) members of boards of education, and (d) professors of school administration. It is likely that the materials have been used to provide training experience in negotiations for teachers as well. Training experiences incorporating the simulation materials have been conducted within time periods as short as one day and as long as fifteen days (at eight hours per day).

Despite this fairly extensive utilization of the materials there has been, to the writer's knowledge, no *comprehensive* and *objective* evaluation of the utility of the simulation materials as a training device. Two assessments which have been made will be discussed at a later point in this section; but neither of these, while objective to a degree, has been at all comprehensive. Thus, most of the information which is available for judging the merits and utility of the simulation materials is purely subjective and is based on the experience of this author and/or on testimony of others who have used the materials.

Subjective evidence is available which bears upon the acceptance of the simulation as a device for general training in the area of collective negotiation. Such evidence indicates that both trainees and trainers have been satisfied that the simulation provided very useful information, insight, and experiences. In no case, to the author's knowledge, has the experience been thought to be worthless or to be a waste of time. It should be noted, however, that one does not normally get negative feedback in a situation in which pride of authorship may be involved. In other words, this author would be unlikely to receive a great deal of negative response to the Game even if such input exists.

As might be expected, the greater the actual experience held by trainees in the area of collective negotiations, the smaller their perceived *personal* utility of the simulation exercise. Simply stated, those who know more about negotiation to begin with find the simulation less beneficial than do less knowledgeable individuals. However, even such "experienced" trainees have typically provided positive responses to the simulation activity.

One other subjective judgment relative to the simulation materials should be noted. They are the only available trainee participation materials which attempt to work at the level of the processes of face-to-face negotiation. A few other materials relevant to these processes exist, e.g., books, films, and filmstrips, but they do not require the active participation of trainees in the learning process.

The available subjective evidence of utility of the simulation does not serve to indicate that the simulation activity actually makes trainees effective, or even more effective, negotiators in actual practice. No evidence on this particular point has been either solicited or received. There has been no opportunity in the author's experience to follow a trainee from the simulation experience into a real world negotiation situation in order to discover if he believed the simulation experience to be useful. Such follow-up studies would no doubt be useful and informative, but they simply have not as yet been conducted.

The task of gaining objective evidence of the actual utility of the simulation is in fact fraught with difficulty. If the criterion for evaluation is to be whether or not the trainees know more about negotiations and negotiation processes after the simulation than they did before it, then the materials can be evaluated. While such evaluation has not been conducted, there is little doubt that the findings would be positive. However, if the criterion for evaluation is to be the much tougher question of whether or not the trainees actually perform better as negotiators than they did before they had the simulation experience, then the evaluation may well be impossible to accomplish. The evaluator in this latter situation would very likely be unable to gain access to the actual data

required for the evaluation. The definition of "better performance" would be most elusive, if possible at all. And the variables
which impinge upon real world negotiations are so numerous,
complex, and difficult to control that any suggestion of a
cause-effect relationship between simulation training and actual
performance would be dubious. Thus, the would-be evaluator is
left with only the input that subjective testimony can provide.

Research Applications

While only two instances (10, 8) of utilization of the Negotiation Game materials in research applications are known, it may be
that the simulation will ultimately have higher utility as a research
device than as a training tool.

One approach to the study of the complex processes of the
face-to-face interaction between the negotiating parties—which is,
of course, an essential element of the total collective negotiations
problem—would be to attempt a detailed analysis of the actual
behavior of practicing negotiators. However, the very difficult
problems of manipulating variables, of obtaining uncontaminated
observations, and of analyzing complex data are imposing obsta-
cles to this research strategy. The use of simulation techniques,
such as the Negotiation Game, appears to be a worthwhile
alternative strategy for accomplishing the needed research.

There is ample justification in the literature for the use of
simulation and other quasi-experimental techniques for the investigation of real world phenomena. For example:

> In many instances, especially in the study of social and psychologi-
> cal phenomena, it is undesirable or even impossible to conduct
> experiments upon real systems. By successfully simulating the signifi-
> cant variables, it is possible to explore such phenomena by experi-
> menting with the simulated system (3).

One of the significant advantages of simulation experimentation is
that it permits the investigator to study processes in a way that
actual-practice situations prohibit. It should be recognized that:

> The natural world has certain disadvantages from the point of view

of observation and theory construction. Certain states of great theoretical interest occur quite rarely, while other states, of little theoretical interest, occur profusely. Certain effects of great theoretical interest are obscured by other effects which are, though powerful, of little interest. And there are always more relevant variables than any observer or any theory could conceivably take into account at one time. Through simulation, such processes may be simplified, measured, and manipulated, so that rare states may be created, reasonably exact replicates ensured, necessary contrasts obtained, compounding factors randomized, extraneous disturbances eliminated, and the processes observed comprehensively, precisely, and more or less at the will of the investigator (11).

It seems obvious that the Negotiation Game and other simulation devices provide an opportunity for the researcher to study problems and systems which would otherwise be impractical or nearly impossible to study. Precedent for the use of quasi- or pseudo-experimental methodologies has been established in education's typically favored research model, the physical sciences.

Generally, it may be said that in many cases judicious pseudo-experimentation may effectively annul the oft-regretted infeasibility of carrying out experiments proper in the social sciences by providing an acceptable substitute which, moreover, has been tried and proved in the applied physical sciences (5).

The potential of simulation devices in formal and quasi-research contexts is rather well established. The Negotiations Game, in the two research studies cited earlier, was used (a) to demonstrate that game theory may be of value when applied to teacher-board collective negotiations and (b) to investigate the effect of negotiator-attitude orientations on the substantive and behavioral outcomes of negotiation. In both cases the simulation was found to be a viable means for the indirect investigation of real-world phenomena.

There is no need to limit the utilization of the Negotiation Game materials to formal or quasi-experimental research activities. Useful "research-like" activities can be conducted with the simulation at the same time that training is being provided. Such "action research" often produces findings which are of high instructional value to trainees. For example, the trainer can, through careful manipulation of the attitude orientations of negotiating groups, contrast the outputs of hardnosed negotiating groups with those of more moderately oriented negotiators. The effect of one very obstinate and/or belligerent negotiator in a group can be illustrated as can the effects of certain kinds of prompting inputs to the negotiators. The effects of time or other pressures on negotiators can be investigated. In sum, the research possibilities provided by the simulation materials are limited only by the ingenuity and resources available to the trainer-investigator.

External Assessment of the Negotiation Game

Only two formal assessments of the utility of the Negotiations Game materials have been made by individuals other than the author. They include a study by Ross (10) at the University of Iowa and one by Cronin and his students (4) at Harvard University. The Ross study was concerned with determining "if the format of [formal] game theory is applicable to the analysis of collective negotiations in education as exhibited in simulation situations [specifically in the Negotiation Game simulation]" (10). The conclusions of this study are largely relevant to the application-of-game-theory question, but two of the findings speak to the question of the Game's utility. They are the following:

1. Eighty-seven percent of the participants (84 school administrators, school board members, and teachers) indicated that the exercise in collective negotiations was moderately to highly simulated [i.e., replicated the real world] (10).

2. The Negotiation Game simulation has relevance to collective negotiations (10).[15]

The Harvard investigation (4) was actually an early field trial of the prototype Negotiation Game materials with students of educational administration in a college-level course situation. The materials were tried in this case without any advice or assistance on the part of the developer of the Game. This investigation or field trial was not conducted for analytic purposes, but rather to identify "bugs" and discrepancies in the simulation materials. While useful information was provided to the developer from this field trial, assessments of the utility of the materials were only incidental. The most relevant assessments of utility were provided by the students involved in the simulation exercise when they were asked to list their "likes" and "dislikes" with respect to the simulated negotiation experience. The responses of the seventeen students involved in the field trial are given, as reported, below.

Liked	Number	Disliked	Number
Participation in bargaining	10	Time limitations	6
Learning about collective	7	Working with partners	2
bargaining		Non-realism	1
Better than cases	4	Confusion in materials	1
Readings	4	Readings	1
Small group insight	3	Tension atmoshpere	1
Strategy sessions	3	Pre-formed positions	1
Realism	1	Lack of Data	1
Materials	1	"No gripes"	1
Working with partners	1		
Serendipity	1		

Other investigations could and should be mounted to illustrate the merit of the simulation as a training device. As is the case with most instructional materials, however, objective evaluations of the materials have been limited. The positive to highly positive testimony of individuals who have used the Negotiation Game is the major evidence upon which one can justify adoption of the simulation in training and instructional settings.

ADDITIONAL TRAINING MATERIALS NEEDED IN THE AREA OF COLLECTIVE NEGOTIATION

Over the past four years the author has had considerable opportunity to work with administrative practitioners and students of educational administration in the area of collective negotiation. Also, he has had opportunities to discuss with professors of educational administration the kinds of training devices and materials that would be useful for instruction in negotiation. As a result of these experiences and inputs, a plan has been formulated which proposes the development of a *total system of instruction* in the area of collective negotiation. This "total system" should include, in addition to an expanded and updated version of the extant Negotiation Game materials, the following instructional devices.

Unit #1—four films which illustrate actual negotiation sessions in progress. With these films trainees can be introduced to the realities of negotiations and will gain insights into the major variations in negotiating behavior. Through observation-discussion of the behaviors, tactical maneuvers, strategies, ethical considerations, and negotiated outcomes illustrated by the films, trainees will begin to develop understandings relative to negotiation processes. At least three distinct instructional uses of this unit are possible. The unit can do the following:

a. Serve as entirely self-contained instructional materials without reference to the total instructional system. Thus, trainers who do not wish to consider the area of negotiations in depth may use the unit as the basic content of their presentation on negotiations.

b. Present a foundation and background for subsequent use of the total training system or for parts of it.

c. Present a review and summary of the activities and learning which results from the use of the total system.

Four devices are suggested for this unit because there are four major classifications or types of behaviors which typically occur in actual negotiation situations. These four are:

a. Hardnosed, belligerent, unyielding, and antagonistic negotiation behaviors exhibited by both sides. The behavior of the negotiators is personally or emotionally oriented rather than task oriented. The device would depict behaviors leading to a walkout, impasse, or other incident which would provide a "natural" close to the presentation.

b. A cooperative behavioral approach by one negotiating team and a belligerent behavioral approach by the other. Changes in the behaviors of each side would be illustrated—usually this involves an increase of belligerency by the cooperative side and a maintenance of belligerency or its increase by the other.

c. Firm negotiating behavior by both sides—concessions are given but not without a struggle. Antagonistic and/or personally oriented behaviors are minimal while problem solving and task oriented behaviors are exhibited.

d. A session in which one of the sides has too many active negotiators (spokesmen), as a result of which the other side can and does use divide-and-conquer tactics with telling effectiveness.

Other situations could, of course, be developed and they would be useful. However, the four listed above appear to be the most representative and typical of real world negotiation situations.

Each of the films should be approximately 30 minutes in length in order that the situation can be developed and a number of points illustrated.

Unit #2—a device which deals with the elements, requirements, and rules of good-faith negotiating, and the generally accepted rules of negotiations. Written materials are available in both of these areas and the final form of this device could be that of a brochure or pamphlet. However, film or audiotape would enhance the impact of these rules for the trainee and would provide for more effective instruction. A series of one- to three-minute vignettes, exemplary of the rules, could appear on a single film or audiotape, or they could take the form of a number of single concept loops. Approximately thirty such vignettes would be required to cover the areas suggested. Examples of the kinds of incidents which would appear in these vignettes include:

a. negotiators exhibiting a "take-it-or-leave-it" attitude
b. insincere or frivolous demands by negotiators
c. failure of negotiators to consider seriously the proposals of the other side
d. one negotiator forcing another into a position from which he cannot retreat without "losing face."

Unit #3—a device made up of two filmstrip-tape recordings, one of which will trace the history of organizational activity and bargaining in the private and public sectors. Major legislation will be described as will landmark decisions of the courts and the state and national labor relations boards. The second filmstrip-tape recording will present ideas and suggestions for the procedures which should be undertaken in preparing for formal negotiations, i.e., pre-negotiations strategies and guidelines.

Unit #4—this device will include grievance-handling training modules or kits. The process of grievance handling is one of the most difficult and least understood areas in the administration of a collectively negotiated agreement. It is important to note that these grievance-handling materials will provide useful training experiences for both teachers and an administrative group which may never be involved in face-to-face negotiations (i.e., principals).

The form which these materials will take is similar to that of a simple written case study or critical incident situation. The materials will be presented in a written format and will provide trainees with background materials describing the terms of a negotiated agreement in a simulated situation as well as the terms of the grievance procedure. To these materials a short written statement of the background, development, and context of particular grievances would be added (including background information regarding the aggrieved employee), as would a formal statement of the grievance. A series of forty to fifty such grievance incidents will be produced. Using these materials, role playing in grievance handling would provide the essence of the training situation, e.g., the "aggrieved party" and perhaps his "representative" would attempt to iron out the grievance with a "responsible authority." Such modules will be designed to present grievance situations at the various steps of the grievance procedure, e.g., first appeal, principal; second appeal, assistant superintendent; on up to final and binding grievance arbitration. In addition to the written materials described above, a few (seven or eight) of the modules will be role-played on film or tape and will be presented with the unit as instructional exemplars or "classics" in grievance-handling technique.

Unit #5—will include series of intergroup or interpersonal interaction incident devices. A series of illustrative film loops or audiotapes will be developed which provide examples of critical incidents or "classic" forms of behavior frequently occurring in negotiation sessions. These devices have as their purpose the demonstration of (and the creation of insight into and understanding of) the commonly recurring kinds of behaviors which occur in small, high stress, decision-making groups.

Incidents selected will illustrate the most common and critical kinds of behaviors which occur in negotiations settings and be such that they relate to, and can be illuminated by, the existing knowledge, literature, and research in relevant behavioral science fields. An example of the kind of incident which might be illustrated is the *fight-flight syndrome;* that is, the tendency of a decision-making group to argue a point, to become angry, and then to back away from the problem and enter into irrelevant action for a period of time.

In addition to the filmed or taped incidents, the package would include written guidelines for their use. These guidelines would in fact serve as a general "teacher's guide" to the materials and could be used by the trainers or their trainees. The guidelines will describe in detail the meaning and implications of the incident depicted on each film or tape and will provide references to the existing literature so that further study can be undertaken by trainees. Having this combination of materials, trainers, both with and without strong backgrounds in the behavioral sciences, will be able to offer trainees an opportunity to delve into those factors of human behavior that are perhaps the most critical aspects of the entire negotiations process.

Unit #6—will provide training in the proper use of contract language and the correct procedures for the development of written contracts. In the existing Negotiation Game, for example, the final agreements are produced in rough prose form. Such rough agreements and the implicit understandings of negotiators must, in actual practice, be put into written, acceptable, and legal contract language. Trainees need to gain experience in writing and interpreting collectively negotiated contracts. Through the use of a programmed text device, trainees will be given detailed suggestions about and examples of good and bad contract form and phraseology. A number of examples of the difficulties which can result from the use of "weasle-worded" clauses, ambiguous language, and loose terminology will be included in this device.

Unit #7—will provide materials in the area of arbitration of impasse. These materials will be presented in a format similar to that of the grievance-handling modules. That is, they will present the facts regarding an impasse situation which has grown out of an advanced grievance and/or deadlock during the negotiation of a contract. Devices will be included in the unit which guide trainees in the preparation of arbitration hearing, and which provide them with experience in handing down decisions; and impasse situations. Perhaps five to ten different arbitration incidents will be presented and, as in the grievance-handling unit, one or two films or tapes will be developed to illustrate "ideal" procedures.

The system of materials suggested above, while it may not actually comprise a "total system of instruction in collective negotiations," would do much to aid professors and other trainers in preparing administrators to participate effectively in, and actively shape the nature of, the avalanche in collective negotiations which appears to be a certainty in public education in the United States.

It should be noted that the units described above, with the exception of Unit #4, have not been developed.[17] They are, at present, simply plans for the development of instructional materials in the area of collective negotiation in education. If the spread of negotiation activity continues at its present rate, the need for such materials will increase and there may well be cause to accelerate the pace of their development.

NOTES

[1] The term "collective negotiation" is used in this chapter to refer to the process in education which has been called "professional negotiations," "collective bargaining," "bargaining," and "negotiations."

[2] The terms "Negotiation Game" and "the Game" will be used throughout this chapter. When these terms are used, they refer to the materials developed by the author while he was a member of the University Council for Educational Administration's "Articulated Media Project." The full citation for these materials is: John J. Horvat, *Professional Negotiations in Education: A Bargaining Game with Supplementary Materials, Instructor's Manual.* Columbus, Ohio: Charles E. Merrill Publishing Company, 1968.

[3] It should be recognized that the only known method for training *skilled* negotiators involves heavy doses of experience which is, in fact, on-the-job training. However, the more training that can be provided in a risk-free situation prior to and during on-the-job training, the less costly and painful the training is likely to be. This need for risk-free training is what prompts the military, for example, to engage in war games, mock battles, and training maneuvers. Through this kind of training, troops can learn many of the key essentials of combat without great loss of life or property.

[4] The *Instructor's Manual* (6) includes all of the materials of the three "Student Use" forms of the Game. Therefore, it is this manual which will be described. The portions of the materials which trainees are given are marked with an asterisk (*).

[5] For the purposes of this descriptive section, the simulation will be considered to begin at the moment when trainees begin to read the background materials and to work together in planning negotiating strategies. In actual fact, the simulation proper does not begin until the two teams face each other and begin to negotiate on the issues.

[6] While the Negotiation Game was developed for use in the training of

educational administrators, there is no reason why it cannot be used for training teachers' organization negotiators. The materials focus on the processes of negotiation and they are essentially value-free in terms of the differences which may separate teacher and board-administrator negotiators.

[7] There exists a large amount of published material in the area of collective negotiations. Two useful bibliographies are available which list and/or describe much of the extant literature. They are: Neville L. Robertson, *Teacher-School Board Negotiations: A Bibliography*. Bloomington, Indiana: Phi Delta Kappa, Inc. (Revised Edition), 1968—contains 715 entries; and John J. Horvat, *Professional Negotiation in Eduation: Annotated Bibliography*. Columbus, Ohio: Charles E. Merrill Publishing Company, 1968—contains 314 annotated entries.

[8] A "team" in the simulation is made up of two, three, or four trainees who represent one of the sides—teachers or board-administration—in the negotiations. Two opposing teams form a negotiation "group."

[9] A negotiating team of less than two members is not functional, while one with more than four members has been found to be too large and unwieldy to be useful in the simulation context.

[10] "Highly pro-labor" and "highly pro-management" are, of course, relative terms. A trainer may find that his group members are all "pro-management" in terms of attitude orientation. Typically, there is a wide spectrum of attitudes within a group even if its members are all school administrators. In attempting to set up more or less "naturally" polarized groups, the trainer simply seeks to pit individuals at the extremes in attitude orientation against each other, whatever these extremes may be.

[11] In longer time periods, e.g., a two-week workshop, caucuses may be fairly lengthy and negotiators may adjourn to work in gathering additional information, planning strategy, etc.

[12] Negotiating teams of three to four members and the use of a single spokesman seem to be "the recommended" structure for negotiating teams in actual practice. For the purposes of training through simulation, the single-spokesman concept is not useful, except where time is available, as a means of demonstrating the advantages of the use of a single spokesman over the free negotiations approach.

[13] When the Negotiation Game materials were first field-tested there was some concern with regard to the ability of trainees to begin negotiating. It was feared that they might just sit and look at each other. This fear proved to be groundless. In all uses of the materials in the author's experience, no difficulty whatsoever has been encountered in "turning the negotiations on." To the contrary, it has been difficult at times to get the negotiators to stop negotiating.

[14] In short sessions (e.g., a one-and-one-half day workshop) it is often impossible to provide time for the analysis of the tapes of the negotiation sessions. In such cases the tape recorder can be omitted and observers can be

Simulation of Collective Negotiations

used instead to provide feedback to the trainees.
[15] "Collective Negotiations" was defined as a process whereby employees as a group and their employers made offers and counter-offers in good faith on the conditions of their employment relationship for the purpose of reaching a mutually acceptable agreement.
[16] The author has developed a limited prototype version of Unit #4–the grievance handling unit.

BIBLIOGRAPHY

1. Bales, Robert F. *Interaction Process Analysis.* Cambridge, Mass.: Addison—Wesley Publishing Co., Inc., 1950.

2. Campbell, Clyde M. "Collective Negotiation." *The Community School and Its Administration,* vol. 1, no. 12 (August 1967).

3. Dawson, R. E. "Simulation in the Social Sciences." Chapter 1 in Harold S. Guetzkow (ed.), *Simulation in the Social Sciences; Readings.* Englewood Cliffs, New Jersey: Prentice-Hall, Inc., 1962.

4. Dunnan, G. P. et al. "Report in Collective Bargaining Game." Unpublished paper. Administrative Career Program, Harvard University, May 1966.

5. Helmer, Olaf & Rescher, Nicholas R. "On the Epistemology of the Inexact Sciences." *Management Science,* vol. 6, no. 1 (October, 1959).

6. Horvat, John J. *Professional Negotiation in Education: A Bargaining Game with Supplementary Materials.* Columbus, Ohio: Charles E. Merrill Publishing Company, 1968.

7. Horvat, John J. *Professional Negotiation in Education: Annotated Bibliography.* Columbus, Ohio: Charles E. Merrill Publishing Company, 1968.

8. Horvat, John J. "A Quasi-experimental Study of Behavior in the Professional Negotiations Process." Unpublished Ph. D. dissertation, The Ohio State University, 1968.

9. Robertson, Neville L. *Teacher-School Board Negotiations: A Bibliography.* Bloomington, Indiana: Phi Delta Kappa, Inc., 1968.

10. Ross, George H. "Game Theory Analysis of Simulated Collective Negotiations." Unpublished paper read at the American Education Research Association Annual Meeting, Chicago, February 8, 1968.

11. Zelditch, M., Jr. & Evan, W. M. "Simulated Bureaucracies: A Methodological Analysis." Chapter 4 in Harold S. Guetzkow (ed.), *Simulation in the Social Sciences: Readings.* Englewood Cliffs, New Jersey: Prentice-Hall, Inc., 1962.

8

The Uses of
Computers in Simulation

Wailand Bessent

Mentioning computer simulation conjures up such esoterica as *matrix manipulation, Monte Carlo Models, Markov chains, stochastic methods,* and *random number generators.* And quicker than you can say, "Boolean Algebra," people who can handle the ideas but not the language panic. Please remain calm. This chapter is intended to introduce the uninitiated to computer-based simulation without invoking either the mysteries of mathematics or unnecessary incantations of the computer.

Such an attempt will, of course, leave much of the story untold, but enough will remain to keep the punch line intact. Best of all, this modest effort will not exhaust the limits of a single chapter, the reader's patience, or the author's knowledge.[1]

In general, the intention of this chapter is to provide the professor, the practitioner, or the student of educational administration with an introduction to computer-based simulations and how they may be useful in training programs or helpful in the management of schools. This narrows the scope of relevant content considerably, since computer-based simulation is an infant art in educational administration.

Specifically, the chapter will be concerned with simulations that may be used (a) for computer-assisted instruction, (b) for research into the operations of systems, and (c) as an operational aid for school district administration—especially in forecasting and planning. Since the constraints of a single chapter do not permit a full treatment of these uses, examples will be given which will illustrate each use of computers for simulation.

WHEN IS A COMPUTER CALLED FOR?

All readers except those who opened the book at this chapter first know that not all simulations require a computer. Cases, in-basket instruments, games, simulated selection, and professional negotiations simulations have been described in other chapters. None of these require any computer-based processing.

When, then, is it appropriate to turn to electronic data processing? Not counting the times when having a computer—like having an electric toothbrush—is nice but not necessary, the simplest answer to that question is to consider computers for processing the simulation under the following conditions: (a) when speed and accuracy are necessary either because of large-volume calculations or because the person engaged in the simulation requires rapid feedback on the results of his performance; (b) when calculations become so complex that doing them by hand takes all the fun out of the game; (c) when a display of the simulation output exceeds the limitations of ordinary printed material; (d) when individualized instruction is an important objective; and (e) when modifications in the simulation need to be quickly accomplished. Let us consider these conditions one at a time with examples illustrating the advantages of being able to turn over to the computer the data handling demanded by simulation. The examples will be treated more fully in a later section of this chapter as we consider some problem types especially pregnant with potential for computer simulation.

How to Save Pencils

There are many occasions when the magnitude of data handling required by a simulation is so great that the high-speed computer is the only thing that makes the simulation feasible. This may be quite apart from the complexity of the calculations, as anyone knows who has attempted some tedious but simple task such as hand-tallying election returns. In situations like this, the extra effort required to build a computer routine for data handling saves many man-hours.

To illustrate the size of the data-handling chores in some instances, let us consider a computer-processed model developed at the Personnel Research Laboratory, Lackland Air Force Base, for simulating the recruitment, promotion, and movement between career fields of Air Force personnel under varying personnel policies (15). A similar procedure could be applied to forecast personnel needs in a large school district.

If, for example, teachers were categorized in terms of nine fields of specialization, three grade (probationary, tenure, and merit) groups, and fourteen intervals of length of service, the resulting 9 x 3 x 14 classification scheme creates 378 possible states. Not all of them are useful since few, if any, merit teachers would become probationary, but if as many as 250 categories were selected as being of some interest, a simulation would require a matrix which would permit the tracking of movement from any of the 250 categories to any other. The resulting matrix calls for a set of calculations among $(250)^2$ or 62,500 elements. Though many of these cells would contain zero values, the calculations require raising the matrix to another power for each year (or appropriate time interval) of the simulation. Pencils, anyone?

For Those Who Can't Wait

Some simulations go better if the trainee is able to get immediate feedback on the results of his responses without hand-carrying the transactions to the computation center. For example, in a simulation of feedback on in-basket items developed at The University of Texas at Austin (1), the trainee sits at a typewriter terminal and types in his actions. His response is evaluated by the computer and the results are typed back to him at his terminal. In this way, he can simulate several actions on the same in-basket item—asking for information, getting the reply, asking for more information, getting a reply, making a decision, getting clobbered by the result, and so on until he either reaches a satisfactory conclusion or goes away for a while, hoping the machine will work on the problem in his absence. It won't.

When the Brain Won't Do

In some simulations, calculations become so complex that even the most determined tally-keeper would burn out the beads on his abacus soon after getting started. But the simulation builder can, with a computer handy, simply specify the *way in which the calculating will be done,* allow the player to feed in his data, and watch all the little lights flash on the console while waiting for the results.

As Strachey (18, p. 72) has pointed out, "There is a limit to the size and complexity of a problem we can hold in our head at one time; it appears that best way to extend our capability is to treat relatively large and complex operations as single units and combine these units hierarchically."

The simulation builder thus may build his program in sub-routines until he has a system of sub-programs which will "divide and conquer" the complex problem. While the structure of sub-programs may be comprehensible, the details of the program may defy immediate comprehension. A good example of this is the simulation of complex systems such as some of the waiting line (queueing model) simulations. In queueing models, the problem is treated as a traffic flow through a succession of service points. As queues are built up, waiting to be processed, traffic flow may be routed to alternate points where the queues are shorter. They may be concerned with such things as the message flow in a school district communications network, customer service installations such as student movement through cafeteria serving lines or availability of student stations in a language laboratory, vehicular flows, or the work flow through a job shop.

In queueing models, it is of interest to know such things as waiting time before entering, the length of lines, length of service time at processing points, the number of turn-aways, total time through the system, and so on at any given time during the simulation.

Computations in the simulated system require generating arrival times, routing each entity through a complex branching of processing points, simulating processing time at each point, and keeping an accurate track of where everything is in the system at each interval—a task that would defy anyone except perhaps a mother with four or more pre-school children. Others will learn to cherish a computer in such moments.

Getting the Results

If the reader has persisted to this point, he will now learn that, besides being fast, accurate, and undismayed by myriad detail or complexity, the computer can also do some clever things by way of displaying the results of a simulation. Of course, the professor with a piece of chalk in his hand may have a certain charm and a great deal of flexibility in presenting his data. But he may run out of chalkboard and patience before he can present all the financial data on a school district simulated for ten years under six proposed operating policies. The computer never wearies of this kind of chore. It offers a number of display modes with varied possibilitites. Let us consider some of the most common display devices.

Most readers are familiar with the standard printed ouput from high-speed line printers that are a part of all computer systems. This printed ouput can display verbal and numerical data in ordinary text and in tabular form and can produce more than one wants in a very short time. With some ingenuity, plots on a coordinate system can also be generated with the typed line. Even primitive graphics can be constructed, although the results wouldn't satisfy Picasso: witness the Christmas messages on printouts pinned on the bulletin board of almost any computation center—the Christmas trees are usually more recognizable than the reindeer.

The printer in non-interactive systems is adequate for output on simulations such as the Personnel Movement simulation described earlier, when the user can afford to wait a day or so for the result and when the result is a long list of numbers printed in tables that he may wish to ponder awhile anyway as he wonders why he ever decided to print out so much detail. Otherwise the simulation will require an interactive system with immediate display of results.

There are also plotting devices which produce more elaborate tracing of plot lines. Most computations centers have at least one operator who has produced a plot of a reclining nude. This, of course, it not the first time a plot has produced a nude.

A similar result for graphic displays can be obtained with a cathode ray tube (CRT) display which can be easily photographed and converted to a microfilm. This is important if the results of the simulation must be preserved—the CRT image, of course, is ephemeral.

A resourceful use of plotting in education is the work of Donald N. McIsaac at the University of Wisconsin. Building on the work of Donald McIntyre, McIsaac has adapted a technique known as *trend surface analysis* to mapping educational variables within a region.

The procedure is analogous to the contour lines that appear on topographic maps showing lines of equal elevation. In the procedure used by McIsaac, the contour lines delineate boundaries within which a variable such as reading achievement has the same expected value. Looking at a school district boundary mapped in this way, the administrator can easily discern the peaks and valleys of high and low achievement.

A mathematical model is employed to generate a theoretical "fit" of a surface over the points used to sample the region (elementary school location, for example). This "trend surface" is based on the equation that results in the smallest errors of predicted values when compared to actual value observed. Contour lines are then drawn on the surface generated and results are plotted on the Calcomp Plotter. The program has many parameters that can be varied by the user and political boundaries can be drawn on the same area plotted.

A statewide assessment of needs in Wisconsin was analyzed by means of trend surface analysis and reported by McIsaac (14).

More interesting results can be obtained with an on-line simulation by means of terminals such as those used for computer-assisted instruction (CAI). CAI terminals now have the following display options: a typewriter which will produce plots, graphics, and special characters; a CRT (equipped with a light pen for a pointing response) which will display graphics and alphanumeric characters; and a random access image projector with a capacity of several hundred frames. In addition, there will soon be audiotape systems in wide use which will permit rapid access to pre-recorded messages; CRTs with vector generated graphics will be widely available, as will colored television screen displays.

These devices will be invaluable for simulations such as in-basket or situational training approaches in which a high degree of realism is desired. With the equipment mentioned above, the simulation could include pictures, facsimile documents, primitive animations, and audio-communications. For example, the personnel selection simulation described by Bolton in Chapter 4 could display such things as application forms, verbal responses to interview questions and a photograph of the applicant.

Some limitations will still exist, however. The on-line computer is not good for producing extensive printed output on a character-by-character printer such as the typewriter. This is offset somewhat by the efficiencies to be gained by having hard copy available. The image projector screen will not provide a very large display, and the size of the cathode ray screen is more limited still in the amount of display provided by a single frame. For these reasons, most simulations in CAI will probably continue to rely heavily on accompanying printed material such as workbooks, manuals, and background material ancillary to the simulations. The author of each simulation must decide what instructional advantage is to be gained by printed materials versus CRT display of instructions and other documentation needed by the user.

Individualized Instruction

A fourth advantage of computer-based simulations is their potential for individualized instruction. When the simulation is intended for instructional use as contrasted with management uses, there are times when a computer-based simulation can be justified even when the problem can be dealt with otherwise. The chief advantage to be gained in instruction is the computer's power for individualization.

For example, in-basket feedback simulation could be handled by a professor handing over requested information and calculating the patterns of response for each student. The data-handling requirements are well within manhandling limits. The advantages to be gained through a CAI approach, however, justify its use.

First, the instruction is self-paced. The student signs on at the terminal according to his own schedule. He works as long as he likes, repeating segments as many times as desired. When he gets tired or uncertain about proceeding, he may sign off and come back later. Upon resuming the program, he begins where he left off, since all his work is stored at his own work space on the disk pack ready for immediate access when he types in his identification.

Second, individualized instruction through computer-assistance can accomplish teaching to a criterion performance. Instead of handing out the assignment for everyone to do as best he can, the simulation builder can specify minimum acceptable performance and continue the instruction until this is reached. In a problem-solving program developed at the University of Texas Computer Assisted Instruction Laboratory, the student may not progress to a higher level in the learning hierarchy until he has successfully solved ninety percent of the test items at a lower level.

Third, individualization is enhanced by being able to track the student through his performance. The computer makes it possible to record his sequence of actions for analysis by the instructor. The resulting record may be used to revise the program to provide additional individualization for future students. This may be done by providing more branches, additional text, or sub-routines for drill.

Fourth, though little conclusive evidence exists, the computer can provide motivation to a higher degree than many other simulations. Part of this, no doubt, is the novelty of conversing with a computer but the challenge of trying to best the machine is one that spurs many human begins on to greater effort. Student responses at the University of Texas indicate that more able students are more likely to respond favorably than those who must struggle to cope with the program. Some indirect evidence of motivation is seen on the students' printouts where they have typed in long comments justifying their actions (all unrecognizable by the program being used). It may be necessary to store some common terms of invective so that the computer can recognize when it being cussed and respond appropriately.

A Programmer's Work is Never Done

The final attempt to answer the question, "When are computers called for?" is that a computer-based simulation is handy when modifications need to be made in the materials that document the simulation. Few simulations reach perfection and most require large amounts of modification. The simulation builder will be tinkering constantly with his model, and revision becomes tedious if printed documents have to be revised. Student manuals and other documents, especially if bound, present major problems if pages need to be altered. Not only is text insertion messy business in printed matter, but copies may be difficult to retrieve, with the result that several versions of printed materials will be extant at once; at least four versions of the Shady Acres in-basket items are being used at present.

This is not the case, however, if the simulation consists of a computer program. Changes in a computer program are readily made and are immediately available for all subsequent users. The student's work is under the control of a computer program which consists of a set of commands or statements that are executed in a prescribed sequence. Both commands and sequence of execution are easily modified. Program revisions may be made by inserting or deleting cards from the program deck, or, in the case of on-line terminals, changes may be made by working in author mode at the typewriter terminal. He simply types insertion or deletion commands, makes the desired changes and the computer immediately updates the program. Printed material required by the program, of course, suffers the same limitations noted above.

FOUR SIMULATION MODELS

A person may classify simulation models in several ways, depending upon his orientation. For example, if he considers the *use* of data, he then differentiates data *generation* simulations from data *reduction* simulation. Or he may note the type of mathematical operations involved and distinguish deterministic from probabilistic models. Others note differences in time orientation and classify simulations as being static or dynamic. Those with an operations research orientation are fond of such terms as "optimizing models," "queueing models," and "gaming models." Finally, one may view the simulation in terms of its intended use: for teaching, research, or management. A comprehensive classification scheme is not attempted here since our interest is in presenting a few examples illustrative of what has been or is being developed with immediate relevance to educational administration.

In brief, simulations will be described that illustrate four approaches:

1. Instructional models based on a deterministic interactive (man-machine) simulation
2. Research and teaching models of administrative decision processes
3. General systems models for management and research use
4. Optimizing models for management use

A Computer-Assisted Instruction Simulation

A CAI approach to teaching administrative decision making has been developed at the University of Texas at Austin (1). The procedure used is a computer-based feedback extension of the in-basket method described by Anderson in Chapter 3.

In this simulation, the computer is used to provide feedback to each response made by the trainee and to evaluate his perform-ance. Let us look briefly at the rationale for the procedure.

Information Search. When a subject is presented an in-basket item for which he does not have adequate information upon which to base some course of action, he must begin seeking information. That is, he has several possible alternatives (some of which he may not perceive), and he must search for the kind of information that will enable him to identify one of the alternatives as being more promising than the others. He might proceed in several ways. He might seek information more or less randomly until he finds that he has enough to decide. Or, he might seek out all the information available and then make his determination. Finally, he might adopt an information-seeking strategy that would optimize his chances for selecting the most acceptable alternative with the minimum amount of information searching. The last-mentioned alternative is the most efficient approach and the one selected for the training model.

The resulting development is a man-machine simulation in which a trainee takes the role of an administrator in an information system and the computer simulates the information by providing feedback of information. To accomplish this, both a model of information search and a computer program for the model were devised.

An Information-Processing Model. Using information in a choice situation involves conducting a search for relevant data, formu-lating rules for evaluating the information, and establishing priority among alternatives. In the prototype problem, the student simulates the decision process he, as principal, would follow in dealing with a request from a teacher, Sadie Crosby, to "do something about" Herbert Ford, a boy in her class who "cannot do the work." She further suggests that he be put back in fifth grade.

This is typical of a choice situation in which alternatives are indentifiable and for which it is possible to obtain information that will reduce the uncertainty of choosing among them. The information is in the form of statements that can be obtained one item at a time upon request. For example, he can ask for test data, grades, have the teacher clarify the problem, confer with parents, observe the classroom, and so on. The problem of conducting an efficient search is to determine what to ask for and in what order it should be requested in order to obtain the earliest possible solution.

Since one item of information may be relevant to more than one of the alternatives and many different combinations of the information may exist, it will facilitate matters greatly if some means of organizing the information in a logical pattern around each alternative is found. Except in the simplest instances, the relationship of information to the alternatives may be obscure unless some intermediate logic is introduced. This may be done by constructing a set of premises for each alternative. The premises may be thought of as decision rules that establish *a priori* the antecedent conditions necessary for the acceptance of each alternative. In Herbert's problem, the student may say, for example, "I will comply with Mrs. Crosby's request if Herbert cannot do acceptable work for the sixth grade, if no way can be found for Mrs. Crosby to deal with his problem in his present assignment, if his parents agree, and if he does not have a severe problem that should be dealt with in special education." In similar fashion, all the alternatives may be expressed in terms of a set of decision rules.

The search for information, then, is guided by seeking the appropriate information items relevant to determining the state of the premises of the argument. In some instances, the premise will clearly identify the kind of information needed. For example, a recurring premise is that no policy exists concerning the action to be taken. The obvious information needed to confirm or reject this premise is a rule or policy.

In other instances, the premise may be a complex one that requires several kinds of information for confirmation. In this event, another set of decision rules must be constructed. For example, the premise concerning Herbert's ability to do acceptable sixth-grade work may be evaluated by requesting information concerning his achievement test scores, his grade reports, conferences with Herbert, evaluation by his previous teachers, and additional information from his present teacher.

The procedure assumes, of course, that there *is* a body of information which, if known, would make it possible to accept or reject an alternative. If not, no rational solution exists. A further complication exists in many situations in which an alternative is partly true or where its truth value is only a probability statement of its being true. These contingencies introduce complexities that were not dealt with in the development of the simulation described above. Part of the charm of a simulation is that the author can control the content of the information provided and hence can avoid situations with high ambiguity. Complexity can be increased as experience with the simulation is gained.

At present, a new procedure is being tested which will allow the trainee to input his own decision rules, including his estimates of the information value of each feedback he receives. In Herbert's problem, for example, the student assigns a numerical value to indicate the relevance of each premise to each alternative. If one can accept the premise concerning Herbert's ability to cope with sixth-grade work, for example, he will be strongly inclined (a value of 10) to accept the alternative of leaving him in the sixth grade. Furthermore, if one cannot accept the premise that Mrs. Crosby can be a satisfactory teacher for Herbert—based on the information he has received—then he is strongly disinclined to leave him in her classroom (a value of -10). This would suggest a third alternative—transferring Herbert to another sixth-grade classroom. Assigning numerical values makes it possible to quantify the decision rules and evaluate the final action; this is an important consideration for computer programming.

A Decision-Making Model for Research and Teaching

A prototype computer-based system was developed by Cullinan and Ruderman (7, pp. 86-143) as part of the Articulated Media Project for the University Council for Educational Administration. Their purpose was to investigate the information processing and utilization patterns of administrators through simulation of an administrative decision situation.

In the prototype, two problems were developed. One concerned the selection of a building site for a school and the other simulated the selection of a principal for a school.

Using a list processing language (MENTOR—a sub-set of LISP), files were constructed from which the subject could request information. In the site-selection problem, the subject assumes the role of superintendent and is given some background material on his school district. He works at a teletypewriter remote terminal where he receives typed information. He has an indexed set of printed documents to which he may be referred during the simulation. As he interacts with the computer, it simulates the answers of staff members to his questions concerning conditions in predetermined categories until he is ready to formulate his decision. The pattern of his information processing may be analyzed to determine such things as the amount of information sought and the pattern of search. The search patterns are not evaluated in terms of correctness or efficiency but are analyzed in terms of differences as correlates of subject attributes and situational effects.

The procedure above was extended in simulation dealing with selection of a principal. This may be thought of as a computer-based version of some of the ideas presented in Chapter 5, although the developments were independent. In this development, the interest was in observing the ways in which different subjects interpreted and weighted information supplied to them. It was designed to gain experience with audiotaped and filmed stimulus materials.

Writen in TELECOMP, a time-sharing language, the program provides the subject with information about four candidates for a principalship. From typical biographical forms, letters of recommendation, and the candidate's own statement (filmed and audiotaped), the subject is supplied information about experience, administrative skills, staff relations, and personality of the candidate. At each step, the subject evaluates each candidate on four criteria.

An interesting feature of this simulation is that subsequent information is modified by the subject's ratings made in earlier steps. For example, if early ratings are low, subsequent information supplied was strongly supportive of the candidate and conversely. The simulation provides a record of the numerical values assigned by the student to the information and to the weights given to various criteria.

Both of these early attempts are being extended and should be viewed as important beginnings in the use of computer simulation to provide a methodology for identifying and analyzing information processes used by administrators in decision making. A more comprehensive model of a school district is being developed by Cullinan and Ruderman in which the trainee will have few constraints in what problems should be dealt with, what information he will seek to clarify the situation, and what administrative actions, if any, are necessary. This comes much closer to simulating the administrator's real life condition where his problems do not come pre-packaged, and where, in his job as troubleshooter, he must decide what trouble needs shooting and what weapons to choose.

A second computer-based simulation for research in educational administration is policy capturing. The general idea of policy capturing is presented in Chapter 5. At this point, let us consider the computer requirements of the procedure.

Briefly stated, the policy-capturing procedure is based on a multiple-linear regression analysis which is used to select the best set of predictor variables to simulate a judge's (or board's) policy for assigning criterion values. Cristal (6), in a light-hearted vein, illustrates the procedure in a monograph entitled *Selecting a Harem and Other Applications of the Policy Capturing Model.* In this fable, the king wanted to delegate the selection of new girls for his harem to his advisors. The Chief of the Royal Psychometricians devised a nine-point scale on which the king's approval of the first three hundred of the new candidates was obtained. Then, characteristics of the girls were obtained on such variables as body measurements, eye and hair color, age, and how much each girl resembled the king's mother. These data were all assembled in a set of predictor variables and the multiple correlation coefficient (R^2) was obtained along with regression weights for each predictor variable. The size of the R^2 indicated how well they had captured the king's policy, and the regression coefficients provided a way of weighting new data on future applicants.

In a less interesting application, Cristal reports successful simulation of an Air Force board assigning grade rating for jobs. They succeeded in identifying a nine-variable system which simulated ratings having a correlation of .92 with the judgments of the board in 3,575 cases.

A similar application in selection of junior college teachers is reported by McBride (13). Using a model with twelve variables typically found in an application form for a junior college teaching position, McBride simulated the selection policies of twenty-eight junior college deans and presidents. On a five-point criterion scale, ranging from rejection to highly favorable, he was able to simulate the policies of the judges eighty percent of the time within one point of their actual judgments. For seven judges (those most consistent in their own policies) *all* the predicted values fell within two units of the actual values.

In a subsequent validation of the model, McBride was able to predict nine out of ten applicants actually hired by a Dean from a pool of twenty-two applicants. He concludes that the procedure is satisfactory for first screening of applicants.

It is easy to see many research applications for the policy-capturing model, since little is known about how judgments are made in administrative decisions. A doctoral study presently underway at the University of Texas, for example, is seeking to capture the policy of administrators in adopting educational innovations.

The calculations require a system large enough to handle a multiple-linear regression program with as many as one hundred variables. Batch processing is satisfactory since computation time is very short in comparison to time spent in getting ready for a simulation and in interpreting results afterwards.

Once it is established, however, the model may be used repeatedly to handle repetitive decisions. In this case, on-line operation would be nice but not necessary.

General Systems Model

A great deal of simulation has to do with the systems characterized by a flow of units of traffic which are serviced at various points and are routed in a way determined by the traffic congestion. For example, most right-thinking men take a service road if the freeway is jammed with a collision, or they seek the shortest line at the bank tellers' windows.

There are several possible applications in educational administration: simulating pupil progress in individualized instruction, language laboratory utilization, use of computer-assisted instruction terminals, or service time in libraries and cafeterias, to name but a few.

The queueing model is termed *probabilistic* rather than *deterministic* to indicate that the result of any two runs will not be identical, but will differ in the same way that drawing two samples from the same population will differ. That is, some operations in the simulation are specified in terms of probability distributions. To simulate the operation of such systems, a model is developed and the computer simulates the flow of events through the system. In this way, the computer provides a means of experimenting with various arrangements under such differing conditions as volume and timing of transactions before building the real system.

There are several challenging aspects to simulating a system of this kind. One is to determine the frequency and spacing of arrivals into the system. This may be done simply by specifying the mean, maximum, and minimum time between arrivals if numbers in the range have an equal probability of appearing, or a function may be introduced which specifies a more complex distribution. It is in this latter event that many of the mathematical mysteries, identified as *Monte Carlo methods,* intrude. Indeed, they are indispensible and the neophyte constructing a systems simulation will have to acquaint himself with them or he will end up building a system with no way to start it up.

Similar problems exist in simulating the length of time each transaction will probably take at each servicing point. In a barber shop, for example, customers may linger longer in the chair of the single lady barber, and both service time and waiting lines will be shorter for the barber who has chronic bad breath. In such cases, the average lingering time and the expected values of other-than-average times must be estimated.

Assuming that the mathematician has done his work, the computer will take over the job of randomly sampling the specified distributions and thereby simulate the arrival of new customers, the routing of each new customer, the waiting in line that results if traffic flow gets heavy, the servicing of customers, and departure from the system of the finished (serviced) product.

The reasons why queueing simulations are not utilized more than they have been reflect the problems encountered in any simulation: the model may be difficult to conceive, the data needed for setting up the probability distributions of necessary variables are not known, and programming assistance may be hard to come by. Even more important, perhaps, is the administrator's practice of waiting until problems occur rather than trying to anticipate them.

Several general system simulators have been developed to make it easier to do the programming for queueing models. A well-known simulator is the General Purpose Simulation System (GPSS) developed by IBM. Much of the programming pain is eased by GPSS since the simulation can be run by coding a set of control cards that specify the attributes of the system. Because of this, the builder can devote all his energy to conceptualizing the logic of his simulation, and the result is conveniently input as parameters on control cards. Anyone who has programmed a queueing model from scratch will appreciate this. Others should try it once for fun.

A similar approach was used in a pioneering development by Cogswell and Associates (4) at System Development Corporation. After a comprehensive systems analysis of several innovative schools they simulated pupil progress in an individualized curriculum. The program, written in JOVIAL, provides a set of operation codes that allows the specification of student characteristics, activities in the systen being modeled, the control of time spent in any activity, and the resources required to process the activities.

The procedure was used to simulate a tenth-grade biology course and a six-year mathematics curriculum in which individuals could progress at their individual rates. The resulting distribution of students at different times makes possible the determination of the resources that would be required under differing ways of constraining the system.

Finding relevance for queueing models in the operation of schools should not be too difficult. Library service, access to counselors, use of language labs, flow of messages from the central office, and pupil flow in individulized instruction are but a few possibilities that come to mind.

Optimizing Models

Another familiar procedure in simulation is to develop a model which not only will simulate the effects of a proposed operation but also will optimize (either maximize) some objective function.

Such operations are usually based on the solution of sets of simultaneous equations and have come to be called linear programming methods.

An example of a school administration-related use may be cited from a school redistricting simulation developed at General Learning Corporation (9). In this model, the problem was to determine attendance boundaries for three proposed middle schools in such a way that requirements for racial balance, building load, and curriculum balance were maintained and the average distance to schools was minimized.

To build a simulation of this kind, a forecasting model must be constructed to simulate the expected enrollment in years for which the simulation is to be run. Again, the computer is useful because it can easily handle the calculations necessary to forecast enrollments depending on the method decided upon by the builder. Also, the solution of the equations specifying the problem is a formidable task and is feasible in large problems only if a computer is available.

James E. Bruno at Rand Corporation has applied linear programming techniques to problems in educational administration. In one such use, he formulated a linear programming model to determine a salary schedule for a school district, The model incorporated the factors desired by both teacher union and school board and allowed inclusion of agreements reached through negotiation.

Bruno's model determined a salary schedule which satisfied the specified requirements and minimized school district costs. The results might not always be acceptable to die-hard advocates of long-established salary hierarchies, but at least they can examine the logical results of their assumptions about salary and bring the resulting schedule into line with public pronouncements about what the district is seeking to reward.

Bruno has also investigated the use of linear programming for devising methods of distribution of state funds to local school districts. Such application would make it possible to take into account available state, local, and federal funds, satisfy the policy constraints placed on the system, and distribute funds in accordance with a criterion of effectiveness such as to maximize state aid to each district.

Several library programs for general application of linear programming are available. For one example, see the Control Data Mathematical Programming System (CDM 3/Linear Programming).

A WORD ABOUT LANGUAGES

Without attempting to consider computer language in any depth, let us mention a few salient characteristics of some of the available languages for simulation. The reader who needs a more thorough introduction to computer languages should consult the critiques of Krasnow & Merikallio (11) or Teichroew & Lubin (19).

The first thing to note is that many of the operations required in simulations can be programmed in almost any language if one wants to go to enough trouble. Since most of us seek to avoid trouble, it is well to pick a language that does the job most efficiently; however, one should note that this is not what usually happens. Most often we end up using the language available to us at our most accessible computation center or the one with which we feel comfortable working.

In general, it is helpful to think of languages that facilitate computation as contrasted with those that are useful for conversational modes. Thus, standbys such as FORTRAN and COBOL (not interactive, but good for input-output) are usable for simulations requiring calculations, while COURSEWRITER is excellent for programming simulations requiring natural language inputs and outputs but is poor for computation.

A relatively new language developed by Iverson (10) is unimaginatively called *A Programming Language* (APL). It is very promising for simulation since it has such functions as a random number generator and a full range of logical operators, and handles vector and matrix calculations with ease. It cannot easily handle extensive verbal data in memory, but this can be overcome partly through an image projector which can store several hundred frames on a filmstrip accessed by the computer. APL is presently available for the IBM instructional system, and a 360 version is being developed.

If many files have to be accessed for rapid retrieval, list-processing languages such as LISP and MENTOR are extremely useful; and if a system simulation is being developed, one should acquaint himself with SIMSCRIPT (12) or SIMULA (8)—languages developed specifically for simulation. Earlier, we mentioned GPSS which is useful for systems simulations, but this is not so much a language as it is a set of simulation sub-routines controlled by the user through parameters on control cards.

Users with no local computation center or those who find it practical to use remote facilities in a time-shared service center will be using such languages as BASIC and TELECOMP, which accept quantitative inputs and are useful in simulations involving both information retrieval and calculations.

A final—and sometimes prior—consideration in choosing a language is its accessibility. Most computation centers will have some languages that are available at all times and others that require special runs. If the user has an exotic language, he must always make arrangements for his runs in advance and sometimes will be allowed to run his programs only at such times as 2:00 a.m. on Sunday. Although these are local problems, they are worth investigating unless one prefers to work at 2:00 a.m.

SOME CAUSES FOR DISENCHANTMENT

All is not unalloyed delight in computer-based simulation. Let us mention a few of the hazards that lie in wait for the unwary.

First, one should be aware of the time and effort required to construct, program, test, and revise a computer-based simulation. It will take at least two times longer (and probably more) than comparable simulation without a computer. Since the development is likely to be expensive, only those simulations that, when developed, will get lots of use are good candidates for computerizing.

Second, some simulations require large amounts of central processor space and, except on large computers, may require virtually the whole system. In these cases, usage is limited to special arrangements. This is true only in certain simulations; an APL simulation, for example, is very small in storage requirements.

Third, the computer is essentially a quantitative data-handling machine, and except for CAI systems or languages with convenient string manipulation capability, the user will find himself changing his model in ways that make it possible to handle inputs and outputs by numbers when natural language would be more desirable. This is a great difficulty in interactive man-machine simulations at present. The history of computer languages has been that they have become more user-oriented and great efforts are being made to achieve more "natural language" capability.

Finally, the programming problem (so deftly avoided thus far) must be faced. Except in rare instances, the man with the simulation urge and the man who can program the machine are not the same person. This means that a programmer must be found who is willing to try to do things the way the model demands rather than the way that is facile for him. This isn't as easy as it may sound.

The programmer has a problem, too, in that his client usually has such a loose grasp of his model that the specifications for the program are hard to pin down. The computer (and hence the programmer) is relentless in its demand for unambiguous instructions on what must be done at every point in the program The result is often that only those programmer-client teams that have a high tolerance for frustration will be able to stand each other beyond the flowcharting stage.

These difficulties are not insurmountable, however, and the outlook is bright. Even a mildly fogged crystal ball reveals a vision of lots of activity in building computer-based simulations for both management use and instruction. The promise of computer technology is so great that simulation, unlike artifical respiration, is not only indispensible when you can't get the real thing—it is sometimes better.

NOTES

[1] Those who want the whole story are encouraged to consult some of the comprehensive works cited in the bibliography: Mize & Cox, 1968; Chorafas, 1965; Tocher, 1963; Naylor, Balintfy, Burdick & Chu, 1966.

BIBLIOGRAPHY

1. Bessent, Wailand. "A Feedback Procedure for Simulation of Administrative In-basket Problems." Paper delivered at American Educational

Research Association Symposium on Feedback in Simulation Techniques, New York, 1967.

2. Bruno, James E. "Minimizing the Spread in Per-Pupil Expenditures in School Finance Programs." Technical paper. Rand Corporation, Santa Monica, California, 1968.

3. Chorafas, D. N. *Systems and Simulation.* New York: Academic Press, Inc., 1965.

4. Cogswell, John F.; Bratten, J. E.; Egbert, R. E.; Estevan, D. P.; Marsh, D.G.; and Yett, F.A. *Final Report; Analysis of Instructional Systems.* Technical Memorandum-1493/201/00. System Development Corporation, Santa Monica, California. 1966.

5. Control Data Corporation. *CDM3/ Linear Programming.* Publication no. 526. March 1963.

6. Cristal, Raymond E. *Selecting a Harem And Other Applications of the Policy Capturing Model.* Personnel Research Laboratory Publication no. PRL-TR-67-1, Lackland Air Force Base, Texas, March 1967.

7. Culbertson, Jack, et al. *The Design and Development of Prototype Materials for Preparing Educational Administrators.* United States Office of Education. Final Report of Project no. 5-0998, Contract no. OE-4-16-014, January 1968.

8. Dahl, O. J. & Nygaard, K. "SIMULA-An ALOGOL-Based Simulation Language." *Communications of the ACM,* vol. 9, no. 9, September 1966.

9. General Learning Corporation. *Final Report of New Haven High School Redistricting Project.* New York: GLC Educational Services Division, March 1968.

10. Iverson, K. E. *A Programming Language.* New York: John Wiley & Sons, Inc., 1962.

11. Krasnow, H. S. & Merikallio, R. A. "The Past, Present, and Future of General Simulation Languages." *Management Science,* November 1964.

12. Markowitz, H.; Hausener, B.; and Karr, H. *SIMSCRIPT: A Simulation Language.* Englewood Cliffs, New Jersey: Prentice-Hall, Inc., 1963.

13. McBride, Galen F. *A Policy Capturing Model Relating to Faculty Selections in Nine Junior Colleges.* Unpublished Ph.D. dissertation, The University of Texas, 1968.

14. McIsaac, Donald T. *Wisconsin Heeds Assessment Study.* University of Wisconsin, 1969.

15. Merck, John W. *A Markovian Model for Projecting Movements of Personnel Through a System.* Lackland Air Force Base, Texas: Personnel Research Laboratory, Aerospace Medical Division, Air Force Systems Command, PRL-TR-65-6, March 1965.

16. Mize, Joe H. & Cox, J. Grady. *Essentials of Simulation.* Englewood Cliffs, New Jersey: Prentice-Hall, Inc., 1968.

17. Naylor, T. H.; Balintfy, H. L.; Burdick, D. S.; and Chu, K. *Computer Simulation Techniques*. New York: John Wiley & Sons, Inc., 1966.

18. Strachey, Chistopher. "System Analysis and Programming." *Information: A Scientific American Book*. San Francisco and London: W. H. Freeman and Company, 1966.

19. Teichroew, D. & Lubin, J.F. "Computer Simulation—Discussion of Technique and Comparison of Languages." *Communications of ACM*, vol. 9, no. 10, October 1966.

20. Tocher, K. D. "Review of Simulation Languages." *Operations Research Quarterly* 15:2, 1965.

21. Tocher, K. D. *The Art of Simulation*. Princeton, New Jersey: D Van Nostrand Company, Inc., 1963.

9

Using Simulation to Conduct Research in Educational Administration

Dale L. Bolton

The first eight chapters of this book indicate rather clearly that the primary use of simulation in educational administration has been for instruction rather than research. This may be due more to the people using the materials than to the technique of simulation itself. For, in spite of Halpin's (21, p. 17) justified plea for a more tolerant and catholic view of various "ways of knowing," many people depend on only one "way of knowing" rather than on multiple ways. With simulation that dependence has been oriented toward experiencing rather than experimenting.

If the simulation used to give individuals initial experiences fails to mirror reality, erroneous views of administration are likely to occur. This appears to be especially true where the simulation is accepted to be reality rather than a model of reality, a problem which may be quite serious where simulations are used repeatedly for instruction. Regardless of whether models are used for instruction or research, there is a tendency to think of them as reality; but the research person is warned about such error; and if he heeds this warning, his contribution to the knowledge of educational administration will be unique.

This chapter will explore some of the problems involved in using simulation for research in educational administration; compare these problems to some of the advantages and needs for research output and illustrate how simulation can be used for research to increase our knowledge of educational administration. A general discussion of the nature of research and scientific inquiry and a consideration of the distinction between testing an idea and obtaining, devising, or generating an idea will be used as an introduction to the more specific discussion of the use of simulation in research.

On the assumption that administration is based primarily on philosophical beliefs, some readers may question the scientific approach to studying it. However, even in the ideological field, perhaps the greatest need is a willingness to test ideas and to compare alternatives as they are implemented. Scientific inquiry, as opposed to common-sense inquiry, is a dynamic process designed not only to answer questions and solve problems; but also to develop more efficient procedures for answering questions and solving problems. In addition, its superiority over other types of inquiry lies in the fact that it is controlled. *Controlled* in this context means that science is efficiently directed toward the attainment of desired objectives.

A clue to how this control is achieved is found in the fact that science often advances by the replacement of a primitive or less adequate model with a somewhat more adequate model, and that model in turn is replaced by a still better one. This suggests a cybernetic cycle spiraling upward. The results of experimentation with simulation often become interesting hypotheses *about* the world which the research person is obligated to test *in* the world, thus suggesting a bridging back and forth between the real world and a model of the real world, as well as a spiraling upward from less adequate to more adequate models.

So the motivation is straightforward—the interest is in answering questions and solving problems regarding educational administration, and in order to do this ideas must be tested. Further, the inquiry process should be controlled in order to more efficiently attain the goals of solving problems and answering questions. The control is accomplished by designing models of reality, determining how these models work, checking conclusions against reality, and modifying the models until they are satisfactory. Educational administration supplies the problem area, the content, and the initial motivation; simulation provides the means for modeling the reality of this content; and science furnishes the process for inquiring.

THE NEED FOR RESEARCH OUTPUT

Potentially, research output can influence educational administration in two ways: (a) by assisting the practitioner in administering educational organizations and (b) by assisting the researcher in studying the administrative process. As far as practice is concerned, the primary benefits from research results lie not in factual conclusions but in the more general concepts clarified or the theory confirmed by the research. Actions are undertaken on the basis of generalizations believed to be true about the world, and research results provide a basis for determining the credibility of these generalizations. Thus, research results assist the practitioner by giving him an indispensable theoretical base on which to make decisions.[1]

Research results benefit the researcher by providing: (a) feedback regarding whether a particular theory explains administrative behavior and (b) clues to how the theory can be modified or how additional research will help to clarify the theory. The research person has the continual problem of investigating particulars in such a way that the results may be generalized to the problems encountered by practitioners. Since research results must be organized eventually into a set of unified concepts or a theory, they are important to the researcher to the extent that they assist him in this synthesis process. Therefore, research results aid the researcher by confirming or disconfirming a theory directly or, failing this, by combining with other results to broaden generalizations.

In spite of the advantages of scientific inquiry, there are times when common sense inquiry is preferable. There are instances when the cost of research and the significance of the problem dictate that decisions be made on the basis of information available (and the concepts and theory which appear to bear on the problem) rather than expending the effort, energy, and money necessary to conduct additional research.

Relationships to the Practice of Educational Administration

For some time, it has been recognized that research (or theory) and practice are not incompatible; however, only recently has it been noted that there is a difference between the standards of productivity applied by those institutions which do research and those which utilize the results of the research. There is a need to turn the attention of the inquirers to research which assists those who are required to develop policy and to manage programs (4).

Results of research conducted in a simulated situation contribute to the practice of educational administration by assisting the practitioner (a) in making decisions that are repeated and routine but which (when cumulated) can have a substantial effect on the efficient accomplishment of the organizational goals, (b) in making relatively unique decisions which are critical to the functioning of the organization but are not made often enough to routinize,[2] and (c) in devising, conducting, and participating in administrative in-service programs.

Let us consider the more routine decisions first. What kind of information is beneficial to the administrator? It should be acknowledged at the outset that information which is descriptive only, which describes administrative behavior in a static situation, or which provides information about a given population of administrators (i.e., the status quo) has very limited value for devising an efficient routine. Much more beneficial is information which tells the practitioner what will happen if certain circumstances are varied, what will happen if the environment is modified or manipulated. In effect, he will benefit from if-then statements which indicate the applicability or generalizability of the phenomenon in question. If a certain schedule is adopted, what is the probability that adequate space will be available for optimum operation (making limiting assumptions regarding student choices, etc.)? If students make certain demands for revised offerings, what is the probability that the contemplated action will lead to student-faculty conflict and what will be the reactions of each group involved? If teacher demands for modified working conditions are met with hard-time refusals by central administrative staff, what is the probability of certain actions being taken by the teacher group?

Since it is difficult to manipulate real educational situations, simulation can assist in the solution of such problems by abstracting the reality of specific situations in a model that can be examined and manipulated. In order to abstract reality, certain simplifying assumptions must be made explicit; only the most important aspects of reality should be included in the model. Then, by operating on the model, the user can draw conclusions which are valid for the real system being controlled or studied. Conclusions drawn from such studies may be difficult to apply to a particular situation for one reason only—the particular situation may be somewhat different from the abstraction studied. Even so, the task of the administrator merely becomes one of making a judgment regarding how similar the problem situation is to the one previously studied—a task made less difficult by the generalizability of the results and the nature of the if-then conclusion.

With both the routine decision and the relatively unique decision, practitioners need to have a conceptual base for dealing with the problems they face. This seems necessary in order to facilitate the goals of the organization and the self-protection of the administrator. In effect, this means that administrators need information (based on research) regarding the elements of decisions which are to be made, viz., the state of the world or the nature of a particular situation, the various alternatives that are available, the probability that certain consequences will occur if particular alternatives are chosen, and the values that can be attached to these consequences. Each of these decision elements can be investigated, and information obtained from research conducted in a simulated situation helps to convince others that certain alternatives are to be preferred for accomplishing the goals of the organization. In the routine decision such information probably is not as important as in the unique decision, since the latter is made infrequently and is potentially more crucial to the accomplishment of goals.

Research results which provide a theoretical or conceptual basis for decision making are helpful also in administrative in-service programs. As a person plans (or participates in) an in-service program for administrators, he may rely on information from his own experience and results from research. Neither of these sources of information should be ignored; but since they represent different avenues of approach, they should be examined to determine how they can be used most effectively.

If internal and external validity were considered in conducting the research, then the results will be generalizable to a variety of situations and will form general concepts or theory which will become the basic content for the in-sevice program. The generalizability of the results indicates their value, making them applicable in many circumstances. But what is the value of the administrator's experience? The great value of experience lies in its utility as examples of the more general principles or theory acquired from the research results. Examples facilitate learning by providing concreteness for generalizations derived from research. Without such examples, the learning of concepts tends to remain at an abstract level and never is applied in practice.

The caution to be underlined here is that experience should not be used to derive the general principles or concepts. Experiences are single events, and to generalize from single events is always dangerous—unless the generalization is treated as an hypothesis rather than a conclusion. Where such is the case, the following cycle is suggested: experience indicates an hypothesis, research is conducted, a conclusion which is stated in general form is reached, experience provides an example for teaching the research conclusion, general concepts learned supply the basis for action.

Research, then, contributes most to the practice of educational administration when it goes beyond mere description and states results in an if-then format, when it investigates phenomena which are directly related to the routinized and more unique decisions that need to be made, and when it becomes an integral part of the experience-research-learning-action cycle of in-service training programs for administrators. Research has not made the anticipated contribution to the practice of educational administrators, but the use of simulated situations for conducting research has not been fully exploited. Simulation offers two benefits not normally derived from other research procedures: (a) it allows the making of if-then statements about relationships among variables and (b) it can be easily coupled with instruction for illustrating the concepts and theory developed.

Relationships to the Development of Theory

The purpose of this section is to explain how simulation can make a contribution to the development of theory in educational administration. However, the emphasis is on the nature of theory, how it is developed, and how it contributes to scientific statements that can be applied to practice. Rather precise definitions of theory have been given elsewhere (20, p. 7; 19, p. 98; 37, pp. 2-7), and it is not the intent of this discussion to repeat those explanations. Rather, the discussion will emphasize three characteristics of theory which may help to clarify the concept more readily than a definition would.

Meaningful observation. The first characteristic of theory is that it provides a way to organize concepts and data so that prior and future observations will have meaning and order. Without a scheme for relating facts and concepts it is difficult to know what to observe or how to analyze or interpret once an observation has been made.[3]

In effect, then, theory is not just the discovery of hidden facts, but a way of organizing and looking at facts in such a manner that learning is facilitated. Learning by experience can be separated from theorizing inasmuch as the latter is more concerned with thinking about what there is to be learned. Experience is direct and immediate, whereas theory may allow vicarious experience through symbolic representation of reality—with subsequent consideration of symbols. It is not difficult to see that simulated situation can also provide a vicarious experience directly[4] but that the theory on which simulation is based allows one to profit from observations made during the experience in a manner that would be impossible were there not some structure and organization to the phenomena being observed.

Prediction. A second characteristic of theory is that it provides the means whereby predictions can be made. If it is good theory, these predictions are better than chance; if it is excellent theory, predictions are maximized in some sense. Thus, accuracy of prediction gives some evidence of the goodness or truth of the theory. The idea that theory allows accurate predictions to be made is compatible with the view that theory attempts to facilitate practical understanding. Coladarci and Getzels (9, pp. 4-5), because they view theory and practice as integral, state that practice can be only accidentally successful without a theoretical dimension. Indeed, if theory forms the basis for prediction, it is tautological to note that predictions will become random without some theoretical basis.

It has been noted that theory supplies a way to organize and relate concepts and data so that meaningful observations can be made. It is this *relating* which makes prediction possible and provides the basis for scientific activity. Mere measurement contributes little to an understanding of phenomena; relating two or more variables does increase understanding and make predictions possible within the framework of the theory expressed. Any activity that is not concerned with finding whether or not there is a relationship between two or more things that vary is purely clerical or on a verbal or descriptive level (25, p. 8). In other words, doing a task without a theory is non-scientific busy work, without purpose or meaning.

An understanding of relationships allows predictions to be made. If these relationships can be established as causal, not only can predictions be made but also the reasons for phenomena occurring can be better understood. Theories stating relationships among variables assist the practitioner or scientist to predict events; if these relationships are causal, an explanation of why the events occur is supplied.

New knowledge.   A third characteristic of theory is that it guides investigations so that new knowledge can be generated. Thompson emphasizes the importance of theory in interpreting both the future findings of the social sciences and experiences in administration; further, he states that probably the most damaging criticism that can be made of any theory is that it does not generate new knowledge (38, pp. 24, 27). Kaplan states a similar view when he emphasizes that theory must not only be modified to fit data unanticipated in the formulation of theory but also must be used to guide the scientist in discovering new and more powerful generalizations (28, p. 295).

In effect, Kaplan is saying that theory is a guide in determining what relationships among variables should be investigated. Further, when relationships are different from those anticipated by the theory expressed, the theory must be modified so that it presents meaningful interpretation of the findings. If this is true, let us explore the place of simulation in theory development.

Simulation. Consider the cycle of events in Fig. 9-1.[5] Enter the figure at Box A, although the cycle can be entered at Box B or D. A theoretical statement is developed which attempts to explain reality by expressing relationships among variables. This statement is an abstraction stated in either verbal or symbolic form and can be analyzed in terms of its implications. These implications are then examined in Box B. In effect, one is saying, "If my theory is correct, I can infer that examination of a model which represents reality (or examination of reality itself) should produce these particular results." Note that the implications of the theory are examined in one of two places: a real situation, or a representation of a real situation. Further, note that the general question being asked is, "Does the explanation of reality that has been devised (theory) explain reality (if this is the choice) or a representation of reality, viz., a model or simulated situation?" If the answer is "no," then the theory must be modified so that the investigation that has been conducted can be explained by the modified theory. In effect, this step (Box C) is a part of the feedback cycle which allows for correction.

If, however, the answer to the question is "yes," then it seems reasonable that the theory may be used as a guide to action in the practice of administration (Box D).[6] The use of the theory in practice becomes a type of field test of the theory; it determines whether the results obtained are generalizable to the the particular situation in which it is being used. The feedback (Box E) from the field test furnishes information that can be used to suggest changes in the theory, to suggest additional problems which need to be investigated or considered when reexamining the theory, or to suggest new concepts that might be incorporated in the theory.

Note that the use of simulation in such a cycle does not by-pass the important stages of theorizing or testing the results of the

268

Figure 9-1
RELATIONSHIP OF THEORY, RESEARCH,
AND PRACTICE IN A CYCLE OF EVENTS

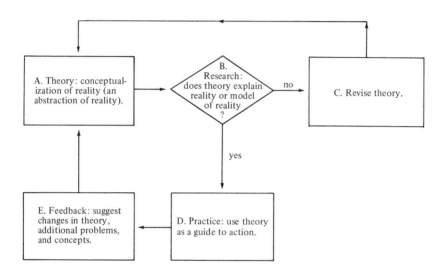

research conducted in the simulation. This procedure is compatible with views of other authors. For example, Schild (34, p. 4) indicates that there are two basic assumptions for the use of simulations in research: (a) the simulation can reflect the important contingencies of real life and (b) these contingencies shape the strategies of the players. Likewise, he indicates that simulation may be used to generate new theoretical propositions. Outcomes suggest a possible framework for analysis, and the framework then allows formulation of more specific propositions. Also, Kaplan (28, pp. 268-69) indicates that hypotheses are often ambiguous and lacking in detail until placed in the framework of a specific model.

The cyclical process described supports the reasonableness of the assumptions made by Schild and, at the same time, the explicitness that Kaplan finds necessary. Also, the separateness of theory, research, and practice shown in Fig. 9-1 suggests that these three functions be carried out by separate people. Indeed, this might be the most efficient manner of conducting the total process.[7] If this is true, however, there must be some assurance that a *cycle* will be sustained, i.e., that the information flow indicated in the figure will be maintained. If, in fact, the information obtained at step D is not given to the person responsible for developing and modifying theory, or if research results are not tested in practice, the cycle will be broken and improvement stopped. Simulated situations form a basis for determining whether theory explains a reasonable representation of reality (where reality cannot be checked directly) and supply research results which bridge the theory-practice gap in a cyclical process.

Nature of Questions Suitable for Investigation

There are wide varieties of questions dealing with administrative processes which may be investigated via simulation. Further, it appears that the content of the administrative task (e.g., curriculum and instruction, staff personnel, school-community relations, or finance) does not limit the use of simulation for research. To go beyond these general statements requires a look at some of the specifics of the administrative process.

Decision making and information processing. Since decision making is critical to the behavior of administrators, it is one of the areas which offers much promise for investigation via simulation procedures. Two aspects of decision making which might be investigated are (a) the conditions which contribute to the selection of strategies to be followed rather than a specific course of action[8] and (b) conditions which affect the estimates of probabilities associated with possible outcomes of decisions made by administrators. Information in either of these areas will be beneficial in teaching administrative processes.

Assuming that the administrator is an information processor who seeks improved ways of processing information, there are a number of questions appropriate for investigation via simulation. For example, given that there are certain "states of the environment" to be sensed, does the administrator possess sensors appropriate to the task? Are his sensors properly receptive to information about his own organization, other organizations, and the larger environment? How can the state of the world be represented internally and made available for retrieval (12, p. 95)? These questions suggest more complex questions—e.g., Do differing conditions yield different responses to the questions posed? Cullinan discusses some of these more relational and comparative studies in his presentation of the advantages of computer-based simulation systems (12, p. 142). Such systems may be used to examine the effectiveness of various file structures and retrieval rules to determine the effect of information displayed in various forms, to evaluate various interactive languages and devices for communicating, and even to assess factors related to individual and team efforts.

Group interactions. Students of small group processes are interested in the most propitious conditions under which decisions can be made in small groups. Through simulation various aspects of small groups can be manipulated to determine what affects their functioning. For example, content of the problem, size of the group, nature of the leader and amount of structure he provides to the situation, types of individuals within the group, and stage of development of the group can all be manipulated within a simulated situation to determine their effect on group productivity and esprit. Several of these variables have been investigated but with populations and settings considerably different from those found in educational administration. Griffin, after his investigation (18, p. 180), concluded that crisis games involving international conflict provide a tool for examining qualitative questions pertinent to group resolution (i.e., questions that cannot be quantified or computerized); however, problems involving international conflict may produce results which differ considerably from those of education.

Conflict resolution. Even so, conflict resolution in education and international relations may be similar in one respect in that they both involve situations that are difficult or impossible to experiment with in reality. Ackoff emphasizes that gaming (as described in the chapter on negotiations by Horvat) should not be considered a substitute for analytic model construction (1, p. 375). Rather, gaming should be viewed as a way of obtaining information that can be used to generate models capable of being analyzed and manipulated.

Ross (33, p. 2) found that the negotiations materials developed by Horvat were generally considered to be relevant to collective negotiations by participants and produced results by teams of teachers and school board members which were different from optimum solutions determined by game theory. The latter result is interesting in that it tends to lend credence to the view that theory developed in one context *does* need to be verified in settings different from the one in which it was developed. In spite of the latter finding, Ross concluded that game theory may still be of value when applied to teacher-board collective negotiations.

One reason for maintaining this conclusion may be the strong view which permeates the literature of gaming and simulation that one of the significant aspects of gaming is its emphasis on conceptual frameworks. For example, Griffin (18, p. 180) maintains that crisis games stimulate thinking that is essential to preparing for dealing with international emergencies. Because the number of contingency plans which might be developed is limited to a few, it is necessary to emphasize concepts, ideas, and notions. Game theory is one conceptual framework that appears to be suited to the analysis of conflict resolution in collective negotiations.

Structural relationships. In the playing of games involving international problems, players gain a more complete understanding of the complexities of international relations and an appreciation of the dilemmas faced by people in decision-making roles (3, p. 9). One of the complexities of such a game is the structural relationships that exist, relationships that are not always completely understood. The principal justifiable use of gaming is to explore stuctural relationships of large complex systems which are not thoroughly understood (1, p. 375).

Certainly one of the problem areas of large school systems in recent years has been the manner in which they are organized for policy making and operation. One of the difficulties in changing one part of the structure of an organization is the effect the change will have on other structural parts. The simulation of large school systems for purposes of gaming should at least require that interrelationships of various parts of the organization be examined. The gaming itself should precipitate hypotheses which can be tested in real situations. As knowledge of structural relations is developed, simulations should become more useful for experimentation—in effect, for determining what happens to certain parts of the organization when structural changes are made in other parts.

Goal setting, establishment of priorities. The structural organization of a school system influences its accomplishment of goals. But the administration of the organization establishes procedures for goal determination and accomplishment. Since a school system may have many goals, and ususally has limited resources for accomplishing them, it is necessary to establish priorities among the goals. Obviously, a knowledge of administrative procedures for establishing priorities and setting goals is necessary since goals provide the basis for the structures and activities of the organization. The concern here is the relationship of goal setting and priority determination to simulation.

It appears that simulations can be established for studying the procedural aspects of goal setting. If so, the relationship of problem and goal items to environmental factors and personalities can be studied to determine their effect on the types of goals established and the priorities determined. For example, do the problems involving poverty and race have different priorities and suggest different goals in large, industrial areas than in rural, agricultural environments? Do cosmopolitan, change-oriented people analyze goal setting for these situations differently from less sophisticated, place-bound people? It may be that goal setting and priority establishment can be considered special cases of decision-making and small group procedures, but it also may be that they have unique factors that must be interpreted outside these better understood processes.

The study of procedural aspects of goal setting and priority establishment in simulated school systems may yield clues to procedures which might be used in establishment of priorities for research and development activities. For example, what emphasis should the national government place on research, development, demonstration, and dissemination? How much emphasis should there be on answering questions of interest to scientists and how much on solving problems being faced by practitioners? No doubt the ultimate use of science comes in the real world where problems exist; but this does not negate the value of scientific endeavors unhampered by the need for decisions and action inasmuch as a hypothesis which is barren today may be fruitful tomorrow. Where the primary justification of federal support of research projects is based on the relevance and applicability of the results to educational practice, i.e., where the contributions to knowledge *per se* are less important that the solving of problems of national significance (4, p. 25) the possibility exists that long-range national goals will be affected adversely. The concern of research which simulates administrative processes should not focus on *what* goals or priorities should be established but on the *procedures* for establishing the goals and priorities. The knowledge acquired in this way may well apply to organizations responsible for research and development activities, also.

Questions unsuitable for simulation. Three types of questions appear to be unsuitable for investigation in simulated situations: (a) Questions which involve self analysis. Introspection might be incorporated into an activity involving simulation, but the contribution of the simulation to the self-analysis (or the reverse) would most probably be incidental. (b) Questions that involve a determination of how decisions are actually made in a real situation. Cautions have been given regarding problems which occur when one begins to think of the simulation as reality itself, and one should be aware that the results obtained in a simulated situation which represents reality can contain only a portion of the constraints of a real situation. For example, it is difficult to develop a simulation that creates the same feelings of threat and pressure as reality. (c) Questions concerned with what *ought* to occur. Exceptions to this may occur if one is concerned with determining what a group of people thought should occur in a particular situation (for purposes of reaching consensus on an issue) or if one is investigating how an individual's expressions of what ought to happen were consistent with other decisions, either prior or future.

POTENTIAL ADVANTAGES OF SIMULATION IN RESEARCH

The generally accepted functions of research are to describe, predict, and control the environment. Description involves measurement, prediction entails correlation among two or more variables, and control generally involves manipulative experimentation to determine causal relationships. The advantages of simulation for research result from the fact that experiments can be conducted on a model of reality.[9] Although all of the advantages of simulation can be obtained through experimentation in real situations, in practice it is difficult to experiment with some phenomena in educational administration.

The use of simulation for research differs from other research in educational administration in two ways: (a) the simulation involves manipulation of analogue models,[10] and (b) the primary entity of interest is human, and it is necessary to measure the performance of individuals in the modeled situation. Simulation itself offers advantages over other types of research, and simulation which uses individuals as the primary entity of interest offers advantages over other types of simulation. Therefore, let us examine some of these benefits.

Measurement of Dependent Variables

The use of simulation for research in eduational administration permits the measurement of dependent variables to be stabilized. Where questions are asked (e.g., via a questionnaire) of administrators who function in widely varying situations, responses are likely to be based on vastly differing interpretations of the stimulus. Although participants in a simulated exercise bring their varying backgrounds to the simulated activity, the stimuli are presented in a controlled atmosphere which helps to increase the reliability of measurement of responses.

Also, control of the simulation by the investigator allows measurement at specified time intervals in the simulation. In real situations, it is often difficult to stop an administrator's decision or problem-solving process in order to measure aspects of the administrative process; however, in simulated situations, this is quite feasible. It is possible to obtain measures of both the information upon which an individual bases his decisions and the outcomes which he expects from his decision-making process. A simulated situation can be coupled to a computer to examine the pre-decisional information search processes of administrators, and their feelings of certainty regarding the sufficiency of the information can be measured at different stages of the information search (23). Also, a computer-based simulation system can be used to obtain knowledge about instructing and preparing educational administrators with the advantage that responses can be gathered in comparable form (12, pp. 136, 143).

Control and Manipulation of Independent Variables

Conducting research in a simulated situation offers three benefits with relation to independent variables: (a) the situation can be controlled so that only those variables of interest need be examined, (b) the variables which are of interest can be manipulated so that causal relationships with dependent variables can be established, and (c) multiple independent variables can be manipulated simultaneously.

Among the advantages of being able to control the independent variable for studying pre-chosen factors is the fact that one can choose variables which appear to be of significance to administrative behavior (because of some theory being examined) and which provide conditions rarely occurring in reality. The obvious advantage of the former is one of the general advantages of laboratory experiments over field studies. The benefit of the latter is discussed less in the literature and appears to be more subtle. [11] Where relatively rare events are of extreme significance to an organization, it is important that they be studied. However, the time of their occurrence may be difficult to predict and their systematic study may be impossible. With simulation, variables can be controlled in such a way that the subject is required to face circumstances which he might never face in cooperative discussion or in solitary meditation. In fact, a value of crisis gaming is exposure to the antagonistic will of another who functions under entirely different assumptions from one's own (18, p. 184). It seems likely that the teacher negotiations game described by Horvat would offer similar benefits, also.[12]

In addition to being able to control rare events in order to expose subjects to them, simulation offers the advantage of being able to manipulate aspects of the events that appear signigicant to the phenomenon being studied. Not only can one manipulate the environment of participants in a simulated activity and control when improbable events will occur, but also the event can be repeated under varying circumstances to determine how certain factors in the simulated environment affect the participants. While certain factors are being manipulated, others are being controlled; thus, causal relationships among variables are established because factors other than the ones being manipulated can be eliminated from having produced the results. Of course, the same advantages can be obtained for non-rare events or events which either presently or ultimately will be faced by practicing administrators.

In chapter seven Horvat discusses the ease with which negotiations games can be modified and indicates that this assists in illustrating desired points and in creating realism. In addition, the ease of modification of any simulation device allows multiple variables to be manipulated simultaneously. Yet the variables manipulated will be fewer than in reality; consequently, the simulation will be more manageable from the standpoint of analyzing what is occurring. This reduction in number of variables raises interesting theoretical questions. For example, one of the common views held by practicing administrators is that virtually complete information about a given situation is necessary in order to make reasonable decisions. Yet if a small number of variables included in the simulated situation precipitates behavior consonant with that expected in real situations, the importance of additional variables becomes questionable. Under such circumstances, the burden of proof is shifted to others to show why those variables which are not included in the simulation are necessary to explain the phenomenon under analysis (34, p. 4).

Control for the Complexity of Studies

Since simulation allows simultaneous manipulation of more than one independent variable,[13] the investigator has more control over and latitude in the complexity of studies he initiates. For example, the investigation of human learning has received much more attention in relatively simple situations than in the more ambiguous, complex situations in which humans find themselves daily (15, p. 91). And this is justifiable since it is important to control the environment to the extent that the investigator is able to make precise statements about what he has learned. Also, he wants to control the environment in order to improve his predictions.

This control over the complexity of the environment improves predictions in two ways. First, it allows effective reduction in variations of so-called nuisance variables which might interfere with the effect of the variables being studied. Reduction in variation of these nuisance variables (which may tend to behave as distractors to human subjects to the extent that relatively random behavior occurs) may increase accuracy of prediction considerably more than increases in variation of the independent variables would (2, p. 117). Therefore, control which reduces the complexity of the simulated environment can improve prediction and aid in understanding the phenomena being studied.

Second, consider the situation where an event or behavior is being affected by several variables, for example four. If an experiment is conducted including only one of these independent variables, then a certain prediction will be made. However, if all four variables are included, the accuracy of the prediction will be increased. Likewise, the single experiment involving all four variables will offer more information for prediction than will four separate experiments involving single variables because the effect of the interaction of all four variables will be known. Therefore, control which increases the complexity of the stimuli affecting participants in simulated situations improves the prediction and thus aids in understanding the phenomena being studied.

We have noted that both decreasing and increasing the complexity of a simulation improve prediction. This is not a paradox since the complexity of the simulation is *decreased* by controlling the nuisance variables while it is *increased* by controlling the number of independent variables being manipulated. Both procedures are useful tools in designing simulated situations for research.

Establishment of Causal Relationships

Much has been said already about the need to conduct research that establishes causal relationships and the potential of simulation for meeting this need. However, this potential is so important that it cannot be over emphasized. To establish causality requires three conditions: (a) evidence of concomitant variation of the independent and dependent variables, (b) evidence that the dependent variable did not occur prior to the independent variable, and (c) evidence which eliminated other factors as causes of the changes in the dependent variable.[14]

Research in a controlled or experimental setting, such as that provided in a simulated situation, produces no advantage over research in a natural setting as far as establishing the first two conditions is concerned.[15] However, it offers considerable advantage over natural settings in eliminating or ruling out other factors as causes. Basically, this is due to the fact that it is difficult to know what is being manipulated by nature and therefore difficult to determine the direction of causality. Although one might systematically rule out a number of variables that could be causing the effect, the fact that nature may have manipulated many other variables—any one of which might be overlooked—means that claims of causality are difficult to make when the investigation has occurred to a natural setting (2, pp. 96, 126).

However, the experiment permits control which nature prohibits and allows one to study and evaluate outcomes resulting from a variety of alternative conditions (14, p. 12). The ability to rule out alternative causes comes from the nature of the experiment, viz., the potential causes, or independent variables, are systematically varied and then other potential causes are controlled by presenting them in a constant fashion or by allowing them to randomly affect the phenomena being studied. Such a procedure does not present absolute proof regarding the cause (or absolutely eliminate other causes), but it does allow one to make a statement about how probable it is that other causes have been eliminated. The investigation in the natural setting does not allow such a probability statement to be made.

Of course, the controls needed in simulation of educational administrative processes depend on the nature of the theory being examined and the way the specific problem has been defined. An illustration of a particular type of problem will indicate the advantages of control for establishing causality. Suppose one is investigating what Cooms and Kao describe as a conjunctive composition model, i.e., one in which successful performance on a task requires a certain minimum on each of several relevant dimensions (10, pp. 6-7).[16]

One might be interested in testing the notion that educational administrators must have a knowledge of human relations principles *and* curriculum theory to function as a leader of a small group assigned the task of solving a certain type of curriculum problem to be presented via a simulated situation. This notion might be based on the idea that knowledge of human relations is required to maintain the group cohesiveness necessary to apply the technical information from the curriculm theory to the problem. In effect, the one component is necessary for group maintenance and the other for task accomplishment. These two components could be systematically manipulated in the teaching process until neophyte administrators attained a specified criterion of understanding. The dependent variable (solution of the curriculum problem) could be controlled so that all subjects were required to perform the same task. Other variables could be controlled by randomly assigning subjects to the treatment groups.

Under these conditions, the simulated setting functions as a means to present a constant stimulus to subjects and to control the measurement of the dependent variable; manipulation of the independent variables and the randomization procedures allow causal statements to be made regarding the effects of the two independent variables and their interaction. If these same variables were investigated in a natural setting, it would be much more difficult to eliminate other possible causes for the leadership behavior of the subjects.

Also, the value of manipulation of independent variables for establishing causal relationships can be seen if one considers some of the questions regarding administrative decision making suggested by Cullinan (12, p. 142). For example: How do administrators weigh and value information? What values and probabilities of outcomes influence courses of action? The knowledge concerning such questions acquired from experiments conducted in simulated situations will be much more beneficial than knowledge acquired via self-report devices administered in a natural setting.

Time Factors

Control over the time when events occur is certainly one of the major values of using simulation for research. Control over time factors allows (a) optional starting of the simulation, (b) compression or expansion of a sequence of events, and (c) provision for dynamic aspects of a process.

Optional starting is of crucial importance to systematic observation and recording of behavior (40, p. 51). This is especially true for rare and significant events since those events which occur often can be observed in a natural setting. For example, the oral expression of an administrator addressing a group of parents or teachers is not difficult to observe because these occasions occur often and one knows ahead of time when they are likely to occur. However, it is much more difficult to know when an emergency may occur, whether it be a small thing such as unauthorized people on a playground, or a potentially larger event such as the initial stages of a student demonstration. When such events are simulated, control over the starting time allows adequate preparation for measurement crucial to research.

Compression of a sequence of events has been well recognized as an advantage of simulation for instruction because it allows one to obtain the experience of several years of decisions in a short period of time (26, p. 27). This benefit is facilitated by the ability to provide prompt feedback to the participant on the results of his decisions (34, p. 3; 31, pp. 36-37). The compression of events which permits instuction to be more effective also aids in research, since the investigator is able to observe and measure more behavior in a shorter period of time. In effect, he can conduct a longitudinal study in a very brief while.

A similar advantage to compression of real time is the expansion of a sequence of events (14, p. 13). This technique is probably not used as frequently in simulation as time compression. Its major contribution to research is interjection of experimental treatments at various stages in a sequence of events. Since the real time sequence of events is stopped so that participants in the simulation can receive instruction, study additional materials, review information received at a prior time, or allow regular activities to intervene (in effect, to allow any treatment of the participants to be interjected at any point in the sequence of events, at the control of the investigator), the total time which elapses for the simulation is greater than the time required for the same set of events in reality.

Much research conducted in a real or natural setting is characterized by the acquisition of data at a single point in time. But one benefit of being able to control events in a simulated situation is that measurements of dynamic processes, i.e., continuing events, can be recorded. McKenney indicates that a business game designed to provide a dynamic planning experience allows data to be acquired on a continuing decision-making process (31, p. 134). Horvat (26, p. 25) describes one of the major advantages of the negotiations games as being the necessity of the players to observe the effects of their behaviors and decisions over a period of time. Since the game is dynamic, the behaviors and decisions made at one period influence future behaviors and decisions in the game. Measuring behaviors at various stages of the process and relating these behaviors to changing conditions precipitated by the behaviors are more advantageous than single measurements at a single point in the process.

POTENTIAL PROBLEMS OF SIMULATION IN RESEARCH

Since one of the benefits of the use of simulation in research is control of stimuli so subjects are treated uniformly, it is natural that a corresponding problem is training personnel in uniform use of the simulated materials.[17] The advantages of controls in simulated situations have been discussed already; this section will deal more extensively with such problems as the realism, scope, expense, and generalizability of results of simulations.

Realism of Simulation

There are ways in which simulation can be perceived as unreal when used for research. First, the simulation may contain non-relevant information which has no effect on the outcome. This may cause the outcome of the simulation to depend on factors on which it has no dependence in reality. Second, the simulation may not include relevant variables, thereby modifying the outcome in comparison with reality. Third, the simulation may include variables which are related to each other in a way that does not conform to reality or is unfamiliar to participants in the simulation. And fourth, quantities of certain components in the simulation may be inaccurate.[18]

It is evident from this listing that one of the problems in developing realism in simulated situations is obtaining sufficient knowledge of reality prior to designing the simulation. Kaplan describes this as a major difficulty which calls for more closure than is usually available to start with (28, p. 288). An investigator needs to know a great deal about the real system before he can presume to simulate it; and if the replication of reality and the means of operating it are not valid, the simulation may be dysfunctional (14, pp. 13-14). Does this mean that the properties of the simulate look like the properties they represent? No, rather it is necessary to meet the stringent requirement that the properties in the simulate obey the same laws as the properties they represent, and this means that the investigator must depend on a theory that tells him how the relevant properties behave (40, pp. 53-54). This lack of precise information about relationships among variables in educational administration has caused problems in simulating administrative processes. For example, a major difficulty is inability to identify an integrated body of knowledge which clearly explains change processes. Part of this lack is attributable to the reward system of academic institutions which discourage inter-disciplinary endeavors, especially those of an applied nature (16, pp. 45, 55).

Maintaining the currency of knowledge on which the simulation is based is a sub-problem of having sufficient knowledge prior to designing a simulation. Since many of the simulations consist of situations which commonly occur in school systems, and since rapid societal and organizational changes cause many of the problems encountered by administrators, the currency of the problems on which the simulation is based is critical to the realism of the tasks being performed. Changes in society and in school systems affect the relevancy of the variables, so the currency of knowledge is important in developing simulation situations for research.

When the efficiency of simulation for instruction is considered, another problem is evident. Too much realism in some training situations may impede learning (29)! The more realistic a problem situation is, the more frightening and overwhelming it may be; whereas, the less realistic it is, the more a person has time to think because he is more relaxed and under less pressure. But what about the effect on a research project? There probably is no generally satisfactory answer to such a question, since so much depends on the purpose of the research. However, what at first may appear to be a defect may actually be a merit. In spite of recognition that a very vivid experience may dull the critical sense of participants, the same sense of involvement may equally dull the critical sense of those handling an actual crisis. Consequently, realism in crisis situations may not be a defect (18, pp. 177-78).

How is the problem of realism resolved in designing simulated activities?[19] Culbertson's (11, p. 2) discussion of the development of the UCEA articulated media project for instructional purposes seems appropriate in relation to research. He indicates the need to identify and use concepts and theories to give meaning to administrative problems represented in "reality oriented" situations. In effect, the nature of reality must be considered by carefully observing real situations; but the aspects of reality to be included in the simulation should be determined by the nature of the theory being tested. If an aspect of reality is not pertinent to the theory being tested, then that component can be omitted from the simulation; this is the implied guideline.

A reasonable gradation between excessive simplicity and complexity can best be attained by experimenting with the simulation itself, i.e., by the use of trial runs and pilot projects which utilize feedback from participants who are familiar with similar real problems to assist in modifying the simulation (1, p. 373). This increases the effort needed to develop simulations but appears to be necessary if appropriate realism is to be achieved.

Another type of feedback which may be helpful in developing realistic simulated situations is the type provided by computer-based systems. Computer-based simulations require exact specifications, objectives, and models for administrative problems to be investigated; in effect, ambiguous computer programs will not run (12, p. 131). While feedback from computers may require more precise specifications of reality for the computer to function, at the same time the added realism may enhance the research.

Scope of Simulation

The scope of the simulation is related to the realism problem. At first glance it may appear that realism determines the scope of the simulation; however, further reflection indicates that the theory which is being tested in the research, and which functions as a guide for the degree of realism needed, also is functioning as a guide for the scope of the simulation. So the purposes and the hypotheses of the research serve the same function as the objectives of instruction, namely, as an initial set of ideas from which the appropriateness of the activities to be included in the simulation can be deduced.

For example, there is the question of whether participants in the simulation should react to the materials independently or interact with each other and then react as a group or individually. Undoubtedly, if one desires to measure the consistency of individuals in making decisions to select teachers, the response to this question will be different from the response if one desires to observe reactions during a negotiations session. The theoretical base is different; therefore, the scope is different. If a group reaction to a problem situation is desired, how large should the group be? Again, since size of the group appears to have some effect on learning in a simulated situation (27, p. 26), it is necessary to examine the theory and the manner in which the results might be applied in order to determine this aspect of the scope of the simulation.

Although simulation offers the opportunity to scrutinize behavior carefully under a standard set of events and a standard situation, the need for expert observers varies according to the scope of the simulation. More observers and/or more extensively trained observers are needed in a saturation approach than in a micro simulation where the purposes may be narrower (13, p. 22).

Another problem of scope which is interrelated with the theory being considered is the nature of the task given to the participants. In an actual problem-solving situation, the decision maker must perceive that there is a problem and identify its nature prior to seeking potential solutions to it (1, p. 53). If the questions being asked by the researcher are such that a problem can be preformulated so that the primary task of the decision maker is to devise alternatives and make choices among the alternatives, the scope of the simulation can be reduced considerably. If the alternatives are provided, the scope can be reduced still further.

A problem of scope which is unrelated to the theory of the research involves allocation of time to rule-learning (31, p. 25). Generally, simulation used for research has more stringent time limitations than simulation used for instruction. In effect, it is more difficult to obtain volunteers for an extended time when the primary purpose of the simulation is research than it is to acquire students in workshops or courses. Consequently, the time limit imposes a constraint on the simulation. In an effort to accomplish as many research purposes as possible within this time limit, there is the natural tendency to reduce to a bare minimum the time allocated to learning the rules of the game or the requirements of the task of the simulation. Of course, if the time allocated to rule-learning is not adequate, then the behavior of the participants may be random or misguided and the results of the the research uninterpretable. A trial run with comparable subjects (advanced graduate students may not be comparable to practicing administrators!) usually is necessary to make estimates of time needed for rule-learning.

Expense of Simulation

Most listings of disadvantages of simulation include the expense of devising and/or operating the simulation. And certainly the absolute cost of simulation activities in education must be considered-not only the cost of the simulation itself but also the cost of the participants' time (18, p. 179)—regardless of whether the simulation is being devised for instruction or research. But cost is a relative consideration and must be compared with costs and results of other procedures (14, P. 14). Whether the simulation is being used for instruction or research, one should attempt to determine the outcomes (i.e., what will be learned) in relation to costs of the various approaches that might be used.

So the absolute cost of simulation may be high, yet relative to cost of other procedures it may be low. Two ideas seem to be implied by this line of reasoning: (a) although simulation may be a costly method of obtaining answers to questions, other procedures (e.g., experimentation in real situations) for answering the same questions may be even more costly and (b) one should not consider using costly simulation procedures for answeing trivial, picayune questions or questions lacking an adequate theoretical base.

In some cases, the fidelity of the simulation is directly related to the cost of the simulation. Yet one should not assume that higher fidelity produces better research results, since simulation frequently is of greatest benefit when real-world values are missing, e.g., the high-risk situation (32, p. 609). In a study which Kersh conducted, he found that a still picture of size 8″ x 10″ was more effective for instruction than a motion picture which approached life size (29, p. 9; 30, pp. 41-42). The realistic projection is more expensive, of course. Where one is concerned with the relative cost of acquiring information, choices must be made among real situations, high fidelity simulation, and low fidelity simulation.

Generalizability

Probably the major criticism of the use of simulation for research is directed at the process of inferring from the simulated situation to a real situation (1). Generally, the problem is considered to be caused by oversimplification of reality, an error easily made since one must simplify in order to simulate. How much one simplifies is the source of the problem (28, p. 180).

Considered in other terms, the problem of generalization is one of providing external validity. The investigator wants to make statements about how people other than the participants in the simulation will behave under conditions similar to, yet different from, those of the simulation. Two factors that jeopardize this external validity are (a), the interaction effects of selection biases with experimental variable(s) and (b) the reactive effects of experimental arrangements.[20]

The first of these factors warns about the manner in which individuals are selected for participation in research using simulation; if it is not possible to infer from the sample to a larger population, the generalizability of the results is quite weak. For example, if the simulation is conducted using advanced graduate students as subjects, it may be quite difficult to generalize to older, more experienced administrators who completed their graduate work at a much earlier date. Likewise, regional differences in populations may be difficult to span.

The second factor warns of the different effect which a given variable (or set of variables) may have upon persons exposed to it under conditions differing from those of the experiment or simulation. For example, the motivations of people may differ in real and simulated situation. Consequently, there is a concern with whether the artificiality of the simulated situation causes individuals to be less ego-involved, and therefore behave differently— reducing the validity as far as research conclusions are concerned (31, p. 115). In what sense, then, might similar reactions be expected in simulated and other situations?

The first of two ways in which these similar reactions may be expected is if there is reasonable assurance that the simulation "represents" or functions as a model of the other situations in which a person might be expected to react. It is conceivable that a simulation might represent reality in the sense that after all of the elements of reality were identified, a proportion of these elements was chosen randomly for inclusion in the simulation. If absolutely nothing was known about the functioning of the phenomena being investigated, such an approach might be reasonable. However, where information is available, one is much more likely to follow ideas such as those expressed in the first two sections of this chapter. Second, if scientific information has advanced to the point where alternative hypotheses have been eliminated, then generalizations may be made more readily.

This latter point is concerned with the general strategy which scientists have used for establishing generalities. It is accepted as a truism that induction or generalization which involves the external validity of research results is never fully justified logically in a neat, conclusive manner. This is due to the fact that the inference which is being made depends upon extrapolation beyond one's sample and beyond the simulated conditions. This being the case, it is necessary to *cumulate* evidence in such a fashion that doubt regarding a generalization is reduced. In effect, it does not matter whether the conditions appearing in the simulation ever appear in real life; what does matter is whether what will happen in a real situation can be predicted more accurately.[21] If inadequate explanations of relationships among variables and how phenomena operate can be eliminated, then predictions can be improved. And this is the function of experimentation, viz., to provide evidence regarding whether a hypothesis (or the theory on which the hypothesis is based) should be rejected or whether it should *continue not to be rejected.* Note that there is no real way in which a hypothesis can be confirmed by the results of an experiment; rather, it merely escapes being rejected. Confidence in the hypothesis and its generalizability increases as it is tested in a variety of ways and continues not to be rejected by the experimental results. In effect, the multiple testings in various situations, and the cumulation of information about the phenomena, reduce the plausibility of rival hypotheses and increase the ability to make real-world predicitons.[22]

EXAMPLES OF RESEARCH WITHIN SIMULATED SITUATIONS

This section is designed to illustrate some of the types of administrative problems that can be investigated in simulated situations. Although several of the illustrations are discussed in other chapters, they are presented here in uniform format so the various bases and procedures can be compared more easily. Individuals who desire to use these studies as examples of advantages of simulation or to examine the problems involved in developing and using the simulations will need to examine the original reports of the resarch.

Study of Elementary School Principalship

The initial and best known study of educational administration using simulation materials was conducted in 1957-1960 as a cooperative endeavor between Teachers College, Columbia University, and Educational Testing Service (22). The study involved many members of The University Council for Education Administration and had a tremendous impact on the use of the in-basket technique for instructional purpose (see Chapter 3). In addition, it opened the way for the user of simulation as a research tool.

Purpose and problem. The major research objective of the project was to determine dimensions of performance in the elementary school principalship and thus to develop a better understanding of the nature of the job of the school administrator. The accurate description of administrative behavior of elementary school principals is essential to the selection and training of principals. An analysis of the description of behavior is essential to developing concepts helpful in understanding the tasks of administration.

Variables involved. Two types of variables were studied: (a) variables that provided information about the subjects—information acquired outside the simulated situation and (b) variables which described the subjects' performances on in-basket tasks. The first type of variable included such measures as age, sex, marital status, social origin, education, experience, professional knowledge, mental abilities, temperament, interests, and judgments by teachers and superiors in the subject's "home" school. The variables in the second category were derived from sixty-eight in-basket items, from unstructured responses to problem situations, and from group interaction and speaking before groups. The responses to the in-basket stimuli were analyzed for content and style and were given an overall subjective rating by scorers.

Objectives. The exploratory nature of this study dictated that a major effort be made to determine factors which accurately described the behavior of the principals involved in the study. In addition to this description process, the study determined inter-relationships among all of the variables involved in the study.

Population, sample. The subjects used for the study were 232 elementary principals from throughout the United States. Thirty-two different school districts were represented, and the sample included 137 men and 95 women.

Method, analysis of data. A standard administrative situation was constructed by simulating an elementary school, and background materials were developed with which subjects could be taught the important features of the school in a day and a half. Special in-basket tests, kinescopes, and tape recordings were constructed to present administrative problems in the simulated school situation. Published tests and specially-devised instruments were used to measure the characteristics and performance of the subjects in their "home" school situations. The use of factor analysis and other correlational prodedures permitted a detailed examination of relationships among all the major variables of the study and unique components of administrative performance.

Outcomes. Ten factors accounted for the performance of the subjects on the in-basket problems, and the relationship of each of these factors to the characteristics of the subjects was determined. The identification of the factors and the relationships to characteristics of principals have implications for the selection, preparation, and practice of administrators.

Teacher Selection

Chapter 4 presented a rather complete description of materials which simulate the teacher-selection process. The brief description here illustrates how the materials were used to manipulate and control variables in such a way that causality was established.

Purpose and problem. This research project was conducted to determine whether the format of information affects decisions made in the selection of teachers. Since decisions are based on information and since the same information may be presented in differing formats, the general problem was to find an information format that does not adversely affect teacher-selection decisions as far as certain selected criteria were concerned.

Variables involved. The four independent variables manipulated were (a) amount of instruction provided on how to process information, (b) number of written documents presented, (c) degree of masking of information, and (d) interview information. Dependent variables used to determine the effect of these variables were consistency of decisions, fineness of discriminations made, time required to make decisions, and feeling of certainty regarding decisions. Factors which were controlled by holding constant for all treatment combinations included assignment situation, supervision situation, evaluation procedure, independence of decisions, physical conditions, time when decisions were made, order of presentation of applicants, order of information regarding applicants, and motivation of subjects.

Objectives. Since the overall objective was to find a maximally useful format (within the limits of the variables examined) for presenting information in teacher applicants, specific hypotheses regarding all main and interaction effects among the independent variables were tested for each of the four dependent variables.

Population, sample. The subjects used for this study were 144 elementary school principals in randomly chosen districts from three countries in the State of Washington.

Method, analysis of data. Descriptive and visual materials were prepared to create a simulated teacher selection situation, an experiment was conducted within the simulated situation by asking subjects to make decisions regarding fictitious teacher applicants, and statistical analyses were made of the subjects' responses to ascertain the effects of the experimental variables. The design of the experiment was a completely randomized 2x2x3x3 fixed model treatment arrangement with measures on all four of the dependent variables; consequently, the basic analysis of the data was done by an analysis of variance for determining the main and interaction effects of each of the four independent variables.

Outcomes. The results indicated that the format of the information did affect decisions. The optimum format consisted of instructions regarding the processing of information, a single summary document, no masking of information, and interviews with audiovisual stimuli.

Varying Expectations for Principalships

In Chapter 5 McIntyre presented information on simulation of the process for selection of administrators, demonstrating how several short simulations could be used for both teaching and research. One of the simulations discussed by McIntyre is presented here to compare the benefits of the research information obtained via this very brief representation of reality with more extensive data-collection procedures.

Purpose and problem. Principals in different school environments behave differently, and there is evidence that the situation does affect their leadership behavior. How much of the difference in behavior is due to influence of the environment and how much is due to selective placement procedures which attempt to match person and situation characteristics is not known. The purpose of this study was to determine whether expectations for principals' behavior in schools serving people of low socioeconomic status differed from expectations in schools for people of high socioeconomic status.

Variables involved. The independent variable was the socioeconomic level of a simulated junior high School; two levels were used, viz., high and low. The main dependent variable was the characteristics of principals considered to be important; 12 discrete categories were used. A second dependent variable was groups of respondents, and five groups were used.

Objectives. Answers to two questions were sought in this study: Do administrators expect the behavior of principals to be different in schools with differing socioeconomic levels? If so, what characteristics are considered to be most important in high socioeconomic areas and which characteristics are considered to be most important in low socioeconomic areas?

Population, sample. The total sample consisted of five sub-groups: Texas school principals (29); Colorado school principals and superintendents (31); Idaho school administrators (18); and two groups of educational administration graduate students at the University of Texas (16 and 14).

Methods, analysis of data. Forms H and L were distributed randomly to the participants. Form H described a junior high school situation in a high socioeconomic area, and Form L described a junior high school situation in a low socioeconomic area. Subjects were asked to complete a twelve-item checklist indicating how important the characteristics were considered to be for the situation represented. Mean ratings for each group were computed for each of the twelve characteristics.

Outcomes. There was general agreement among groups of the importance of the characteristics. The tendencies indicated by the data are that school administrators regard intelligence, breadth of interests, grade-point average, appearance, conservative political stance, and innovation to be more important for principals in schools serving areas of high socioeconomic status. Conversely, they regard large physical size, strict discipline, liberal political stance, love for children, and high controlling supervision of teachers to be more important for principals in low socioeconomic areas.

SUMMARY

The use of simulation for research offers the opportunity to test ideas about problems in the real world of educational administration by designing models of reality, determining how these models work, checking conclusions against reality, and modifying the models until they are satisfactory. Educational administration supplies the problem area, the content, and the initial motivation; simulation provides the means for modeling the reality of this content; and science furnishes the process for inquiring.

Research ouput can influence educational administration by assisting the practitioner in administering educational organizations (by providing concepts helpful in interpreting the world and in making decisions) and by assisting the researcher in studying the administrative process (by providing feedback and clues about theory which is being examined). The types of questions suitable for investigation via simulation do not appear to be limited by the content of the administrative task. They include such aspects of the administrative process as decision making and information processing, group interactions, conflict resolution, structural relationships, and goal setting and establishment of priorities. Questions which appear unsuitable for investigation in simulated situations include those involving self-analysis, a determination of how decisions actually are made in a real situation, and what *ought* to occur.

The advantages of simulation for research result from the fact that experiments can be conducted on a model of reality. Although all of the advantages of simulation can be obtained through experimentation in real situations, in practice it is difficult to experiment with some phenomena in educational administration. The use of simulation for research permits the measurement of dependent variables to be stabilized, the manipulation of multiple independent variables simultaneously—and the consequent establishment of causal relationships, the control of variables which are not of interest to the theory being examine, the control of the complexity of the study, and the control over the time when events occur.

Potential problems in the use of simulation in research include realism, scope, expense, and generalizability of results. In addition, training personnel in the uniform use of simulated materials is a potential problem with relation to controlling the stimuli presented to subjects.

The examples of research in simulated situations discussed in this chapter include a large research project designed primarily to measure administrative behaviors of elementary principals and to relate these behaviors to characteristics of the principals, a project designed to test the efficiency of differing procedures for training people in small group processes, a project which demonstrates how variables in the teacher-selection process can be manipulated and studied, and an administrator selection simulated activity which can be completed in a very short period of time and can be replicated inexpensively. These examples were presented in parallel format to facilitate an understanding of differences among studies which have been conducted primarily to describe administrative behavior, to establish relationships among variables so predictions can be made, or to determine causality so the environment can be controlled.

This chapter contains logical arguments and empirical evidence which are compelling for conducting experiments in educational administration in simulated situations. The viewpoint that educational administration is too complex for study via experimentation (i.e., that there are too many variables to contend with) is weak and may be nothing more than a "blanket rationalization of our ignorance as to what experiments to perform, and how to go about performing them" (28, p. 166). Simulation offers the opportunity to model or represent reality in such a way that beneficial experimentation can occur, and the use of the results should afford much greater understanding of the behavior of administrators and the environment within which they work.

But even if one accepts the view that experiments need to be conducted in simulated situations, he should heed certain cautions. He should be reminded of what some have called the law of the instrument—give a small boy a hammer and he will find that everything he encounters needs pounding. Not all administrative problems require extensive research efforts, and fewer still are of such theoretical and practical significance that they warrant realistic simulation and manipulation of variables. Problems which are investigated via simulation should be subject to the same general strategy as other research, i.e., the potential benefit from the information received should outweigh the risk if the information were not available.

Another caution which the discussion in this chapter has emphasized is the *necessity* of coordinating research conducted in simulated situations with application of the results in actual practice. Feedback from such coordination causes the theory on which the research is based to be modified and simulated situations to be made more real. For, although one ought not to be too concerned about creating unreal simulations, he should be quite concerned about creating unreal relationships (40, pp. 59–60).

Still another warning is issued against becoming interested in the simulation for its own sake and not as a representation of reality.

This is most likely to occur if the correspondence with reality is difficult to establish; when this happens, the researcher is likely to use the simulation for non-research purposes, such as instruction and demonstration of ideas (1, p. 373). This is merely a warning to be aware of the shift which occurs in purpose when one discontinues using a simulation for research, not a deprecation of instruction.

This discussion must not omit comment on two concerns which are of significance to all research in educational administration, viz., the implementation of research results and the conditions needed for adequate research to be conducted. Much has been written recently about different models for moving from "pure" research to implementation and most of these models involve the use of specialists who function between the research person and the practitioner. (The county agent in agriculture is the most common analogy used.) This proposal has merit and should be given a fair trial to determine its effectiveness; but it should not be the only alternative considered for testing, inasmuch as it has some potential weaknesses which might be avoided by using other procedures. For example, Ackoff (1, p. 408) argues that nonscientists responsible for implementation tend to modify applications in such a way that the test of the research results is made useless. He proposes that the researcher's role should be similar to that of an architect, i.e., active supervision of implementation.

If the architect model is to be tested as a viable alternative to the county agent model, the reseacher must seriously consider changes which have been needed for some time. For one thing, the research person must be much more competent than he has been in the past for his research must now be relevant as well as convincing. He can no longer plan his research in isolation from the people who will implement the results, and he cannot shove to someone else the responsibility for dealing realistically with the implications of his research—someone who understands it less than he does and who is less ego-involved in its being carefully implemented. Another change that will be needed is the careful training of more researchers. This change, combined with the need for high competency of the researcher, implies that the selective recruitment of people to conduct research in educational administration must be much broader than it has been previously. It is not at all clear that teaching or administrative experience in the public schools is essential to this research task, for example, and such prerequisites to research positions should probably be eliminated.

If more and better-trained research personnel are needed, this means that greater financial resources must be allocated to solving problems in educational administration. This is implied in all serious discussions of research which seeks to solve real problems and improve practice, because significant problems require conditions which are considerably beyond the individual person's effort. At least three critical conditions must exist for attacking a significant problem (8, p. 16): (a) appropriate acceptance and motivation by agencies involved, (b) staff available for long-term application to the problem, and (c) funding not only to support the staff but also to make any necessary physical and organizational changes within the setting in which the problem exists. These conditions indicate the need for concentrated effort by a number of agencies and people if ideas are to be generated, tested, and implemented. But anything short of this kind of effort is role playing and a delusion and should be recognized as such.

The problems of educational administration are complex, but this complexity is not unique and does not imply that rigorous research techniques (including experimentation) are inappropriate to the development of knowledge necessary to the solution of the problems. The simulation of reality can play a significant role in research efforts designed to solve administrative problems in education. The discussion of this chapter has identified some of the reseach needs related to both theory and practice, specified some of the advantages and problems of simulation, and provided examples of how simulated situations have been used to conduct research in educational administration.

NOTES

[1] See, for example, Coladarci & Getzels (9, p. 5); Campbell, Charters, Jr., & Gragg (7, pp. 172, 179); and Campbell (6, pp. 279, 301), for discussions of the administrator's need of concepts and theories which assist him in reflecting on the problems which he faces and on which he must take action.

[2] Herbert A Simon (36, pp. 5-8) describes these two types of decisions as *programmed* and *nonprogrammed* and discusses traditional and modern procedures for making them.

[3] Jacob W. Getzels (17, p. 235) emphasizes the need for developing theory in educational administration that will give meaning and order to observations and will help to specify what types of observations need to be made. Getzels and Coladarci (9, p. 8) discuss the tool-like character of theory when it assists in creating order out of what may appear to be a disorganized situation.

[4] Some might argue that the experience in the stimulated situation is not vicarious but real. However, the very function of simulation is to represent reality and readers have been cautioned about the dangers of thinking of the simulated situation as reality. This does not deny the legitimacy of the emotions or thought processes during a simulation, but it should be recongnized that these occur in a model which *represents* reality.

[5] This figure is an adaptation of one used by James N. Holmes (24, p. 15).

[6] The cycle could have been made more complex at this point by dividing Box B into two seprate parts: either research is conducted in reality or it is conducted in a simulated situation. If research was conducted in a simulated situation, one might then branch into the real situation prior to proceeding to Box D. However, a primary reason for using simulated situations is that some research is impossible to conduct in a real situation. For clarity, the additional step has been omitted.

[7] Roald Cambell (6, p. 175) notes that the construction of theories requires time which is unavailable to the practitioner, skills which he normally does not have and "an aloofness from the press of events which he cannot afford."

[8] The selection of a strategy is, of course, the selection of a course of action, but differs from the specific course of action in that it is a procedure or rule which permits a specific selection in a specific context once additional information is known.

[9] For a good discussion of the general uses of simulation and the relation of simulation to other uses of models, see Russell Ackoff (1, pp. 351-64).

[10] An *analogue* model uses one property to represent another; for example, a road may represents the terrain of a given geographical area. Simulation in educational administration uses pictures, word descriptions, drawings, charts, etc. to represent the elements of a real school situation. An analogue model is different from an *iconic* model (involving a transformation of scale, such as a model airplaine in a wind tunnel) or a *symbolic* model, where the symbols represent quantities as in mathematical models. Science uses all three and generally uses the analogue and iconic to develop the symbolic since it is more precise for manipulation. However, the first two are easier to understand; therfore, they are used more in the initial development stages of a discipline and for instruction.

[11] Zelditch, Jr., & Evan (40, p. 49) and Griffin (18, p. 76) discuss the importance of this idea. Also, Griffin emphasizes the point that one should study situations in order to become better informed and not simply because of the high probability of their occurrence. He states that in international politics improbable things happen with alarming consistency—a state of

affairs some might find comparable to educational administration.

[12] McKenney (31, p. 134) and Cullinan (12, pp. 127-28) discuss some of the advantages of being able to control variables in a simulated situation, and Cullinan gives examples of such variables in investigations of decision making.

[13] Actually, manipulation of multiple independent variables also has depended upon the development of experimental designs and their statistical analysis. Likewise, the use of high-speed computers has aided the analysis of complex data coming from such experiments (see Cullinan, 12, p. 136). Simulation has provided the means for controlling and presenting stimuli to subjects in various forms analogous to the way they appear in reality.

[14] See Clair Selltiz et al. (35, pp. 83-88) for an expanded discussion of this point.

[15] It is not intended to imply that experiments cannot be conducted in real situations—as contrasted with laboratory or simulated situations. However, experiments in real situations are different from investigations of relationships which occur among variables in a *natural setting,* undistrubed by systematic manipulation by an investigator.

[16] For example, consider a person who takes a history test in French. He must know enough French to be able to read the questions, but the French does not allow him to answer the questions. Likewise, no matter how much history he knows, he must have a knowledge of French to understand the questions. Each factor is necessary, but neither is sufficient. This is the model assumed when state laws require an individual to have a scholarly degree (say a master's degree is a subject-matter field) before he can become an administrator. Being a scholar is considered necessary to being a good administrator. If the state also requires teaching experience, then each of the components must be satisfied; an excess of either is not sufficient to compensate for a lack in the other.

[17] Michael Inbar (27, p. 26) discussed the differential impact which the players' predispositions have on the outcomes of games. He indicated that these predispositions are influenced by the person in charge of the session; consequently, it is important that sessions be properly handled by the the person in charge. When the simulation is being used for research, this means the sessions must be controlled either to maintain uniform treatment or to vary the treatment systematically.

[18] This discussion was adapted from Ackoff's indentification of ways a model may be in error (1, pp. 139-40).

[19] Blalock (2, p. 8) indicates that the basic dilemma of any scientist is how much to oversimplify reality. The scientist wants to select models that are simple enough to aid conception of the phenomena, yet realistic enough to acquire accurate predictions. Ackoff (1, p. 372) indicated that there is a great temptation in gaming (simulation involving human participants) to enlarge the model in order to capture the "essence" of reality but this temptation should be resisted in order to aid in interpretation of the data.

[20] Campbell and Stanley (5, pp. 174-207) discuss problems of internal and external validity with relation to experimental and quasi-experimental research designs. The discussion here of generalization from simulated situations borrows much from their views.

[21] See Kaplan (28, p. 170) for a discussion of this point.

[22] Examples of the testing of validity of simulated situations are given by Kersh (30, p. 75) and Utsey (39, pp. 9-10). Kersh concluded that concepts learned in simulated classroom situations transferred to the actual classroom, and Utsey found that experienced teachers and student teachers transferred skills (in the diagnosis of reading problems) learned in the simulated situation to their own classrooms. However, it will be noted that each of these studies deals with a phenomenon learned in the simulation and attests to the validity of simulation in only one manner. These studies do not provide evidence regarding whether behaviors *learned in reality* will be exhibited in a simulated situation.

BIBLIOGRAPHY

1. Ackoff, Russell L. *Scientific Method: Optimizing Applied Research Decisions.* New York: John Wiley & Sons, Inc., 1962.

2. Blalock, Hubert M., Jr. *Causal Inferences in Nonexperimental Research.* Chapel Hill: The University of North Carolina Press, 1961, 1964.

3. Boocock, Sarane S. "An Experimental Study of the Learning Effects of Two Games with Simulated Environments," *American Behavioral Scientist* X, 2 (October 1966): 8-17.

4. Boyan, Norman J. "Problems and Issues of Knowledge Production and Utilization," in Terry L. Eidell and Joanne M. Kitchel, eds., *Knowelge Production and Utilization,* Chapter 2. Columbus, Ohio: University Council for Educational Administration and University of Oregon: Center for the Advanced Study of Educational Administration, 1968, pp. 21-36.

5. Campbell, Donald T. & Stanley, Julian C. "Experimental and Quasi-Experimental Designs for Research on Teaching," in N.L. Gage *Handbook of Research on Teaching.* New York: Rand McNally & Co., 1963, pp. 171-246.

6. Campbell, Roald. "Implications for the Practice of Administration," in Daniel E. Griffiths, ed., Behavioral Science and Educational Administration. Chicago, Illinois: The University of Chicago Press, 1964, pp. 270-302.

7. Campbell, Roald; Charters, Jr., W. W.; & Gragg, William L. "Improving Administrative Theory and Practice: Three Essential Roles," in Roald F. Campbell and James M. Lipham, eds., Administratice Theory as a

Guide to Action. Chicago: Midwest Administration Center, the University of Chicago, 1960, pp. 171-189.

8. Carter, Launor F. "Knowledge Production and Utilization in Contemporary Organizations, in Terry L. Eidell and Joanne M. Kitchel, eds., *Knowledge Production and Utilization.* Columbus, Ohio: University Council for Educational Administration and University of Oregon: Center for the Advanced Study of Educational Administration, 1968, pp. 1-20.

9. Coladarci, Arthur P. & Getzels, Jacob W. *The Use of Theory in Educational Administration.* Stanford, California: Leland Stanford Junior University, 1955.

10. Coombs, C. H. & Kao, R. C. "Nonmetric Factor Analysis," Engineering Research Bulletin, University of Michigan 38(1955): 63.

11. Culbertson, Jack. "A General Description of the Articulated Media Project," in *The Design and Development of Prototype Instructional Materials for Preparing Educational Administrators.* USOE Project No. 5-0998, Contract OC-4-16-014, January 1968, pp. 1-17.

12. Cullinan, Paul & Ruderman, Robert. "A Prototype Computer-based System," in *The Design and Development of Prototype Instructional Materials for Preparing Educational Administrators.* USOE Project No. 5-0998, Contract OE-4-16-014, January 1968, pp. 86-147.

13. Cunningham, Luvern L. "Simulation and the Preparation of Educational Administrators." Unpublished paper read at the International Intervisitation Conference, University of Michigan, October 1966.

14. Dawson, Richard E. "Simulation in the Social Sciences," in Harold Guetzkow, ed., *Simulation in Social Science: Readings.* Englewood Cliffs, New Jersey: Prentice Hall, 1962, pp. 1-16.

15. Dill, William R. & Doppelt, Neil. "The Acquisition of Experience in a Complex Management Game," *Management Science* 10(1963); 30-46.

16. Downey, Loren. "Prototype Instructional Materials and Processes for Preparing Administrative Personnel to Understand and Cope with Planned Change," in *The Design and Development of Prototype Instructional Materials for Preparing Educational Administrators.* USOE Project No. 5-0998, Contract OE-4-16-014, January 1968, pp. 43-85.

17. Getzels, J. R. "A Psycho-Sociological Framework for the Study of Educational Administration," *The Harvard Educational Review* XXLL, 4(1952): 235-246.

18. Griffin, Sidney F. *The Crisis Games: Simulating International Conflict.* New York: Doubleday & Co., Inc., 1965.

19. Griffiths, Daniel E. "The Nature and Meaning of Theory," in Daniel E. Griffiths, ed., *Behavioral Science and Educational Administration.* Chicago: The University of Chicago Press, 1964, pp. 95-118.

20. Halpin, Andrew W. "The Development of Theory in Educational Administration," in Andrew W. Halpin, ed., *Administrative Theory in Education*. Chicago: Midwest Administration Center, The University of Chicago, 1958, pp. 1-19.

21. Halpin, Andrew W. "Ways of Knowing," in Roald F. Campbell and James M. Lipham, eds., *Administrative Theory as a Guide to Action*. Chicago: Midwest Administration Center, The University of Chicago, 1960, pp. 3-20.

22. Hemphill, John K.; Griffiths, Daniel E., & Frederiksen, Norman. *Administrative Performance and Personality*. New York: Bureau of Publications, Teachers College, Columbia University, 1962.

23. Hickey, Michael E. "Pre-decisional Information Processes in Teacher Selection." Unpublished doctoral dissertation, University of Washington, Seattle, Washington, 1969.

24. Holmes, James N. "A Theory of Sociocybernetics and its Application to Educational Administration." Unpublished doctoral dissertation, University of Washington, Seattle, Washington, 1966.

25. Horst, Paul. *Factor Analysis of Data Matrices, Part I*. Seattle: University of Washington Press, 1963.

26. Horvat, John. "The Development of Prototype Materials in the Area of Professional Negotiations in Education," in *The Design and Development of Prototype Instructional Materials for Preparing Educational Administratiors*. USOE Project No. 5-0998, Contract OE-4-16-014, January, 1968, pp. 18-42.

27. Inbar, Michael. "The Differential Impact of a Game Simulating a Community Disaster," *American Behavioral Scientist* X, 2 (October 1966): 18-27.

28. Kaplan, Abraham. *The Conduct of Inquiry*. San Francisco, California: Chandler Publishing Co., 1964.

29. Kersh, Bert Y. *Classroom Simulation: A new Dimension in Teacher Education*. Final Report, Title VII Project No. 886, National Defense Education Act of 1958, Grant No. 7-47-0000-164, Oregon State System of Higher Education, 1963.

30. Kersh, Bert Y. *Classroom Simulation: Further Studies on Dimensions of Realism*. Final report, Title VII Project No. 5-0848, National Defense Education Act of 1958, Grant No. 747-0000-288, Oregon State System of Higher Education, 1965.

31. McKenny, James L. *Simulation Gaming for Management Development*. Boston: Graduate School of Business Administration, Harvard University, 1967.

32. Obermayer, Richard W. "Simulation, Models and Games: Sources of Measurement," *Human Factors*, VI, 6(1964): 704.

33. Ross, George H. "Game Theory Analysis of Simulated Collective Negotiations." Unpublished paper presented at the annual meeting of the American Educational Research Association, Chicago, 1968.

34. Schild, E. O. "The Shaping of Strategies," *American Behavioral Scientist* X, 3(1966): 1-4.

35. Selltiz, Claire; Jahoda, Marie; Deutsch, Morton; & Cook, Stuart W. *Research Methods in Social Relations.* New York: Holt, Rinehart & Winston, Inc., 1959.

36. Simon, Herbert A. *The New Science of Management Decision.* New York: Harper & Row, 1960.

37. Suppes, Patrick. *Set-Theoretical Structures in Science.* Stanford, California Institute for Mathematical Studies in the Social Sciences, Stanford University, 1967.

38. Thompson, James D. "Modern Approaches to Theory in Administration," in Andrew W. Halpin, ed., *Administrative Theory in Education.* Chicago: Midwest Administration Center, The University of Chicago, 1958, pp. 20-39.

39. Utsey, Jordan. "Simulation in Reading." Unpublished paper read at the National Reading Conference, December 1966.

40. Zilditch, Morris, Jr. & Evan, William M. "Simulated Bureaucracies: a Methodological Analysis," in Harold Guetzkow, ed., *Simulation in Social Science: Readings.* Englewood Cliffs, New Jersey: Prentice-Hall, 1962, pp. 48-60.